IMAGES
of America

Juneau and Sauk Counties

1850–2000

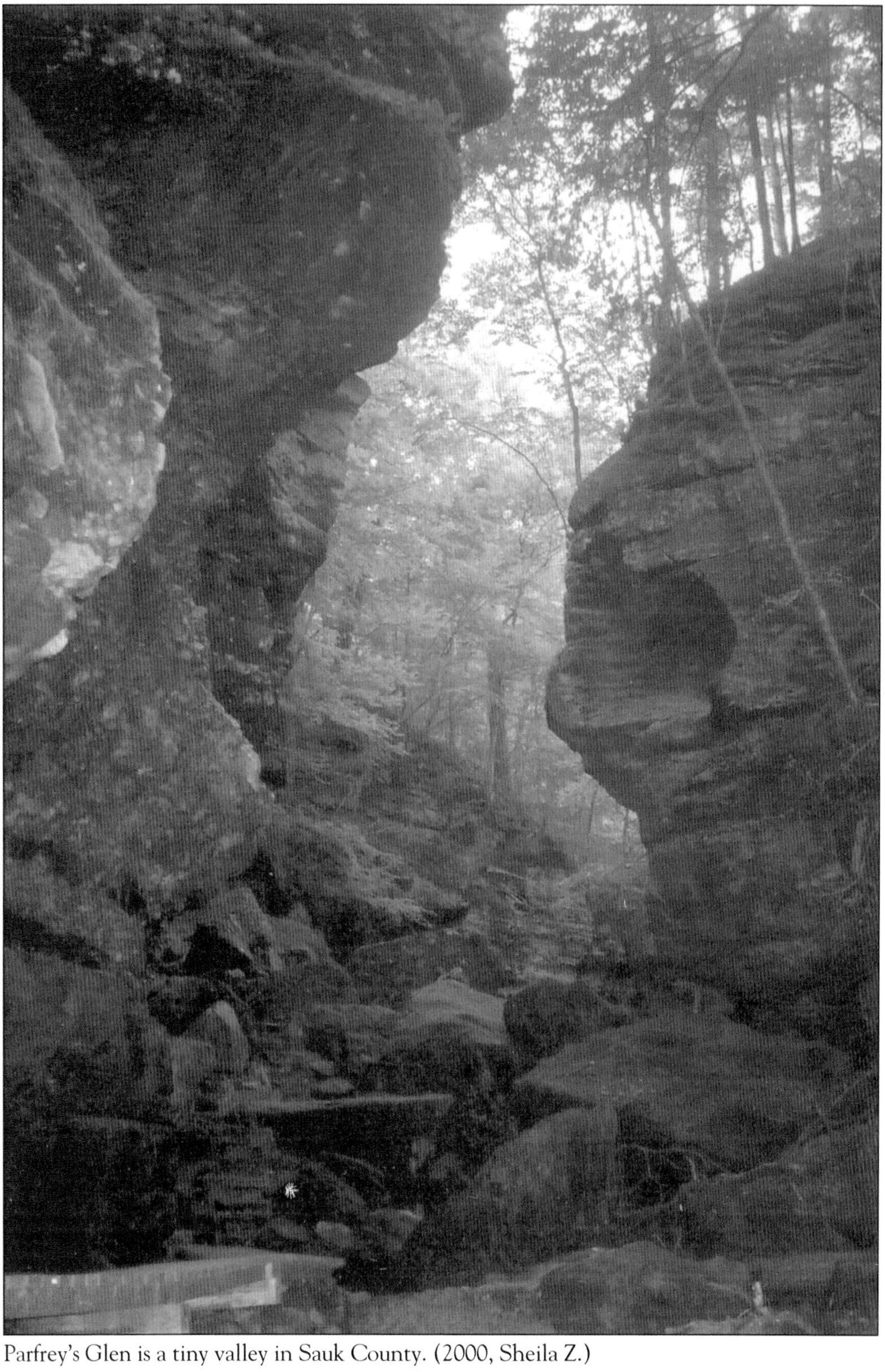

Parfrey's Glen is a tiny valley in Sauk County. (2000, Sheila Z.)

IMAGES
of America

JUNEAU AND SAUK COUNTIES

1850–2000

Jacqueline Ann and Sheila Z.

ARCADIA
PUBLISHING

ISBN 978-0-7385-1938-8

Published by Arcadia Publishing
Charleston, South Carolina

Printed in the United States of America

Library of Congress Catalog Card Number: 2001094991

For all general information contact Arcadia Publishing at:
Telephone 843-853-2070
Fax 843-853-0044
E-mail sales@arcadiapublishing.com
For customer service and orders:
Toll-Free 1-888-313-2665

Visit us on the Internet at www.arcadiapublishing.com

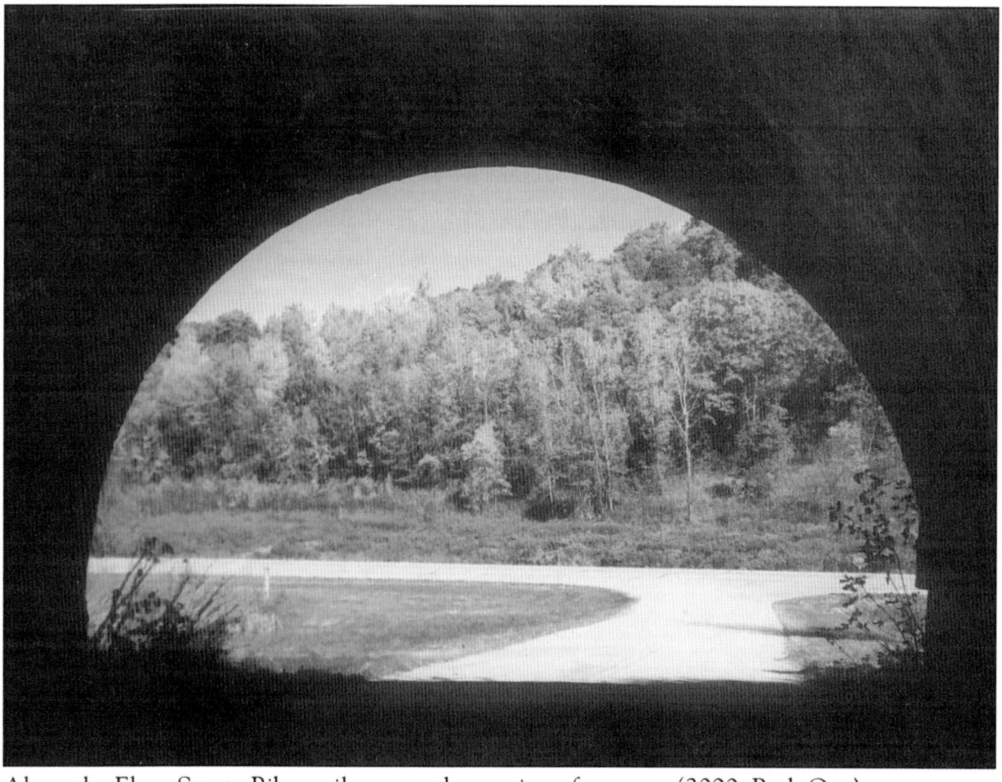

Along the Elroy-Sparta Bike trail, we see the passing of seasons. (2000, Barb Ott.)

Contents

Sauk County

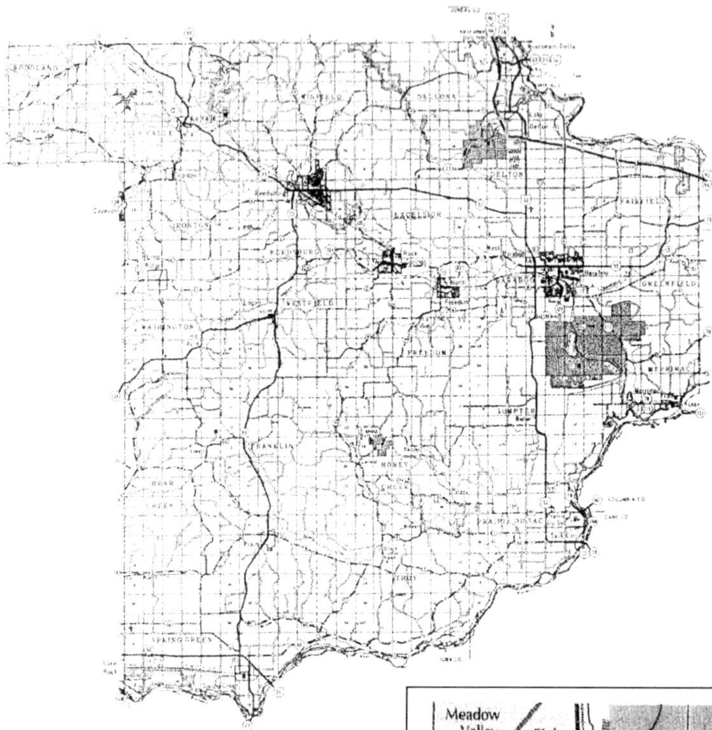

Juneau County

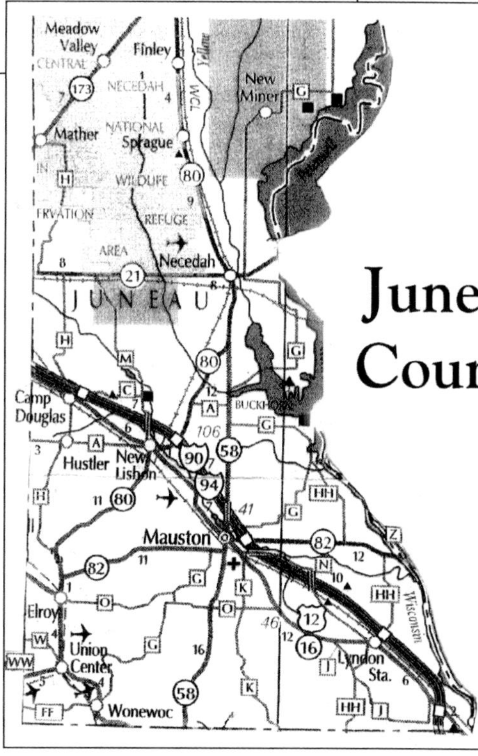

INTRODUCTION

Our spirits fill with the glory of your rocky bluffs.
We tremble with awe at your green valleys,
Sweeping across the countryside to join the hills.

The people struggled to survive. Many of them didn't know how to farm, but farming was necessary for survival; so they learned. Lumbering was an accessible but dangerous industry, and many lumberjacks are buried on the riverbanks. Still, they persisted. Living conditions separated the weak from the strong. Tuberculosis ran rampant across the land. The flu epidemic of the First World War knocked on almost every door. Doctors were in constant demand.

Shacks grew into houses. Schools held both eager and reluctant students who were sometimes pulled for labor. Churches appeared. The settlers needed God.

Along the rivers, in the woods, on hills overlooking valleys, the people found food for the soul. The land and the people became interwoven, and patterns began to emerge.

The people came from different cultures, but they gathered and contributed their values, attitudes, and dreams into the consciousness of the community, village, and farm areas that came to be the counties of Juneau and Sauk. Their poets whispered of inner peace, houses at rest.

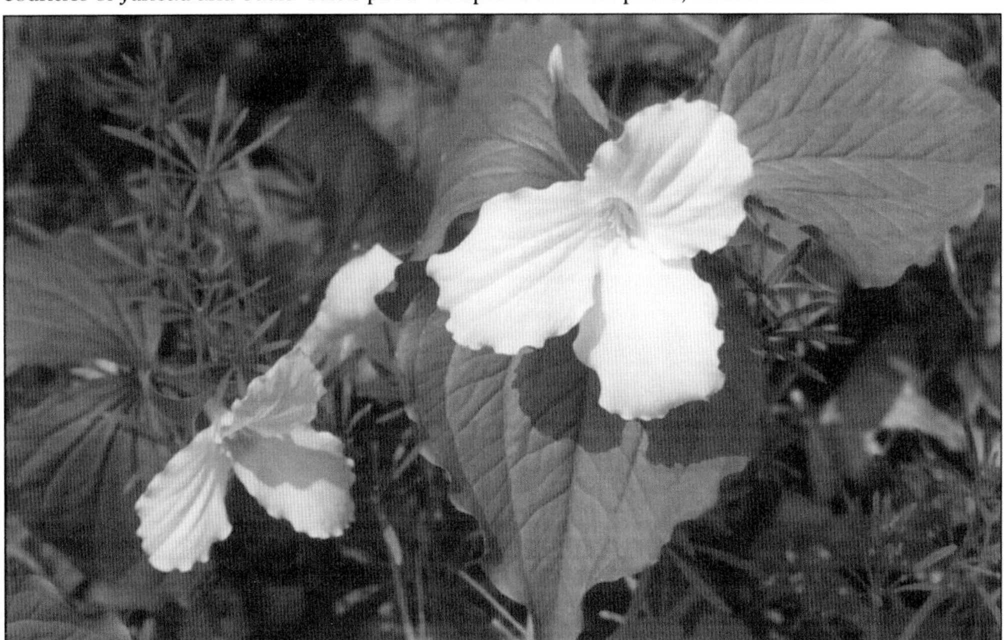

Trilliums, protected wildflowers, stand saluting the sun. (2000, Barb Ott.)

Our families walked the paths of county history.
Homesteaded, voted for statehood.
Brawled through the twenties, survived the thirties.

Men and women came together to chart a true course and to keep the land safe.

The rivers have always been a gift, offering transportation, power, food, recreation, and enticement. The roads and railroads arrived and became partners for progress.

Businesses and industries appeared, some to die, some to flourish.

The people learned to survive the winter and embrace the spring. Their space, their bonding with nature teaches them, time passes, change is a constant truth, actions have a consequence. In the middle of winter, they see the beauty in the snow. They asked, "What's for the common good?" And when the answers evolved, people gave.

The roots of the people grow deeply into the soil. They know the riches of their land.

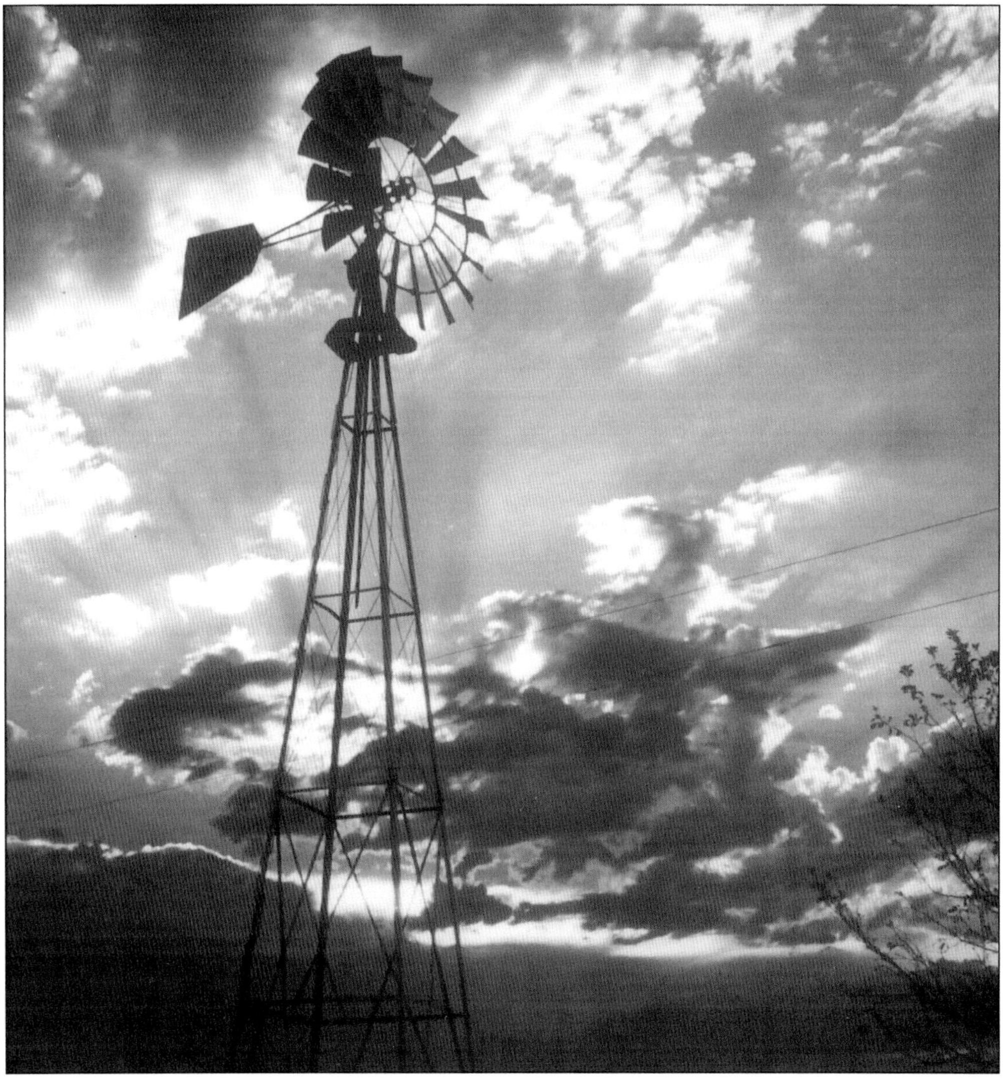

A restored windmill on Jim and Barb Ott's farm, County G in Juneau County.

One

The People

Over the surface of the land,
We see the shadowy outlines
of the people.

The early settlers needed courage and fortitude. Many became farmers for the first time. They had to learn to work with nature and to develop new skills often by trial and error. There was a high demand for self-sacrifice. The family community had to supply the labor force and spiritual and emotional support. The first goal was survival.

Juneau and Sauk Counties, with great variety in plant life and animals, encouraged an appreciation of nature's beauty. This area demanded creativity and teamwork to survive harsh weather and encouraged the reflections and understandings that come from bonding with nature.

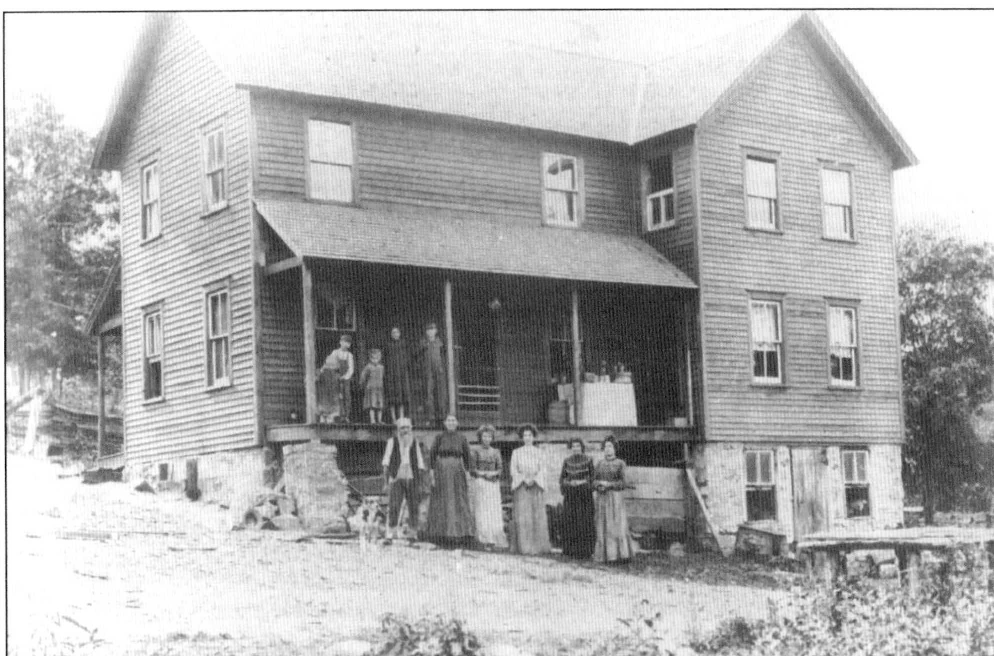

John Deitzman and Greenberry Henricks were Civil War buddies. Greenberry stayed with the Deitzmans, and helped John build this house. Everyone enjoyed the front and back porches, the many windows, and the space for a big family. Mary Deitzman was thrilled with her new home—the first frame house in Sauk County. (Late 1800s, Hazel Owen.)

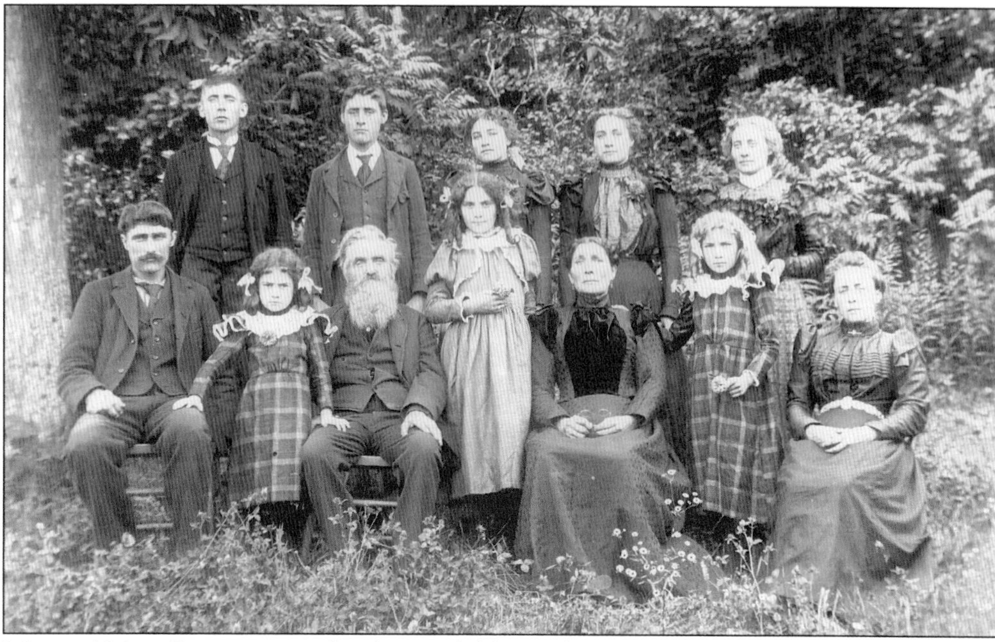

John and Mary Deitzman raised eighteen children. Eleven of the children were born to them. Cholera, dysentery, and fever claimed the lives of three of their children. They worked from dawn to dark for family survival. Mary was John's third wife. His first wife died of fever, leaving two children. The second wife died giving birth to their fifth child. (1896, Hazel Owen.)

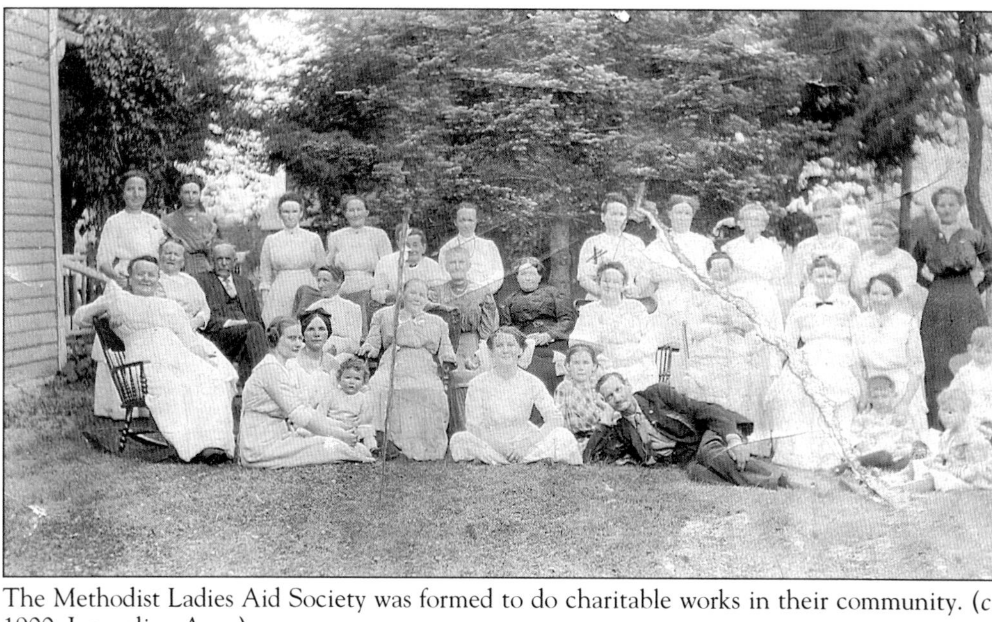

The Methodist Ladies Aid Society was formed to do charitable works in their community. (c. 1900, Jacqueline Ann.)

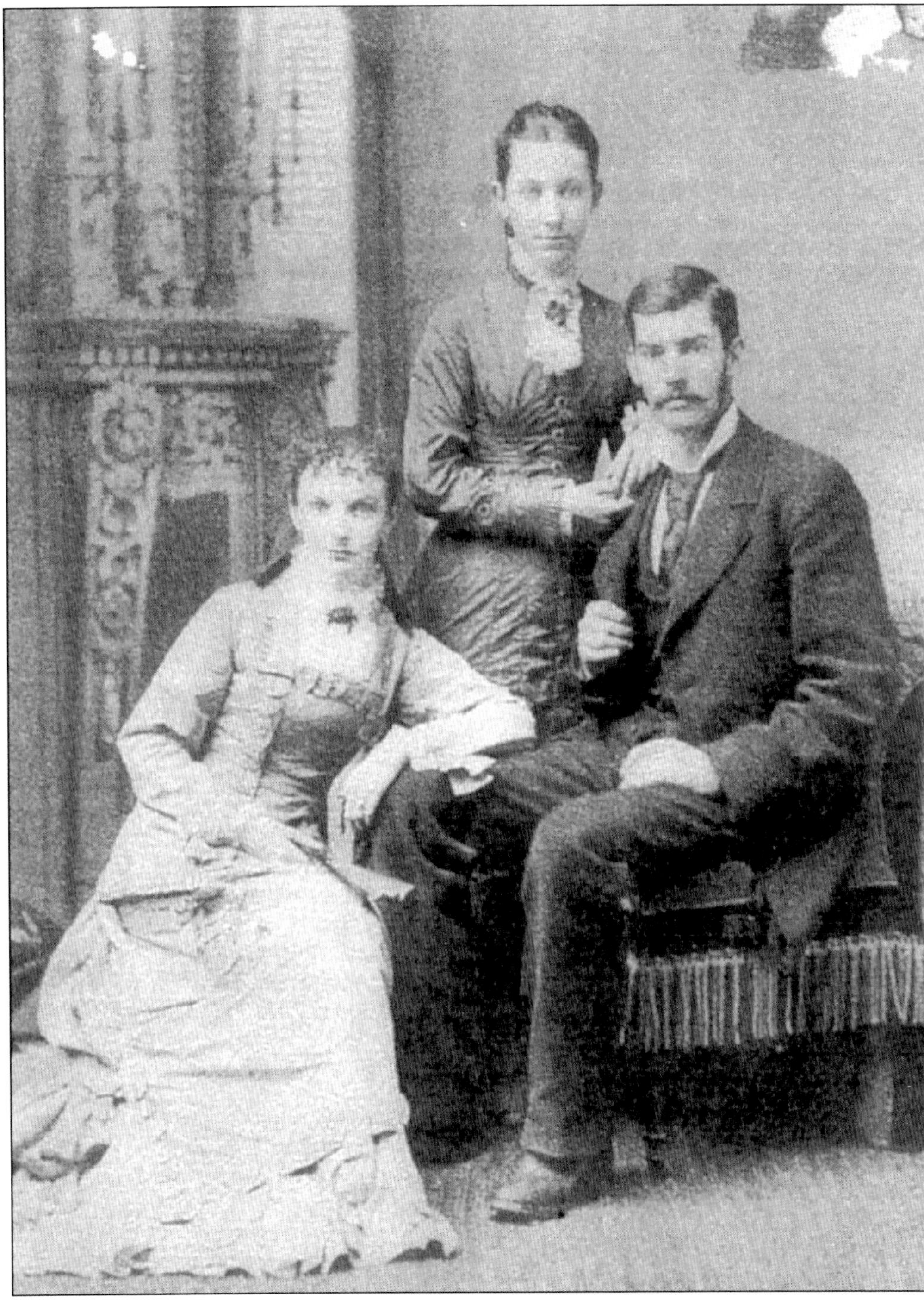

The young people in Necedah's first high school graduating class, 1878, were attractive and very well dressed. They were John T. Kingston Jr., Emma Weston, and Josephine Sarles. *History of Northern Wisconsin, 1881* tells us that Necedah was *the* important lumbering town in northern Wisconsin. Thomas Weston, Eliphalet Miner, and John T. Kingston controlled the lumbering company.

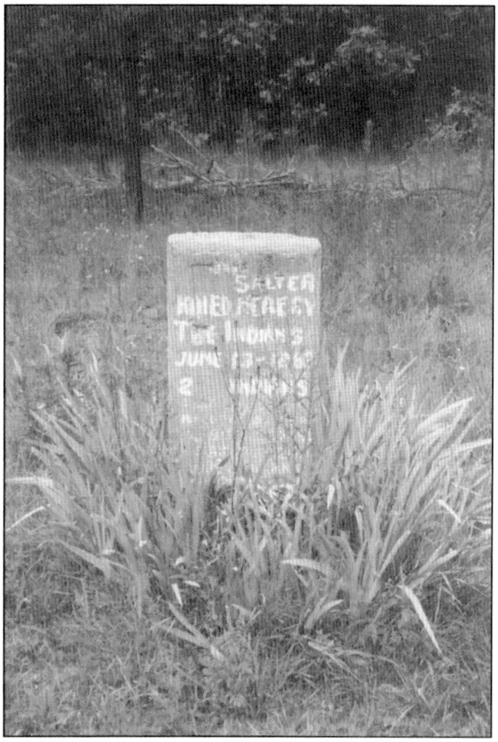

"Hell's Delight," a grog shop between Mauston and Necedah, belonged to George "Daddy" Salter. It was June 13, 1863, a beautiful day to work outside. George traveled about 3-miles away from his shop and home to work in the fields. On this day, two American Indians approached the homestead while he was gone. Emma Salter, strong in spirit and body said, "No, no, I won't give you anything!" The Indians killed Mrs. Salter. Two chairs pushed against the wall made a crib for her baby, left unharmed. Some pies were stolen. An itinerant German, George told the story of the two Indians. "I'll kill every Indian I capture," he vowed. He captured two Indians. He cut their heads off and stuck them on poles in front of his shop. (Sheila Z.)

The Gardner family came to homestead a farm near Reedsburg in 1852. Pictured here are the sons of Elisha and Phoebe Gardner, from left to right: (back row) John Wesley, Fletcher Welcome, and William Serinus; (front row) Lorenzo Obed, Elisha Henry. Lorenzo became a prominent farmer and agriculture leader in Sauk County. His farm was near the old homestead. (Norma Scott.)

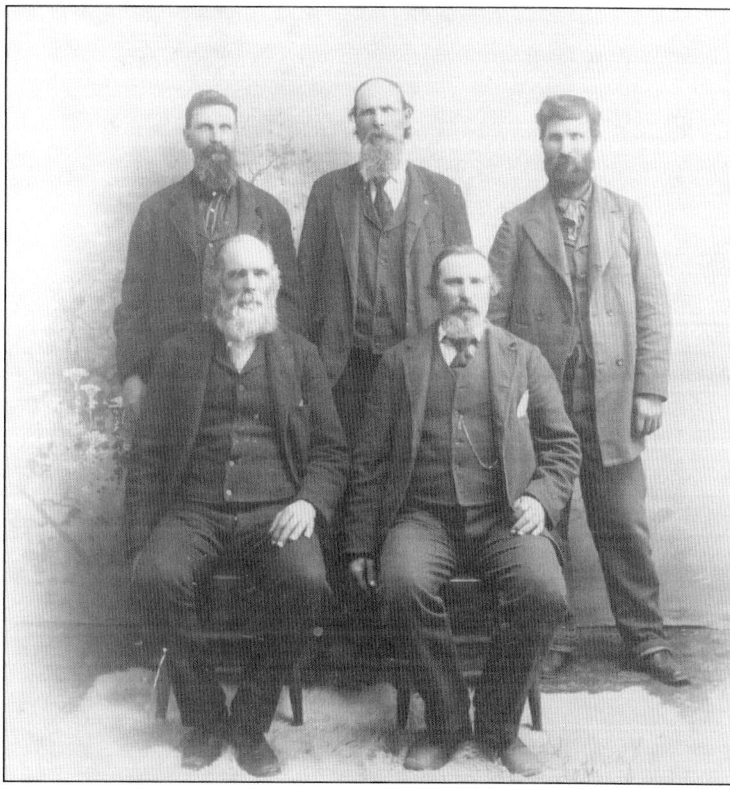

In 1895, a young schoolteacher named Hannah May Thompson lived near Wonewoc. She shared her life and hopes through her diary. Hannah's dreams would not come true. She died, at the age of 26, in Chicago. A family mystery bloomed when her brother went to Chicago and couldn't find the funeral. (Norma Scott.)

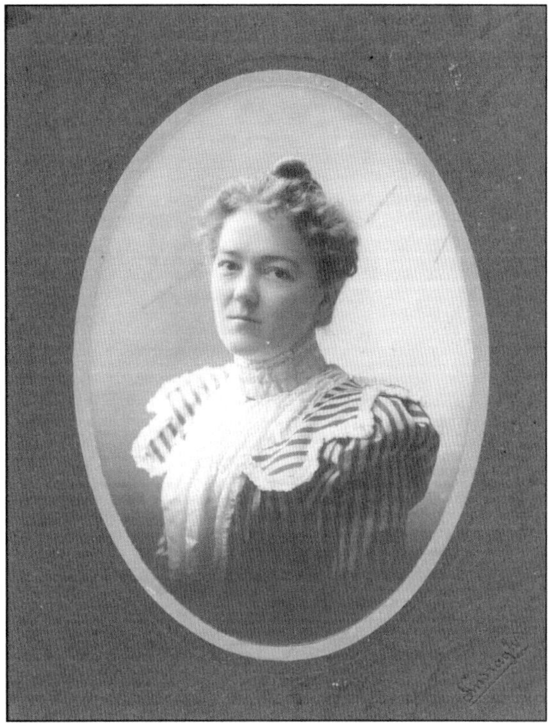

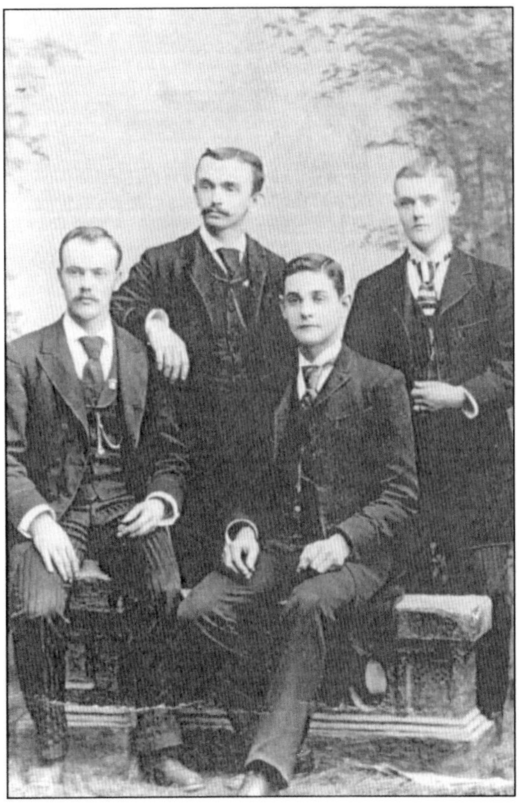

Robert Lader Scott spent most of his adult life in Baraboo, Sauk County, and the LaValle area. He enjoyed telling his family about an adventure he had as a young man when he went out to see the West. Robert worked for a farmer who occasionally drank too much. The farmer's wife asked Robert to plow a cornfield. While he was plowing, two men came riding through the knee-high corn. They stayed for supper, and slept in the dug out where Robert slept. In the morning, he asked the farmer's wife who the men were. She said, "Jesse and Frank James." They often stayed over night. Pictured here from left to right are as follows: (sitting) Robert Lader Scott and unidentified; (standing) John Wesley Scott and unidentified. (c. 1900, Norma Scott.)

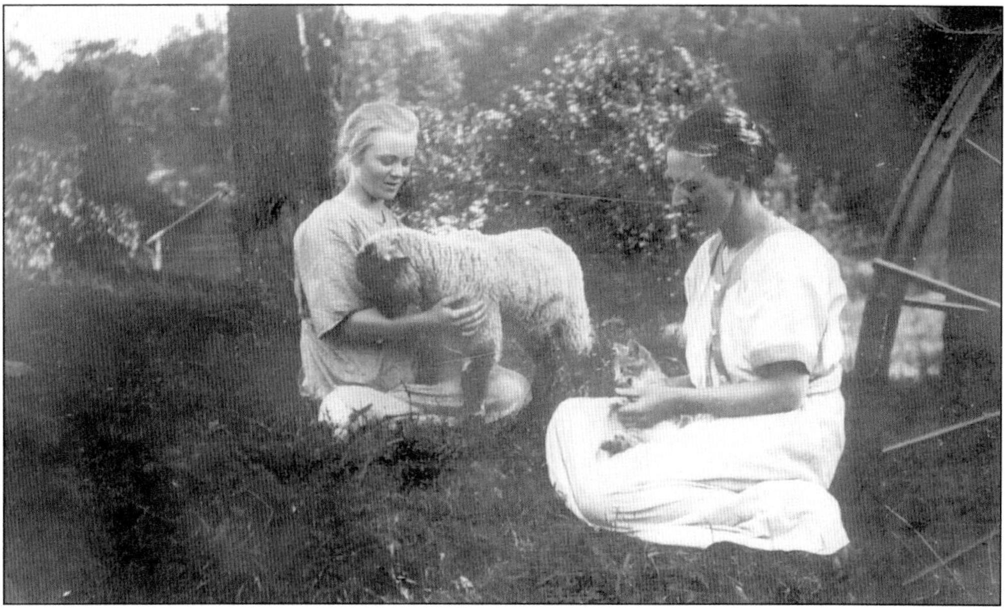

Ruth Albertson is pictured here, holding one of the sheep kept by her family in the fenced-in area of lawn around their farm home. The sheep kept the lawn trimmed and were raised for their wool. Olga Albertson, who was married to Ruth's oldest brother, is pictured cuddling a little kitten. Both young women enjoyed the company of the farm animals. (1919, Claire Ness.)

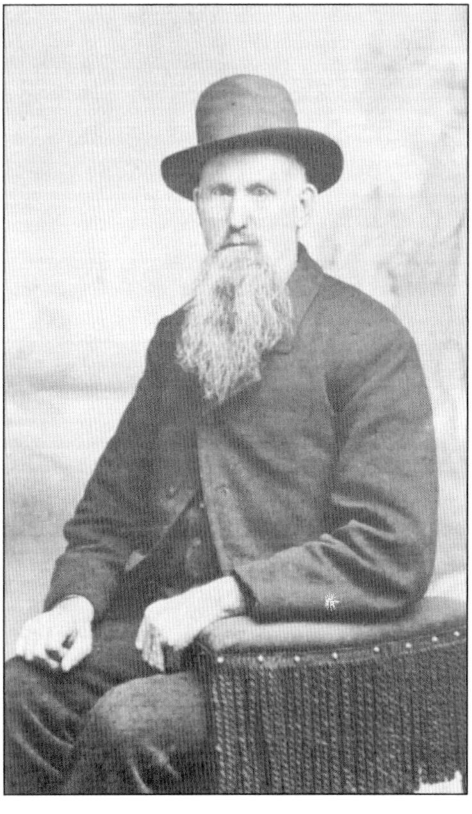

On September 30, 1864, James Douglas, his daughter Ann Eliza, and friend "Amp" Chamberlain left a work train and walked one-quarter of a mile to Chinaman Rock. They started Camp Douglas, a wooding camp, to make and sell cordwood. Ann Eliza was the first person to marry in Camp Douglas. She married John Singleton, who came to the wooding camp from Maine. The Camp Douglas of today is 1/2-mile east of the Douglas wooding camp.

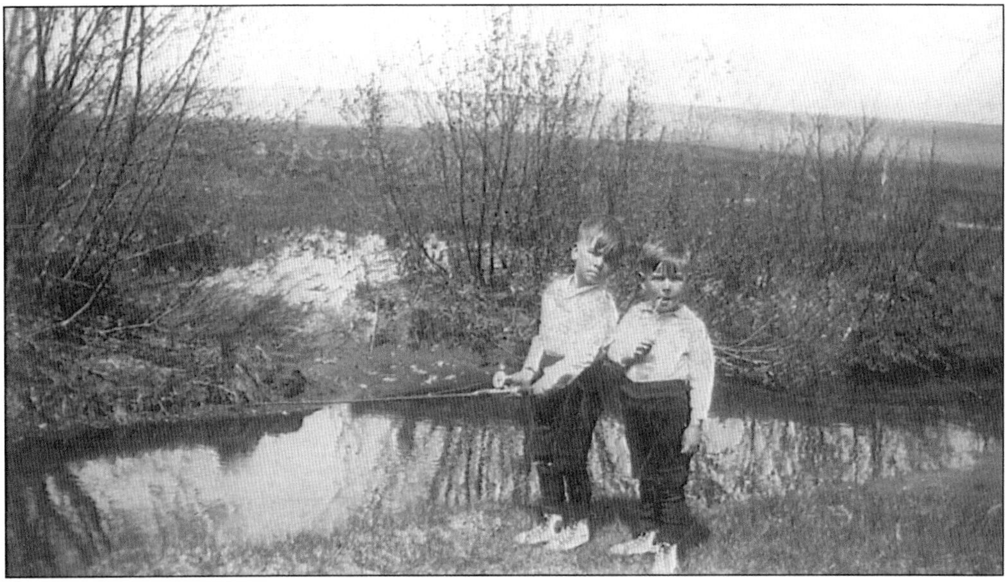

Junior and Harry Wright are pictured here fishing in Lyndon Creek, *c*. 1930. No snacks, just weeds to suck on. (1930, Harry Wright.)

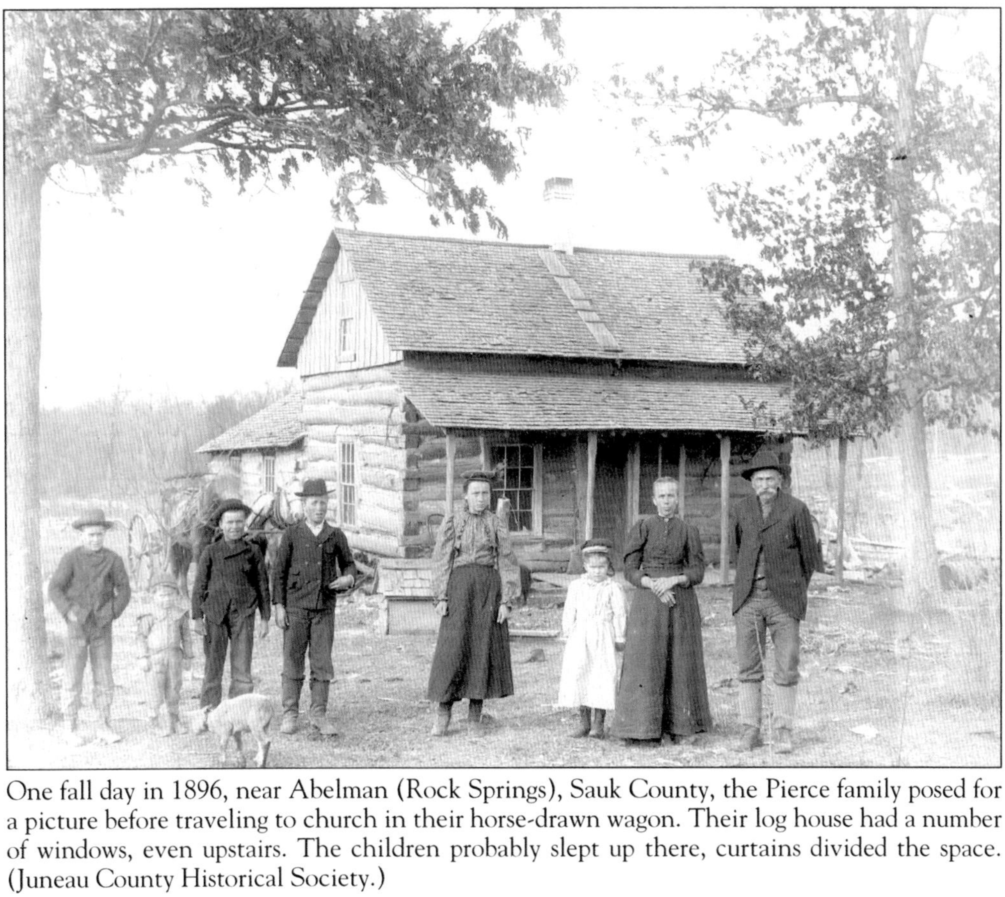

One fall day in 1896, near Abelman (Rock Springs), Sauk County, the Pierce family posed for a picture before traveling to church in their horse-drawn wagon. Their log house had a number of windows, even upstairs. The children probably slept up there, curtains divided the space. (Juneau County Historical Society.)

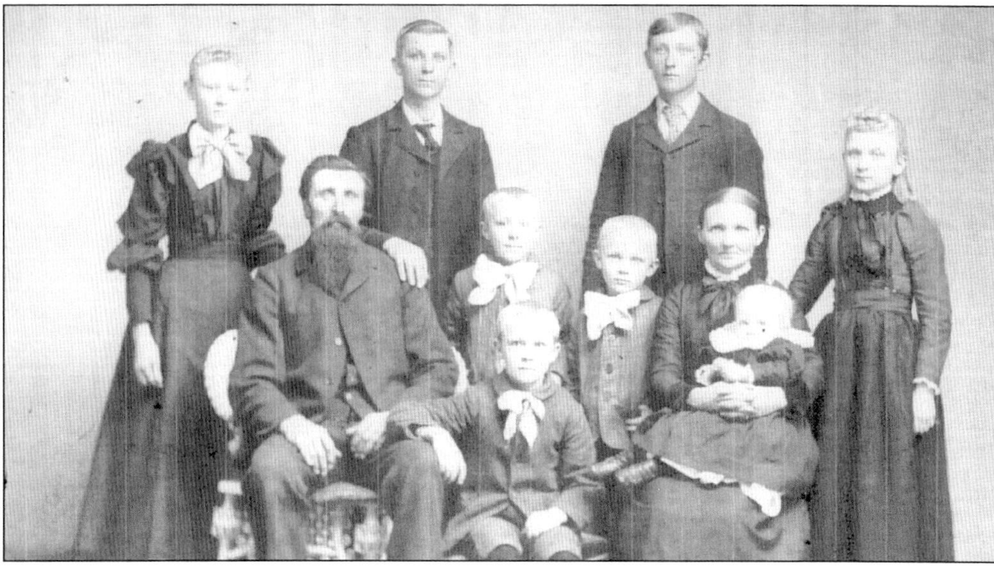

Ole Albertson came from the Suldal Area in Norway. He was happy to meet a beautiful girl, Mata Nelson, in the Lake Koshkonong Area, who was also from Norway. They married in Juneau County in 1873. Ole needed a farm and found 110 acres about 3-miles south of what is now the village of Hustler. He wanted those acres. They reminded him of the land he left behind in Norway. Delighted when a neighbor lent him $700, Ole bought his land. He built a log shack for himself and Mata and all the family they would have. Later, Ole built a frame house around the log shack. The family is pictured here: (back row) Clara, Henry, and Nils; (middle row) Ole, Otto, Albert, Mata, and Annie; (front row) Sam and Ruth. (1893, Claire Ness.)

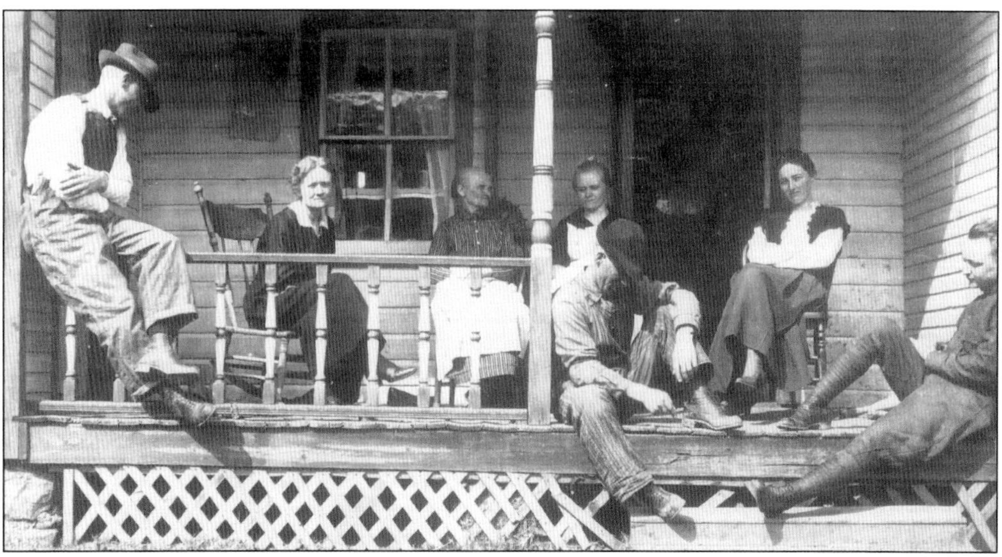

A World War I soldier, who was also a cousin, came to visit the Albertson family. They relaxed on the front porch of their farm home, 3-miles south of Hustler. The family is pictured here, from left to right: (front row) Otto, Albert, and Nels Knutson; (second row) Ruth, Mata, and two unidentified people. Mata's husband Ole died of Tuberculosis in 1903. She was the matriarch of her family. Otto and Albert farmed all their lives on this land purchased by their father. (1917, Claire Ness.)

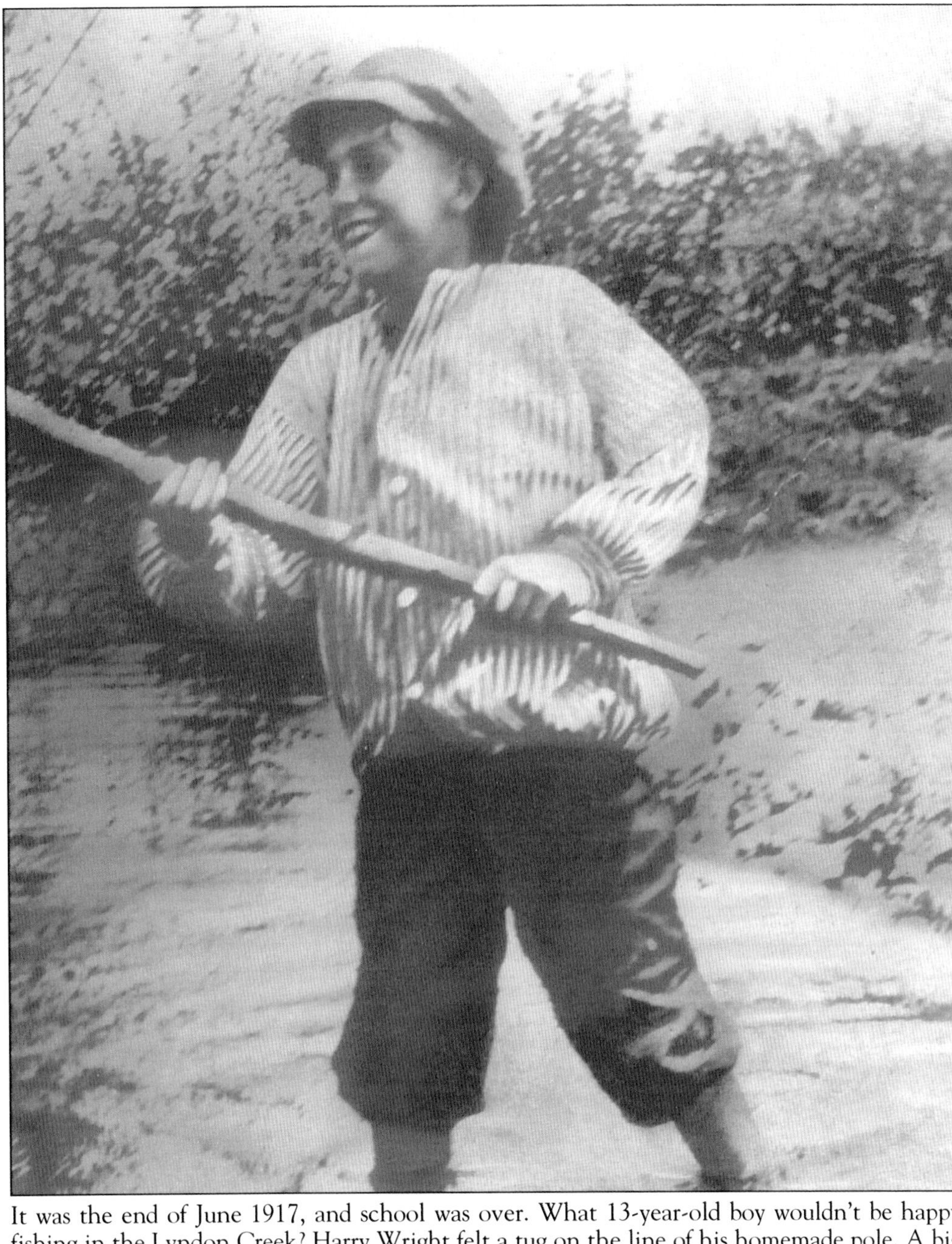

It was the end of June 1917, and school was over. What 13-year-old boy wouldn't be happy fishing in the Lyndon Creek? Harry Wright felt a tug on the line of his homemade pole. A big one! Mama would be happy tonight, especially if he got another. He wiggled his toes in the creek's sandy bottom, knowing he would not need to wear shoes till September. In August, Harry and his brother Neal would go wild berry picking. Two days later, both boys would be seriously ill with the flu, which swept through Juneau County during World War I. Neal would hear his parents say, "We won't have to worry about Harry any more." Harry died in bed on the farm, about one-quarter of a mile from Lyndon Station. Two older brothers survived the front lines in the Battle of the Marne, World War I, 1917–1918. The brothers didn't know Harry was dead until they came home. (Jacqueline Ann.)

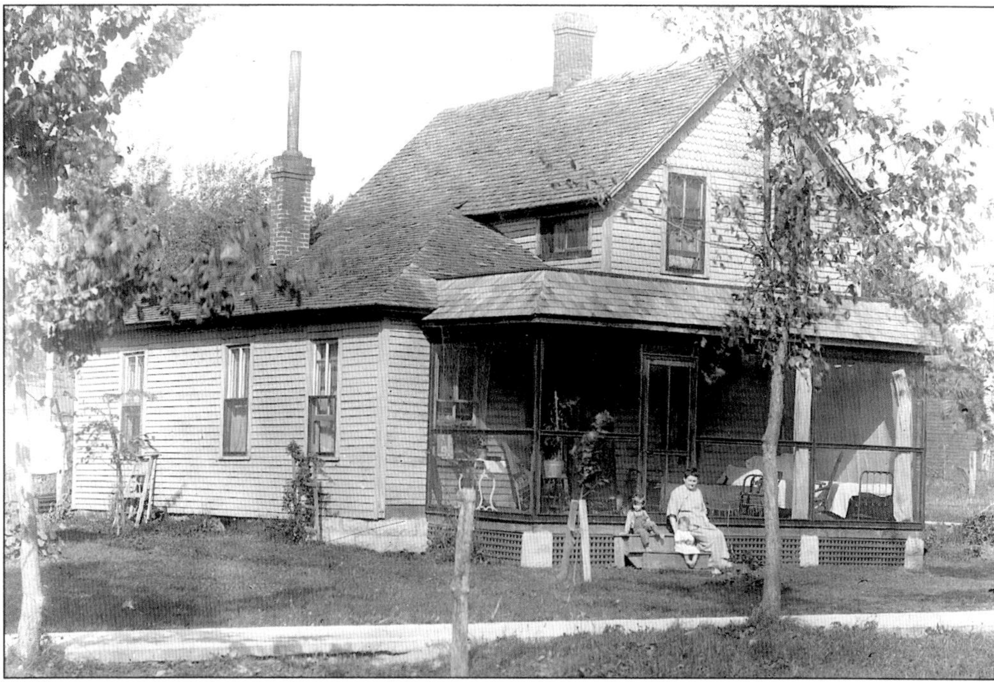

A young mother, just 32, died on this porch, on the cot with the white blanket. She left five children. Nellie Nichols, worried about the care her husband would be giving her children, refused to stay at a sanitarium near Madison. Her mother is pictured here sitting on the steps of their Mauston home with two of Nellie's children. Prayers, good food, and fresh air did not save Nellie's life in 1922. (Jacqueline Ann.)

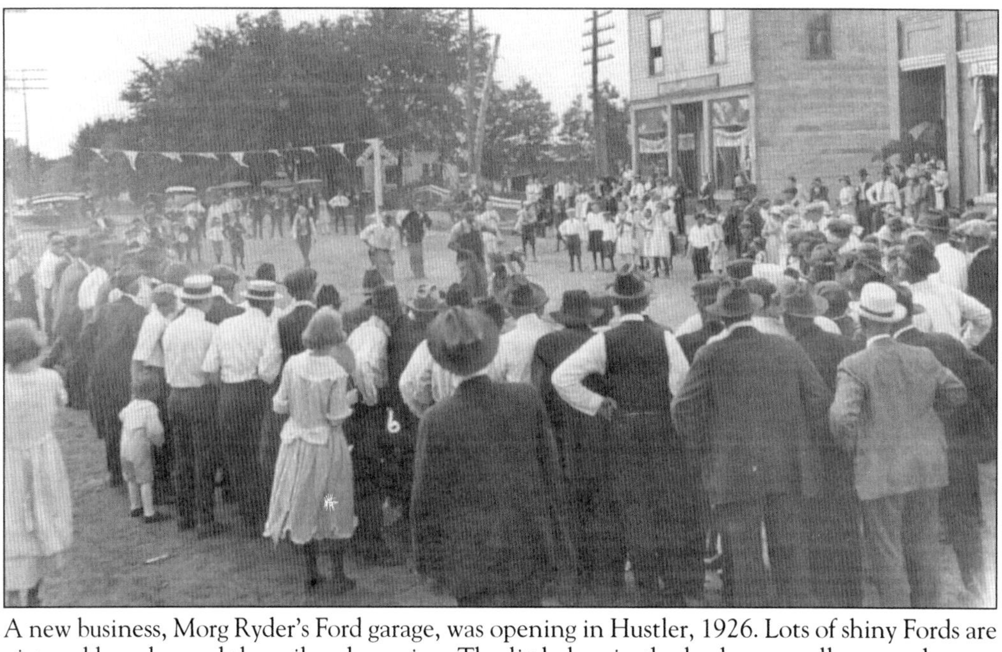

A new business, Morg Ryder's Ford garage, was opening in Hustler, 1926. Lots of shiny Fords are pictured here beyond the railroad crossing. The little boy in the back row really wanted to see his papa win the gunny sack race, but his big brother blocked his view.

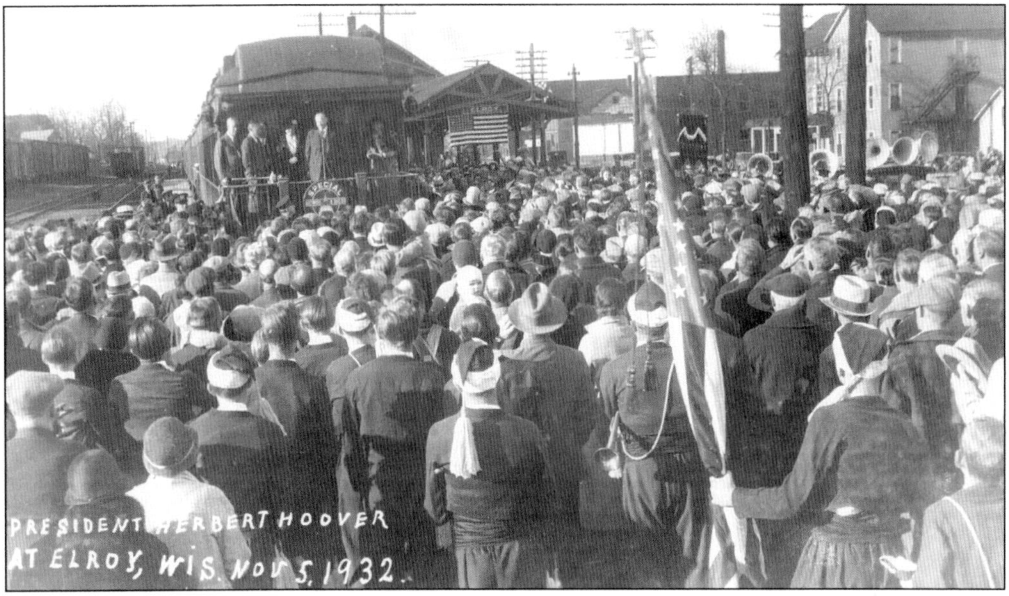

Elroy, a small, unpretentious town in western Juneau County, has great community spirit. The people are proud of who they are and where they come from. They believe in themselves as a community. On November 5, 1932, on his campaign trip around the country, Herbert Hoover stopped to give recognition to the importance of towns like Elroy, which make up the foundation of the United States. (1932, Elroy Historical Society.)

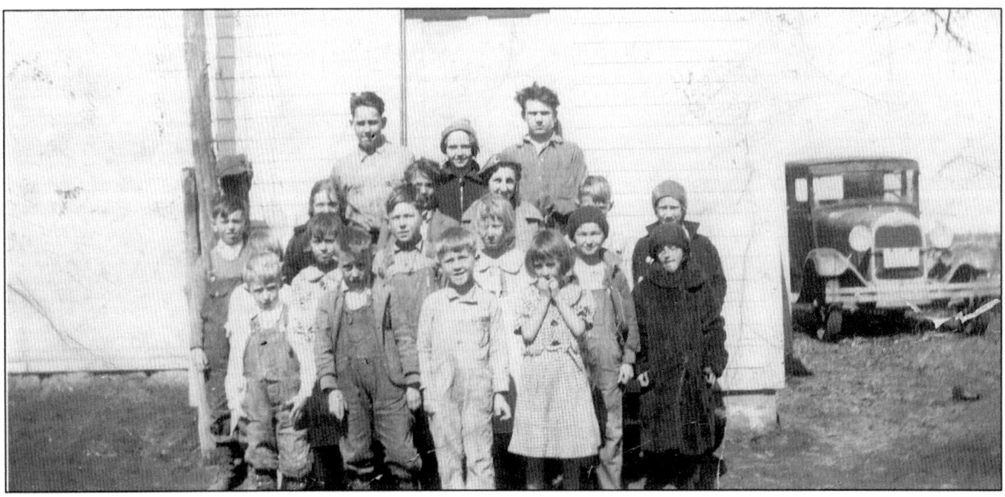

These children in front of the Big Dells School loved their teacher, Miss Mary Timm. She took them on field trips in her Model T. One might think they'd need a bus. Oh, no—double sit, stand on the running boards, hang on—everyone goes! Pictured here are as follows: (front row) John Hall, Henry Hajek, Richard Rogge, and Irene Hajek; (second Row) Francis Hajek, Joe Cauley, Mary Hajek, Dutchis Swab, and Mildred Weber; (third row) Russell Doherty, Swab, unidentified, unidentified, Clarence Hall, and Swab; (back row) Kenneth Cauley, June Cauley, James Cauley, *c.* 1934. From 1936–1939, Gertrude Taylor of Lyndon Station taught at Big Dells School. Pug Hall, who lived across from the school, started the fire for her every morning. Gertrude drove from Lyndon Station to Big Dells. In the winter, the roads were bad, and she broke the track. Her former students say, "She was a good teacher." (Henry Hajek.)

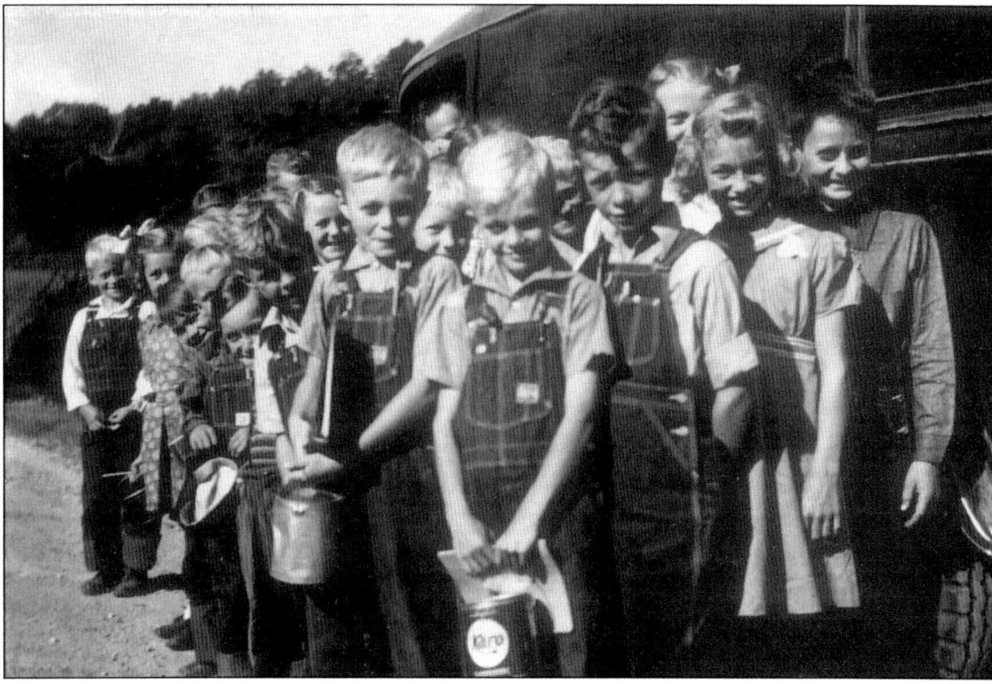

The children waited by their bus to go to Tunnel School. They must have had a wonderful teacher; they seem so happy to be going. The bus was a converted beer truck with wooden planks along each side. Blankets covered the planks. Sometimes it seemed a little dark inside because the only windows were at the windshield and the rear of the truck. Mom packed lunch in the Karo syrup cans. (c. 1937, Claire Ness.)

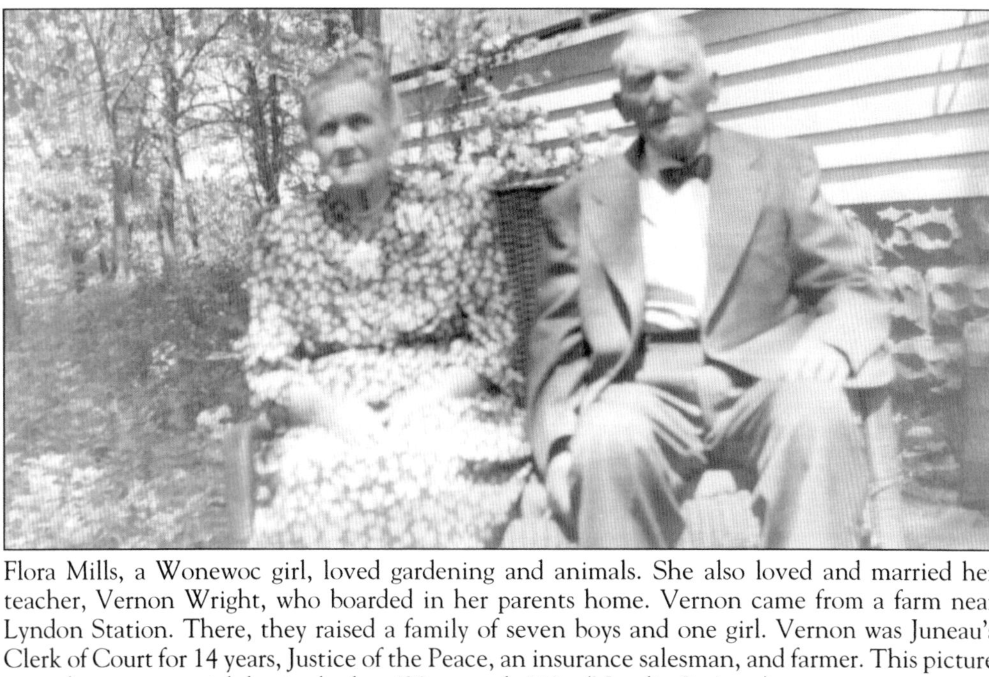

Flora Mills, a Wonewoc girl, loved gardening and animals. She also loved and married her teacher, Vernon Wright, who boarded in her parents home. Vernon came from a farm near Lyndon Station. There, they raised a family of seven boys and one girl. Vernon was Juneau's Clerk of Court for 14 years, Justice of the Peace, an insurance salesman, and farmer. This picture was taken on a special day in the late '30s or early '40s. (Natalie Steiner.)

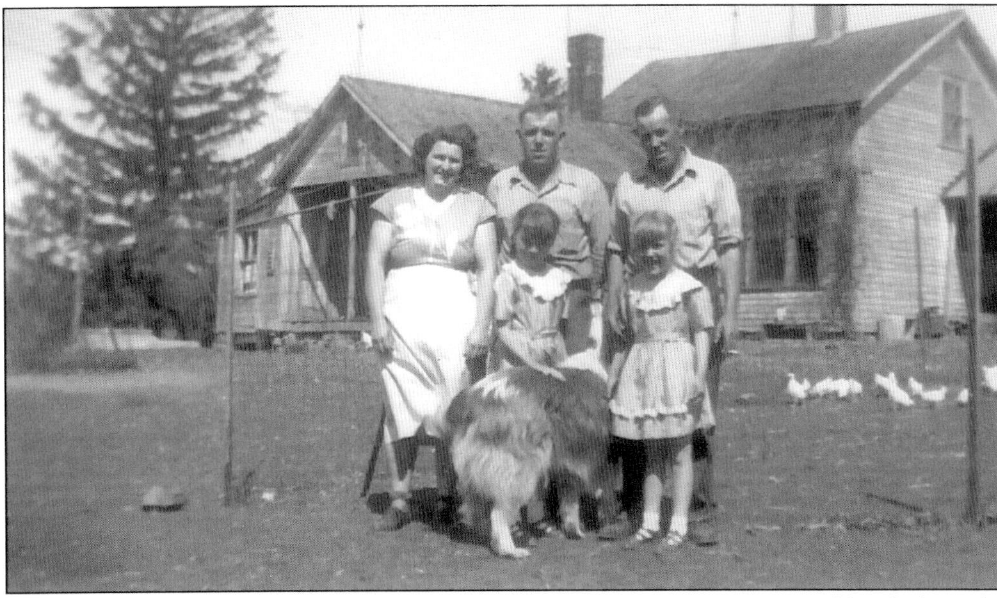

Hazel and Roy Owen remodeled this 140-year-old house (about 170 years old today). Rufus (Roy's brother, pictured right) helped. Marjorie and Marie, Hazel and Roy's daughters, also tried to help. The girls burned down the outhouse as their parents put a new bathroom in the house. The Ballinger family homesteaded this land on February 11, 1817. The Owen family was the sixth family to own the farm. Because the barn was about one-eighth of a mile from the house, the chickens had a room attached to the wood shed, which was connected to the house. A room for the hogs was attached to the chickens' room. Roy and Hazel put up new accommodations for the animals and removed their rooms. (1951, Marie Geitz.)

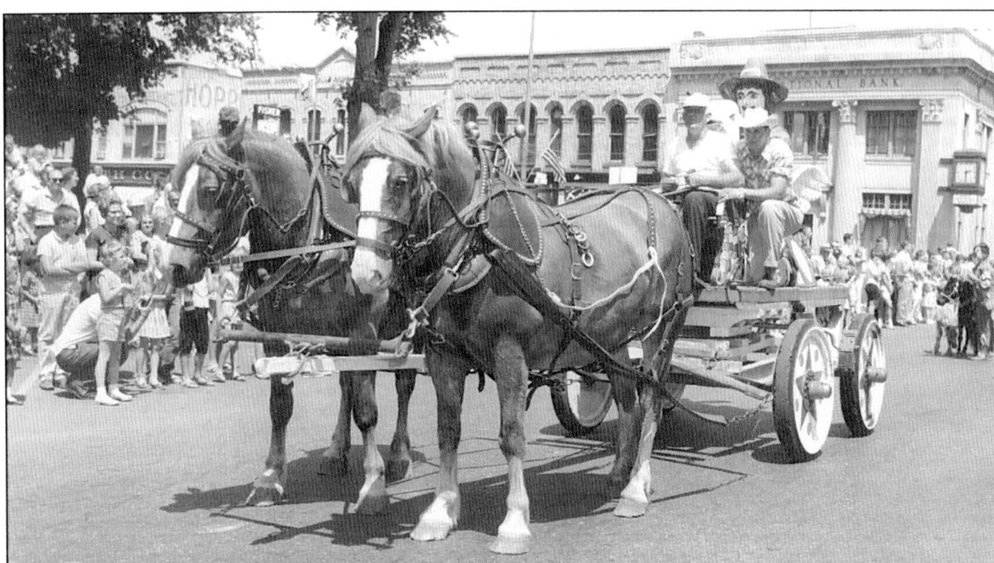

Roy Owen's hobby was driving and caring for his team of Belgium horses. He and his wife Hazel thought the Belgiums were the best part of the Baraboo parade in 1975. Folks often saw Roy and Hazel driving their team around LaValle and the surrounding countryside. They bought the horses when they were eight months old and always kept them together. (Hazel Owen.)

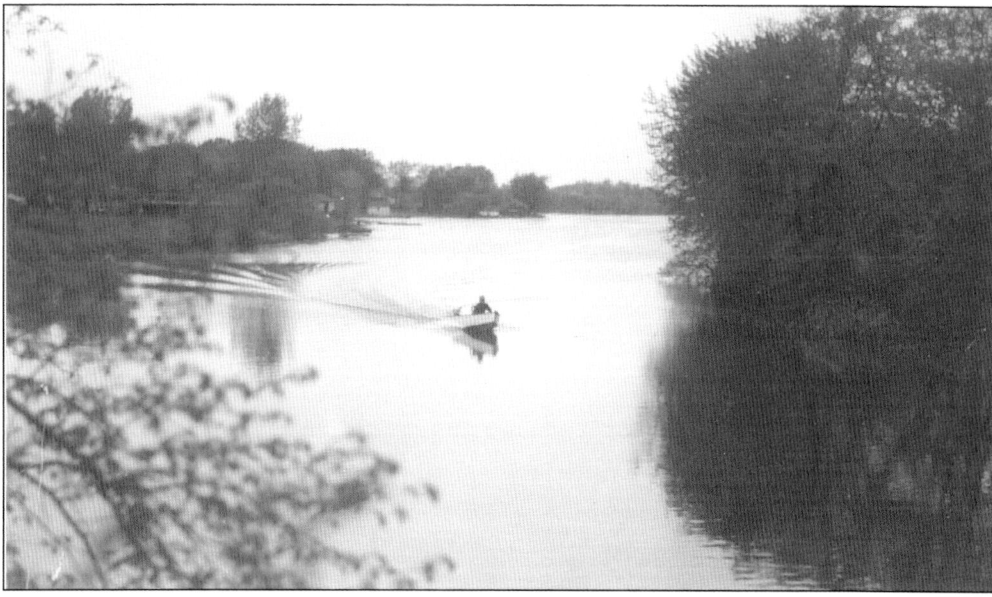

Murl Briggs was born on November 11, 1885, in Juneau County and loved the Lemonweir River. Every day, weather permitting, he went up "The Pike." The fish community offered him sunfish, blue gills, small and large mouth bass, crappies, northern, walleyed pike, perch, rock bass, sturgeon, suckers, bullheads, red horse, and dogfish. Murl never threw away a fish and never ate one either. He cleaned them and gave them away. The Lemonweir is a picturesque river meandering southeast across the southern part of Juneau County into the Wisconsin River. (Jacqueline Ann.)

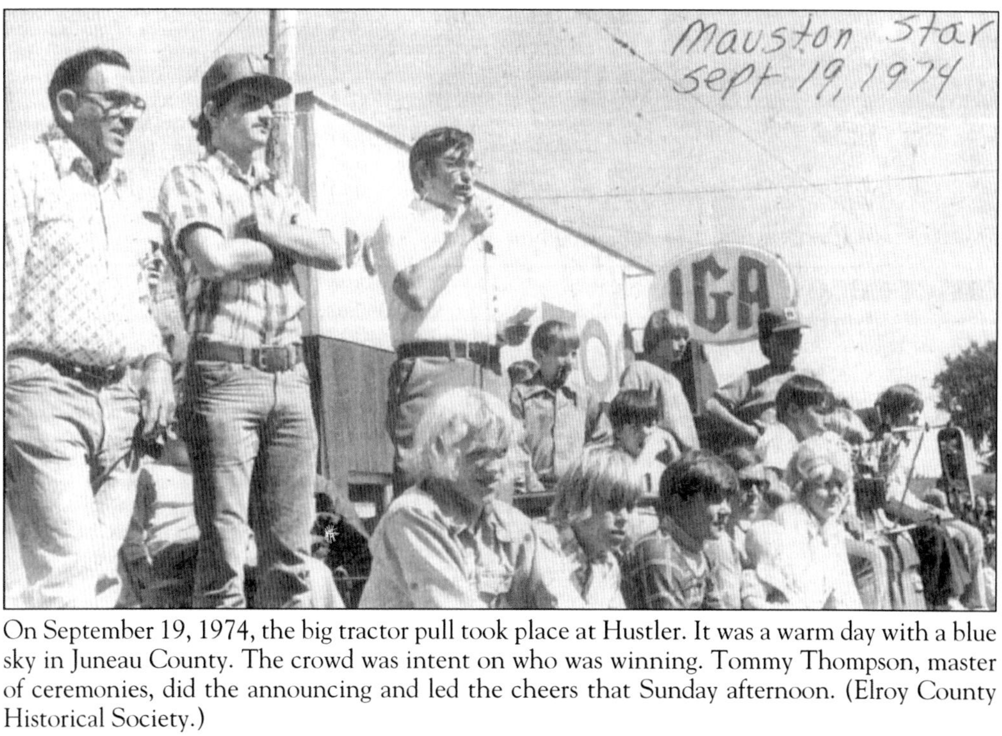

On September 19, 1974, the big tractor pull took place at Hustler. It was a warm day with a blue sky in Juneau County. The crowd was intent on who was winning. Tommy Thompson, master of ceremonies, did the announcing and led the cheers that Sunday afternoon. (Elroy County Historical Society.)

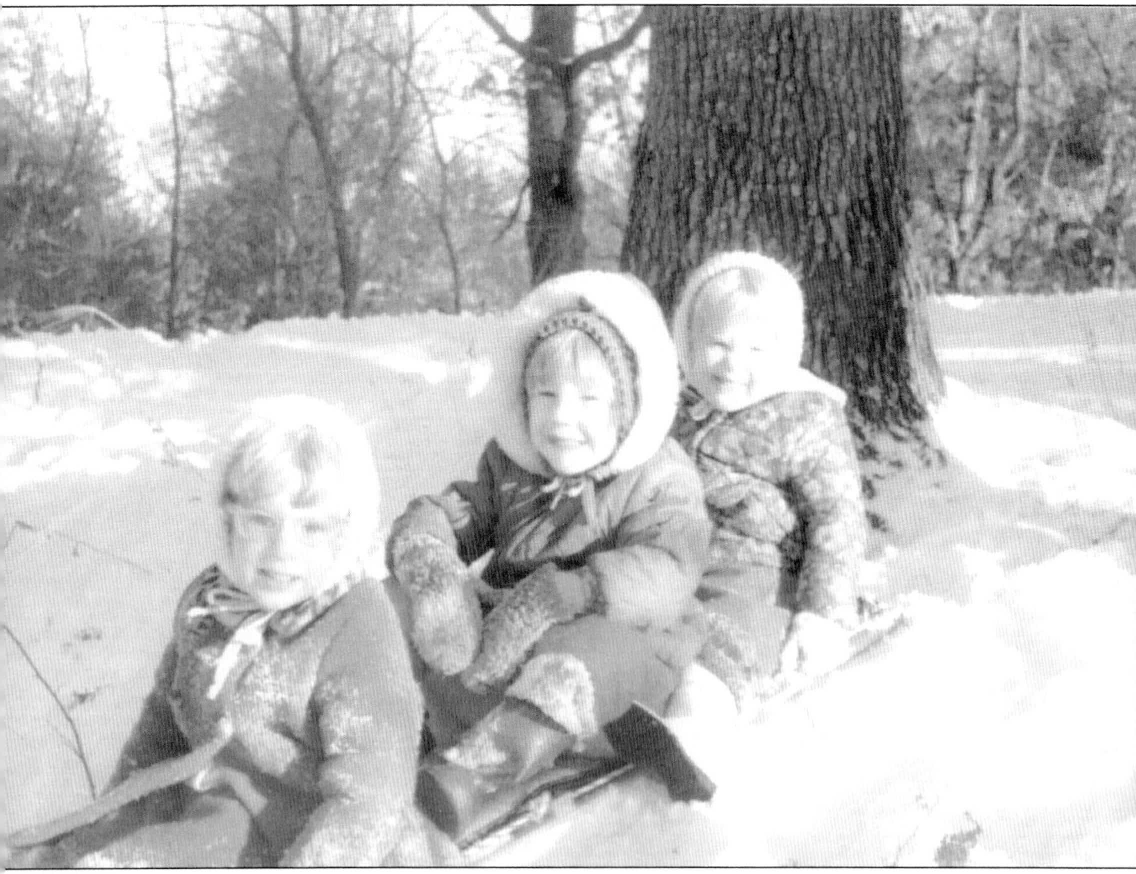

The girls, Lynn, Kristi, and Sheila Geitz, were thrilled by the first snowfall of 1970. Mom got the toboggan out and helped with the boots and zippers. The sun was bright, the air was crisp, and the girls were warm in their padded winter clothes. The air carried giggles and happy little-girl voices. (Lynn Geitz.)

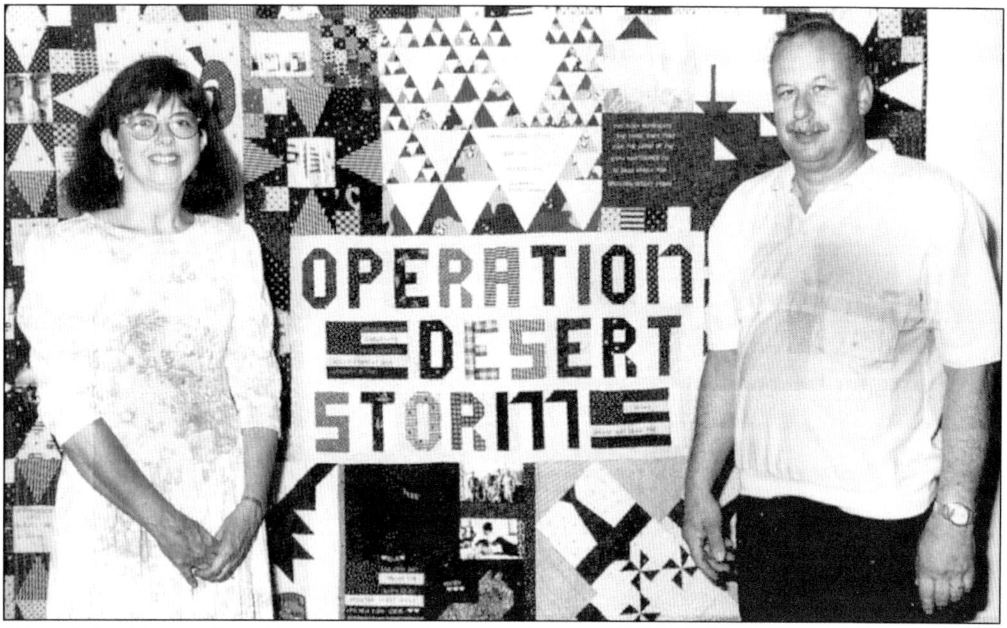

When John Diny of Reedsburg went to Saudi Arabia, Linda, his wife, made a quilt, putting her love and pain into each block to tell the story of what was happening to her and to John. The fabric had stars, stripes, and plaids in red, white, and blue. The blocks showed ships carrying cargo, planes flying the troops, and the Christmas she spent without him. (1995, Sauk County Historical Society.)

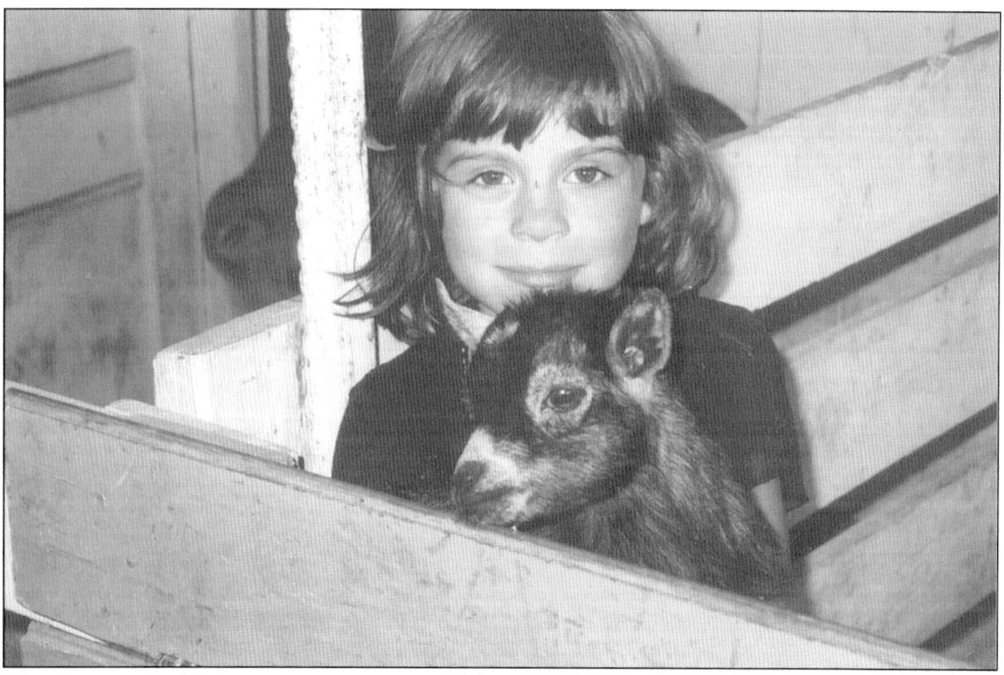

The desire to hold the pygmy goat caused Charitee Logan Seebecker to sneak into the little goat's pen. It was a special moment for the five-year-old girl at the Juneau County Fair, 2000, in the small animal barn. (Sheila Z.)

Two

VILLAGES AND TOWNS

All of life's lessons can be learned,
In your villages and towns.

Sites were chosen by white settlers for the same reasons that Indians had previously chosen them. Towns were formed near rivers for transportation and power, near woods for building materials, game for food, and good soil for crops.

When the settlers first came, they lived in log shanties or in (or under) their wagons. Their first homes were log cabins. If there were sawmills near providing lumber, frame homes could be built.

Schools and churches were the first community buildings built by the settlers.

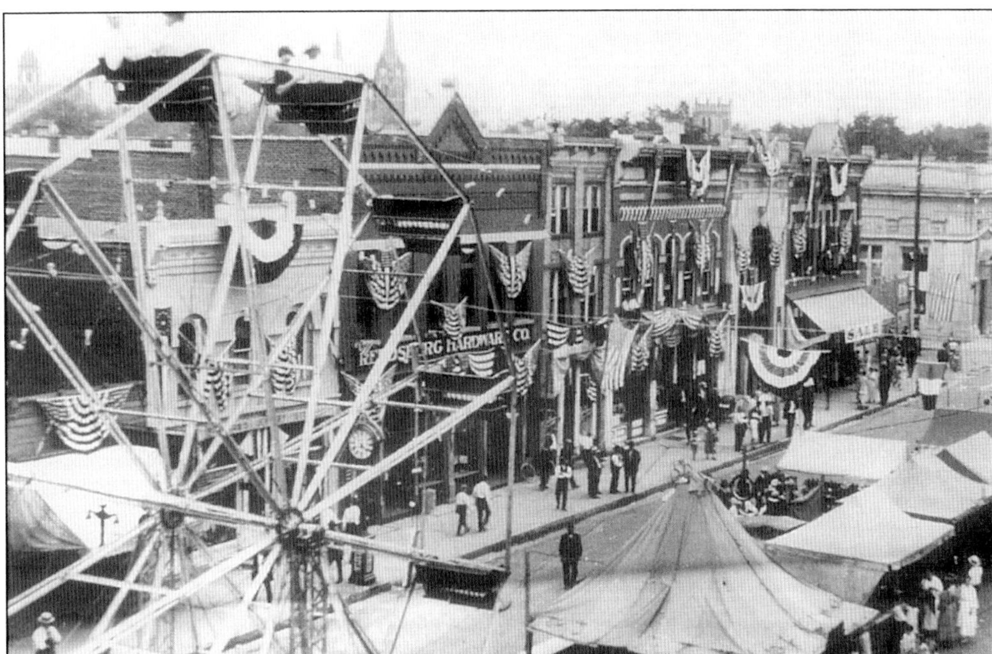

A Reedsburg firemen's celebration is captured in this photograph. (1924, Reedsburg History Committee.)

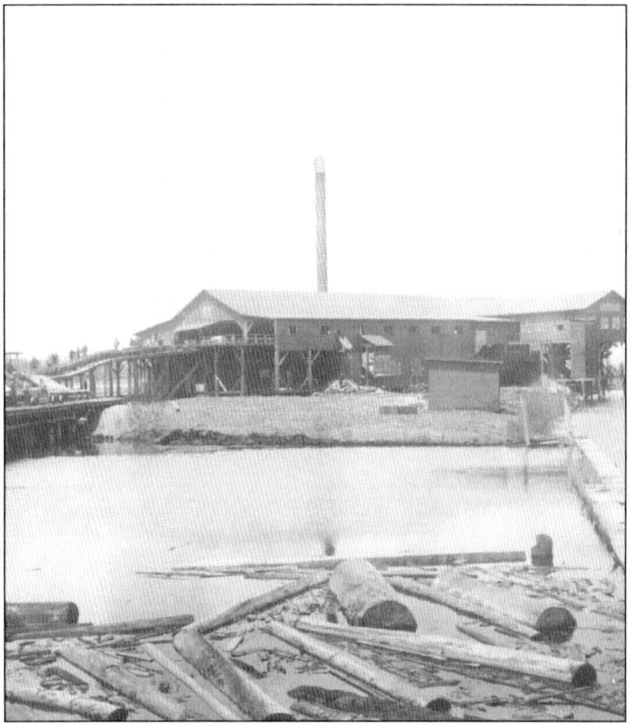

Tom Weston began building the Tom Weston and Company Sawmill in 1848, and it was completed in 1849. Necedah was built around the mill. Tom Weston, Eliphalet S. Miner, and John T. Kingston controlled the lumbering Company. Joseph Babcock took control of the company and used its influences to aid him in his election to the United States Congress. When the supply of lumber ran out, the company became a real estate operation specializing in the sale of drainage district lands and other cutover properties. (Juneau County Historical Society.)

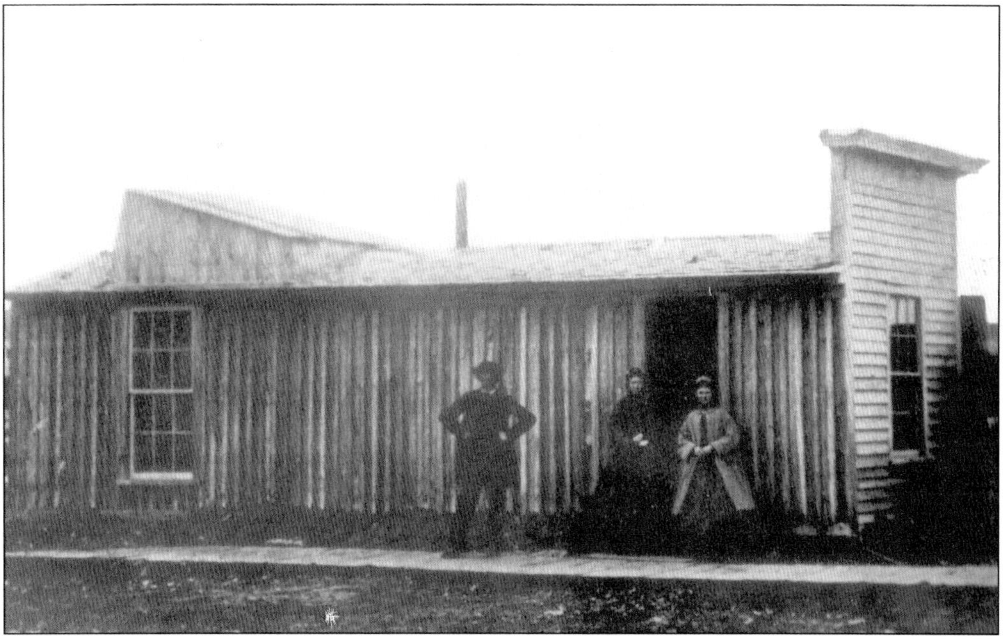

This is the first photography studio in Mauston, with board sidewalks and dirt road. The board sidewalks could be a hazard to children who seldom wore shoes in the summer. Slivers were common, and knotholes were filled with pitch. On Halloween, pranksters tipped sections of the sidewalks up. Property owners would often need to repair their sidewalks at this time. Children would search the sand below the sidewalks for stray coins. (1854, Juneau County Historical Society.)

Henry Gardner Briggs married Josephine Sarah Delap on December 24, 1882. This is their wedding picture taken at a photographer's studio in Mauston. Josephine was 17, and Henry was 29. He managed a lumber company in Mauston and built many homes there. Josie frequently advised young women in her family: "Twenty-five is young enough for a woman to marry. If it's the right man, it's enough time, if it's the wrong man, it's more than enough time." (Jacqueline Ann.)

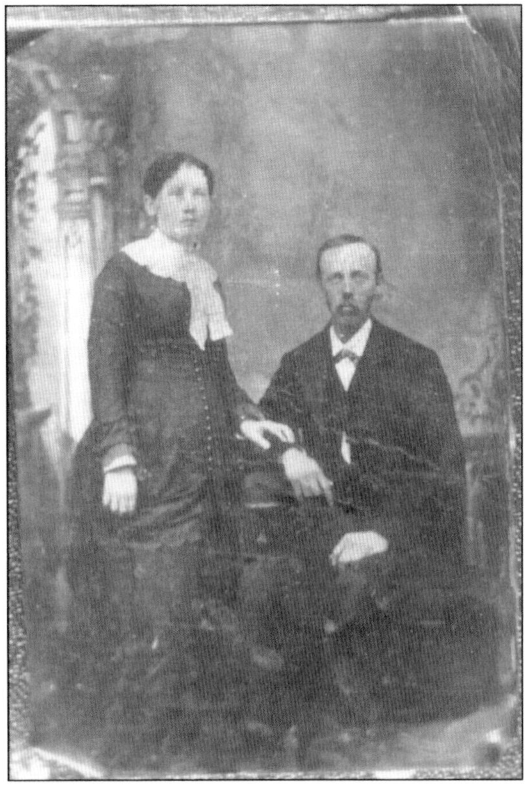

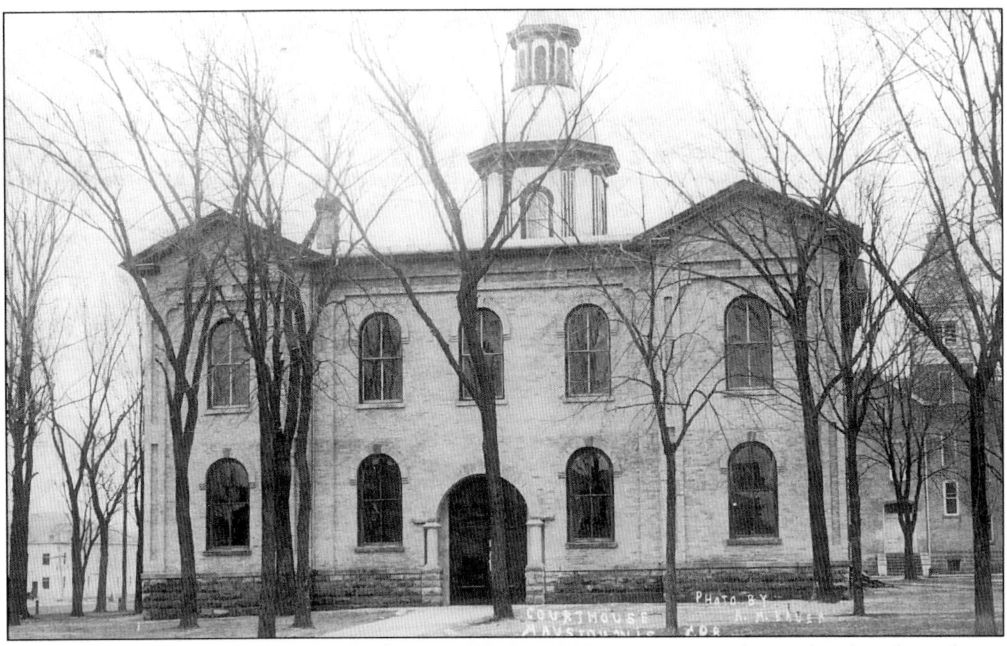

The Mauston Court house was built in 1875. In 1890, an octagonal wooden bandstand was built on the courthouse square. During World War I, young women sang war songs from the stand. A new courthouse with a county jail on the top floor was built in 1941. (Juneau County Historical Society.)

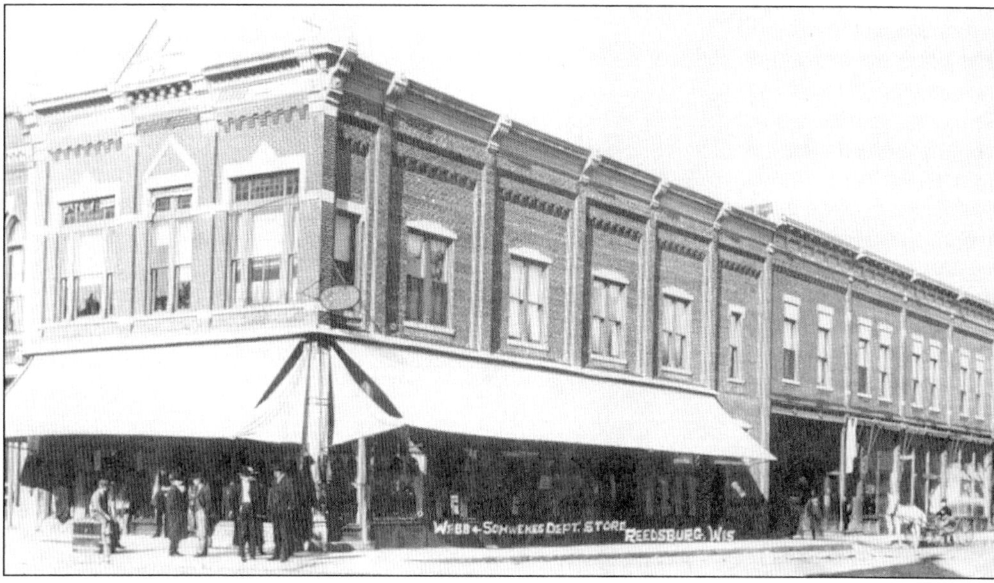

The general store was the most important business in a village. Residents of an area sold their products and supplied their needs through the general store. Schweke and Webb's Big Store in Reedsburg was the biggest store in Sauk County in the 1880s. (Reedsburg History Committee.)

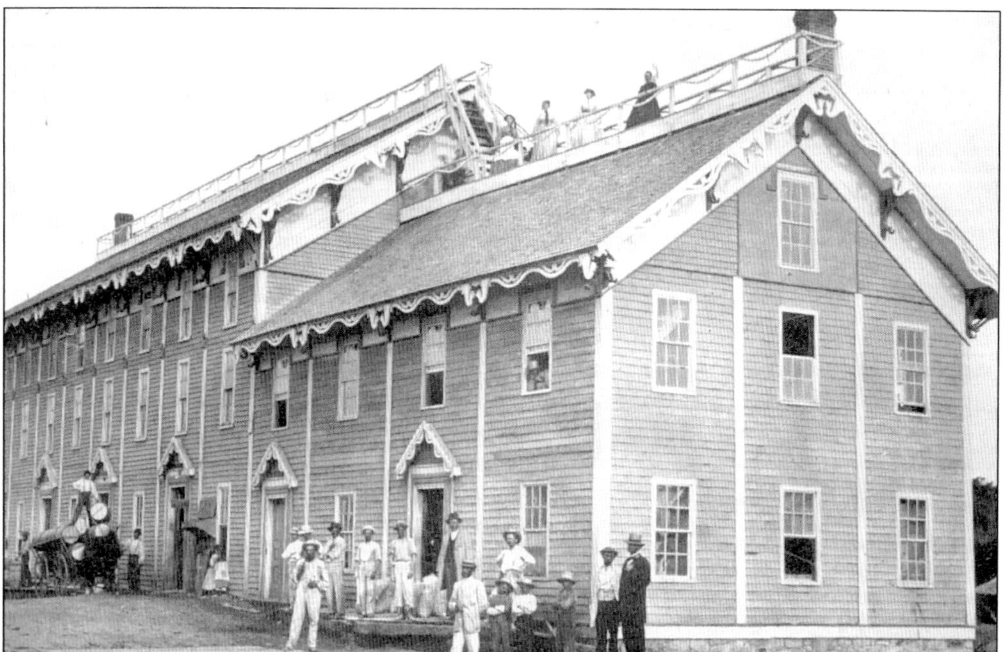

The Bassitt Mill at Baraboo was appreciated by the farmers of that area. Wheat was the first and most important crop until the late 1870s. The farmers brought their wheat to the Bassitt Mill and shipped it into the Baraboo stores, helping the economy. (1855, Sauk County Historical Society.)

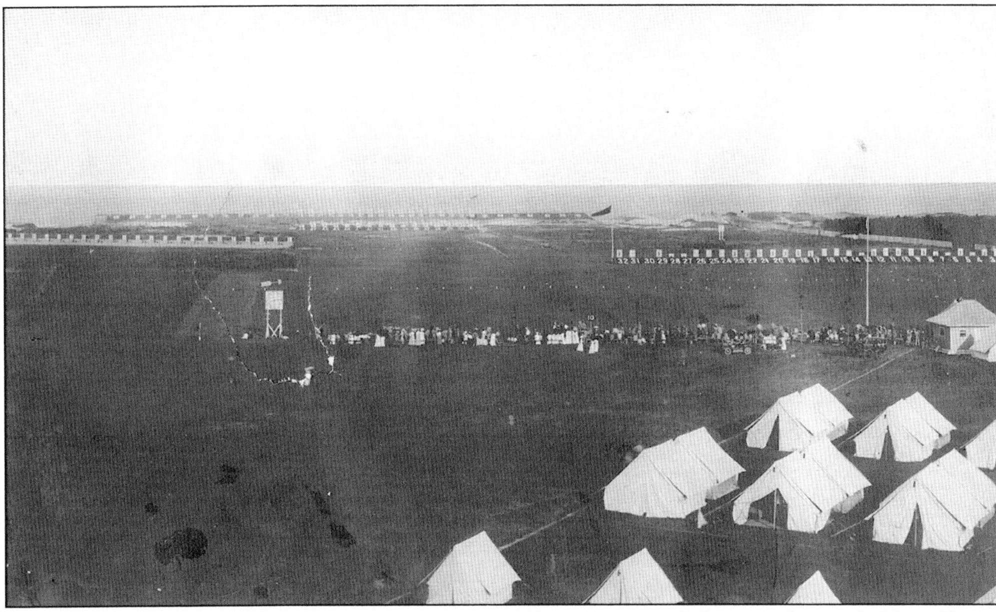

This is the small arms firing range at Camp Williams, 1909. Adjutant General Chandler P. Williams used personal funds to buy 440 acres to be used as an encampment site for regiments of the National Guard of Wisconsin to train and practice with their weapons. At Camp Douglas, a village 4-miles away, volunteers cleared brush from a 100 by 600-yard strip to create the first firing range. The first military group to use the camp did so in 1888. (Claire Ness.)

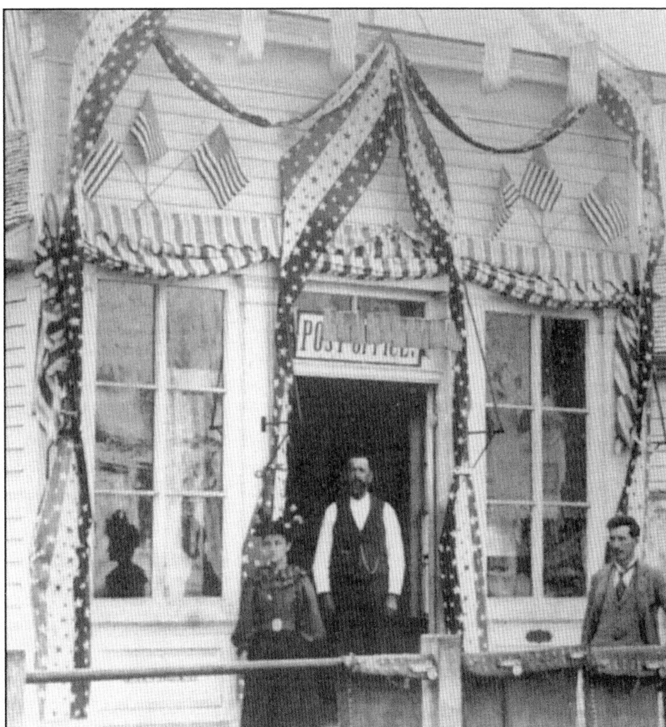

Most of the early settlers in Sauk City came from the east. These pioneers were accustomed to having postal service, so obtaining a post office in their village was a great achievement. (1890s, Sauk County Historical Society.)

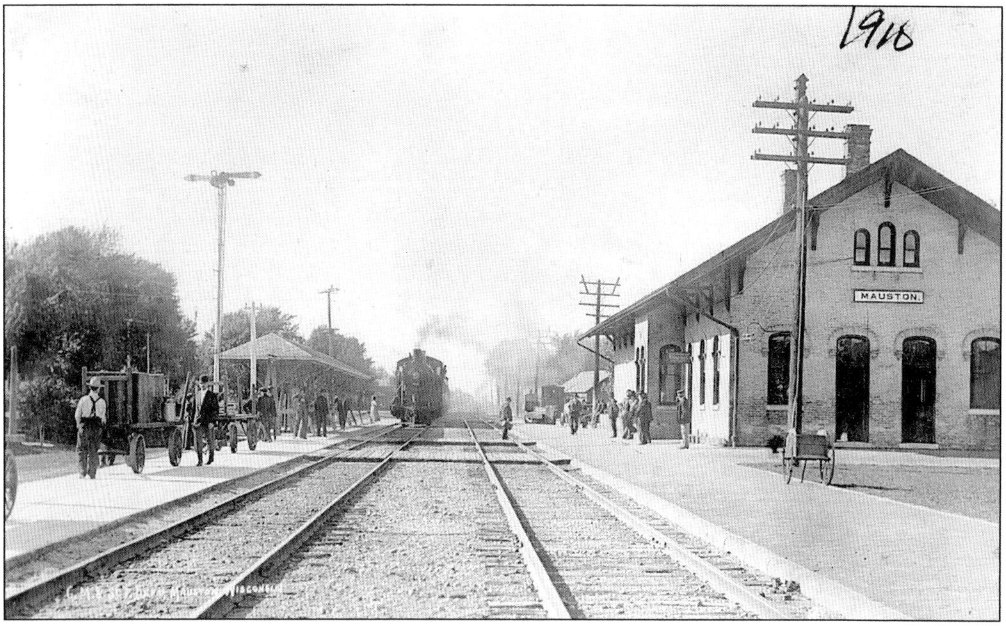

An important cream-colored, brick building, the Milwaukee Road Depot was at the hub of the city of Mauston. The station agent set the "regulator" timepiece daily after the correct time was wired to him. Townspeople set their watches by the station clock. All raw materials and manufactured items came to Mauston by rail in the late 1800s and early 1900s. Large stacks of lumber sat by the tracks. Hops, wheat, and potatoes were stored in sheds by the tracks, and animals and fuel also had their place near the tracks. (Juneau County Historical Society.)

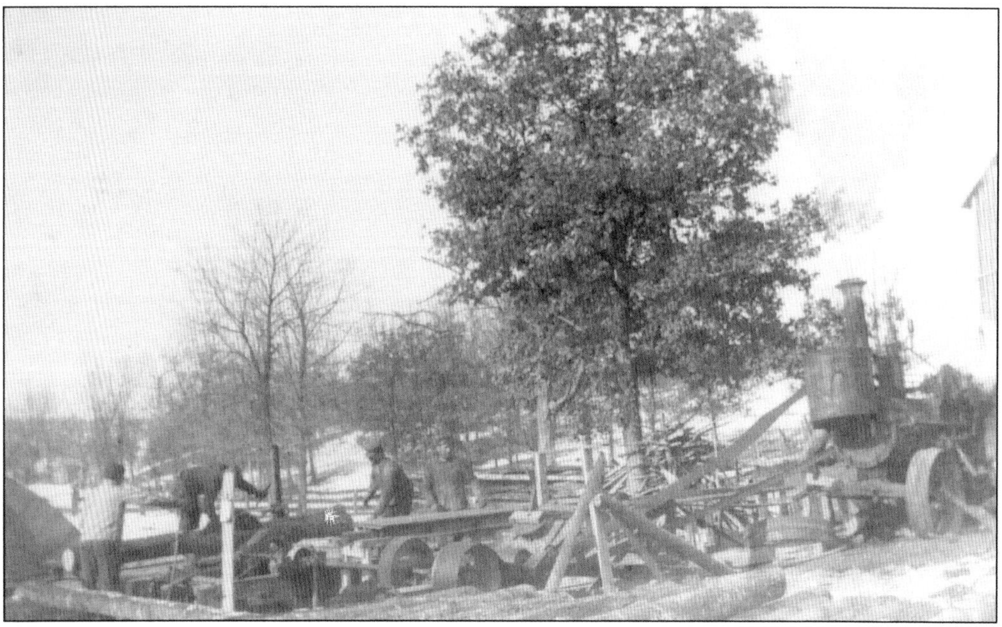

Early settlers were always concerned about building their schools and churches. Their children needed an education, and everyone needed spiritual direction. The men pictured here are cutting and sawing logs for the Carr Valley Church. (1900, Hazel Owen)

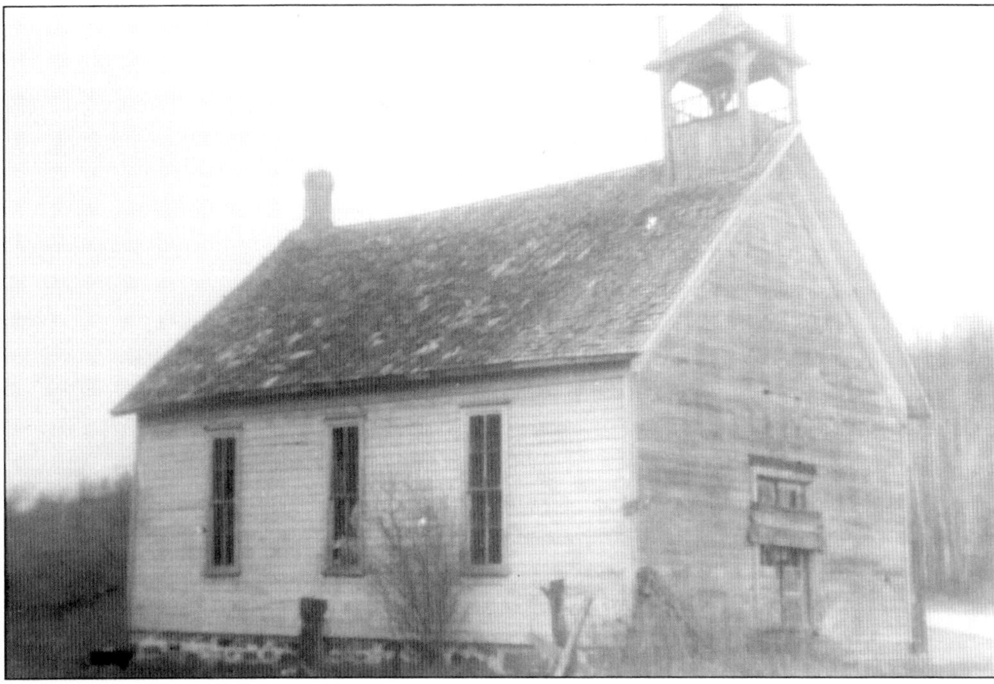

John Deitzman donated the land for the Carr Valley Church. He and other volunteers built the church *c.* 1900. It was a Methodist church with a capacity of about 90 people. When the church was no longer in use, the land once again became part of the farm from which it had been taken. (Hazel Owen.)

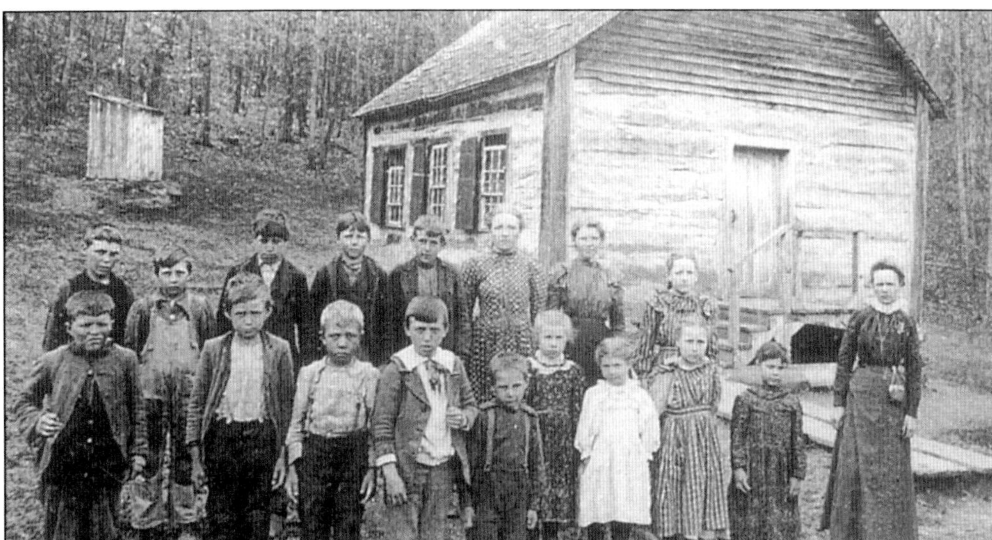

The first community building that the pioneers would erect was the public school. This school was named Fernside because of the fern-covered hill behind it. Each Arbor Day, the teacher and children had a clean-up day, raking the leaves and trash into piles and burning them. On Arbor Day, *c.* 1926, the busy children and teacher got the burning trash too close to the school, and the building burned down. The community built a new and better school. (1900, Sauk County Historical Society.)

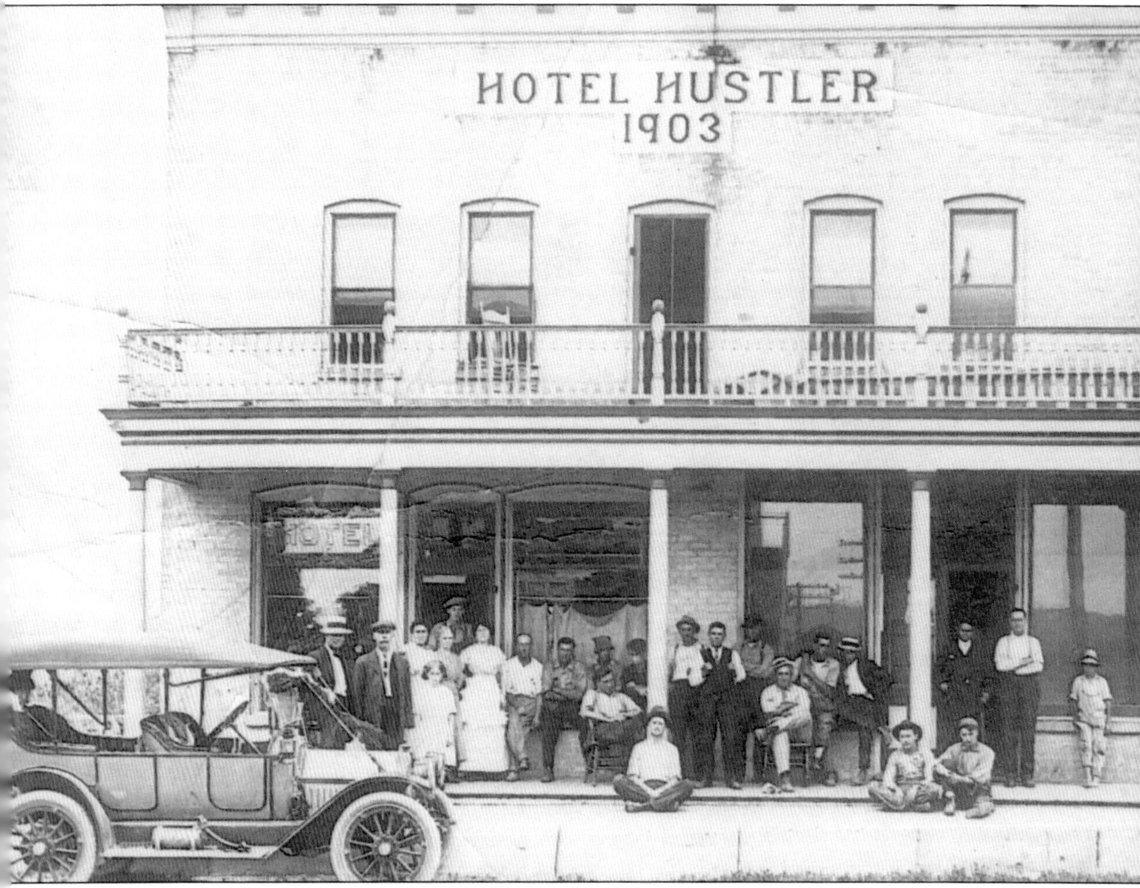

The Hustler Hotel was near the railroad tracks. Passengers from the train went to the hotel or to a nearby tavern if they wanted coffee or lunch, and then hurried back to the train. Hustler got its name because the town's early business people were such hustlers. (1903, Claire Ness.)

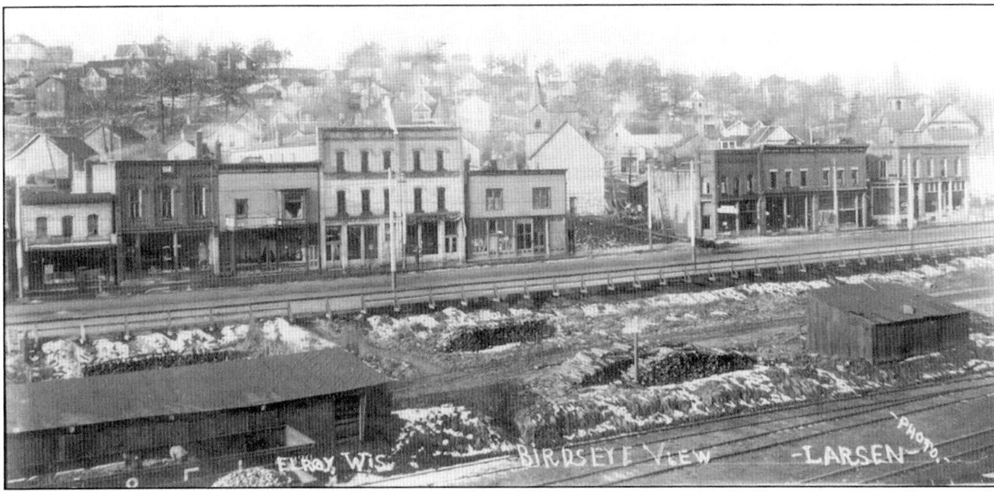

In 1909, Elroy, Wisconsin, was a small town nestled in the hills of Juneau County. Pictured here is Main Street with Second Main Street behind it. Main Street faces the railroad, the hub of the community. The steeples of two of Elroy's seven churches can be seen behind the empty lot and to the right. Ice cream socials, band concerts, and patriotic programs often were held on the vacant lot. A path went from the lot to the Methodist Church and other places on Second Main Street. (Elroy Historical Society.)

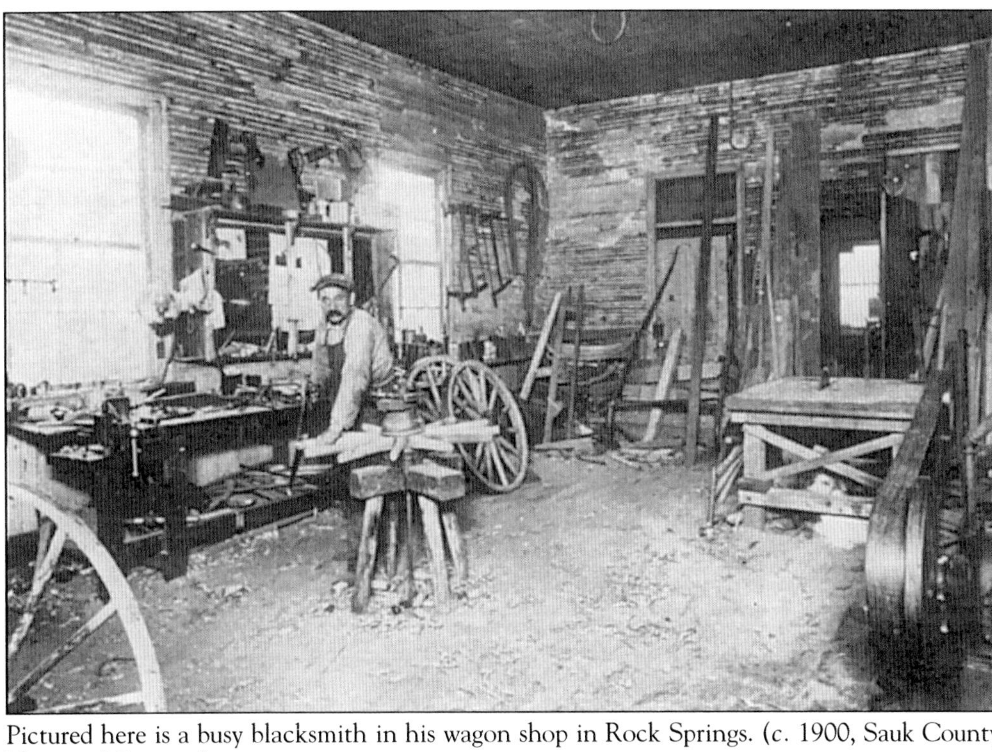
Pictured here is a busy blacksmith in his wagon shop in Rock Springs. (c. 1900, Sauk County Historical Society.)

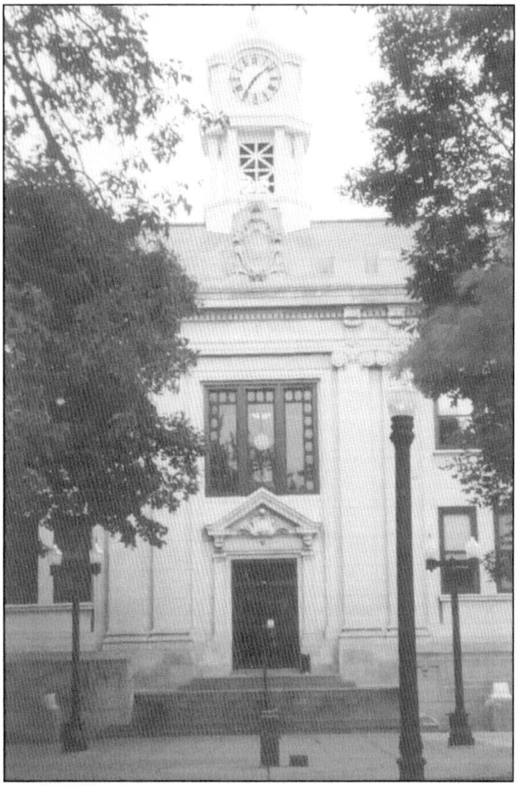

This is the entrance to the Baraboo Courthouse, which sits on a square of land in the downtown area, surrounded by streets and businesses. It was built in 1906. When more room was needed for Sauk County business, an addition was added in 1963. The jail was part of the addition. Another addition was needed, so a large, modern building called West Square was constructed across the street from the courthouse. It was ready for use in 1995. Reedsburg was the original county seat of Sauk County. (Jacqueline Ann.)

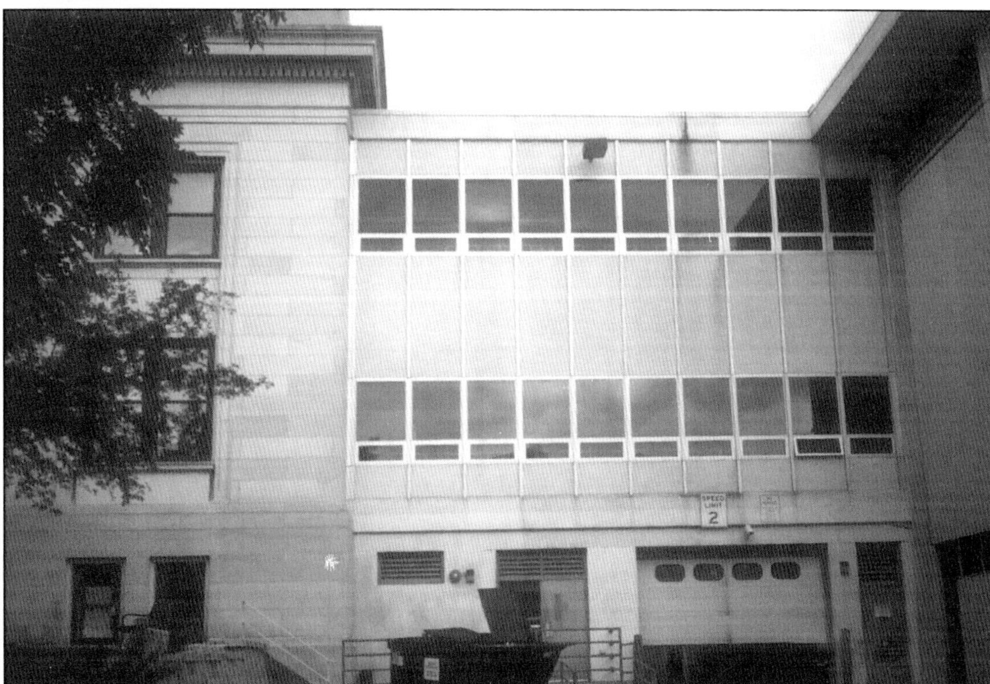

The addition that was added to the Baraboo courthouse in 1963 is the section of the building, pictured here, where the two rows of windows begin. (Kathryn Wu.)

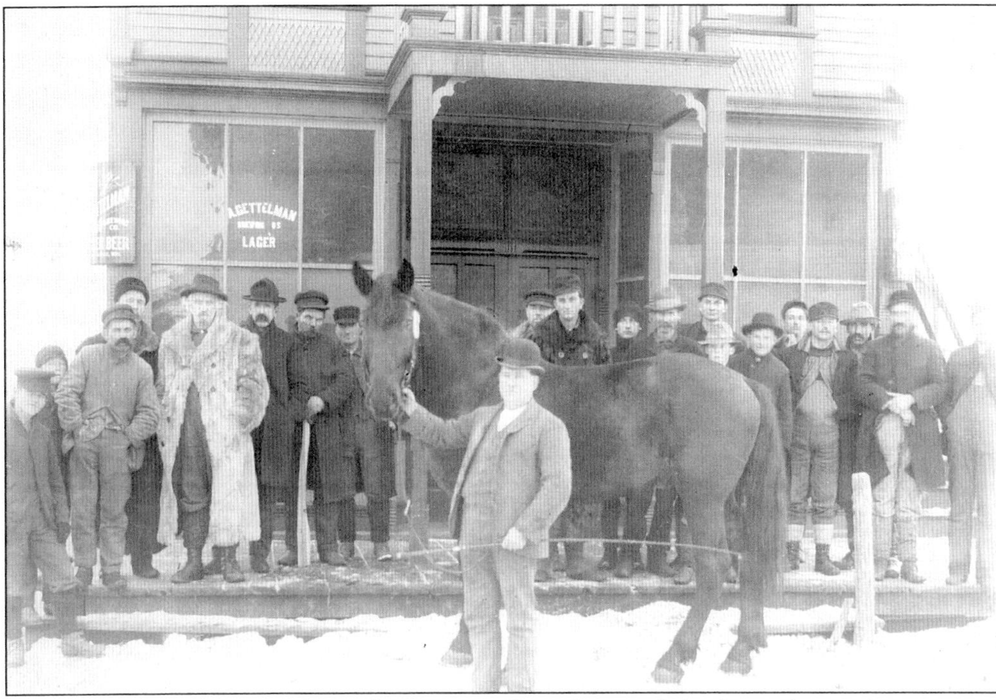

We don't know what story this Irishman was telling about with his horse, but we know it must have been a good one to lure all the patrons out of the saloon in Lyndon Station. Notice the man in the buffalo coat. (1910, Juneau County Historical Society.)

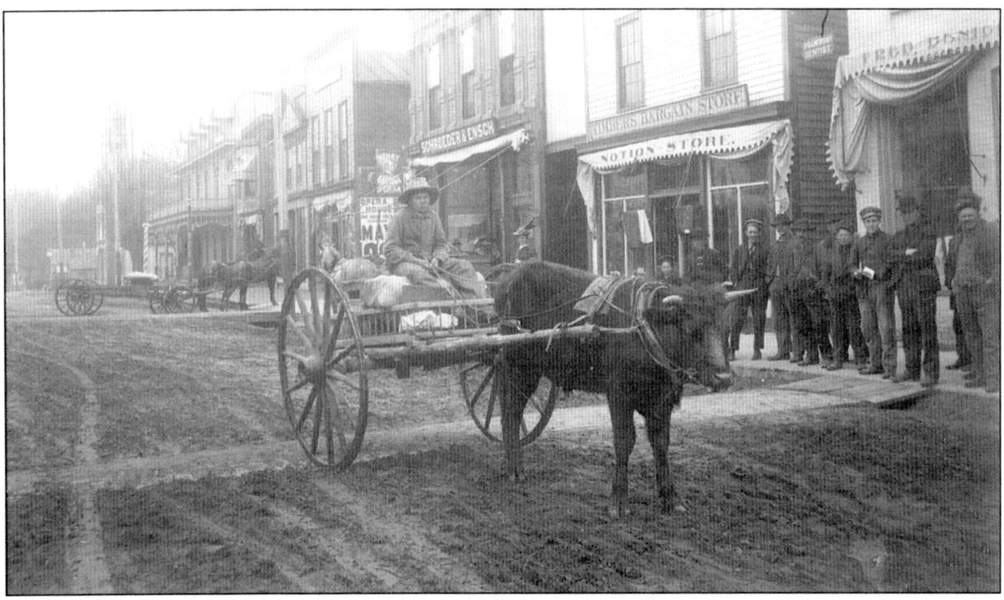

Pictured here is one of the last ox carts on State Street in Mauston, 1912. The first settlers used oxen more than horses because oxen could live on wild fodder, and if times became hard, oxen could be used as stew meat. Horses worked and traveled faster than oxen, but some farmland had to be used for their feed. As the farmer became more prosperous, he switched from oxen to horsepower. (Juneau County Historical Society.)

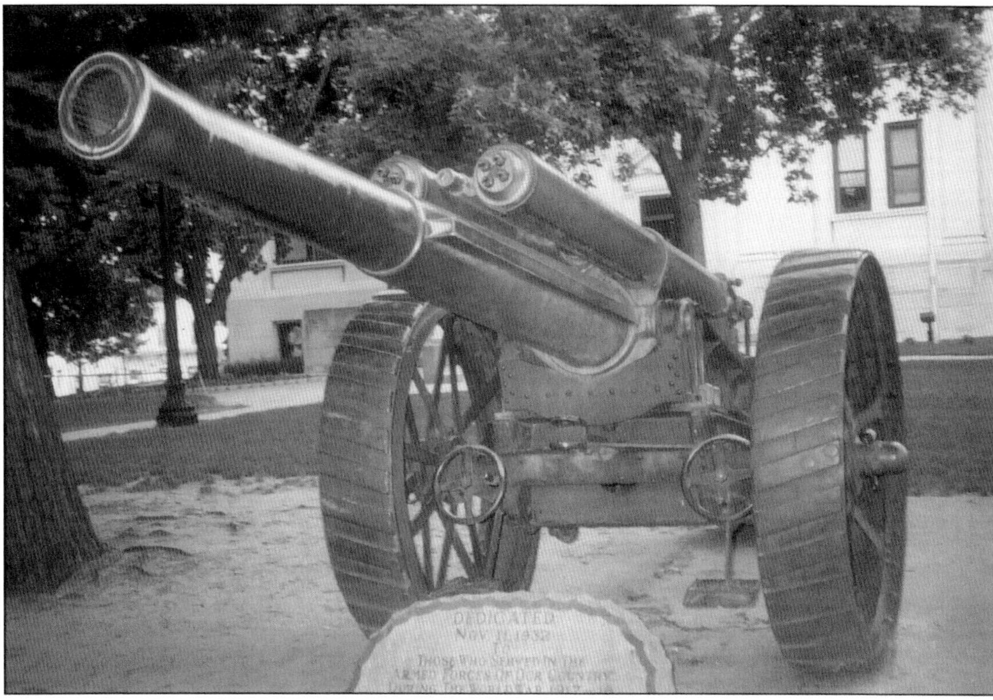

A cannon is pictured here in front of the old courthouse at Baraboo. The big gun is a memorial to the armed forces of World War I, dedicated by disabled veterans of the World War, Chapter Eight, Veterans of Foreign Wars, Post 2336. (1917, Jacqueline Ann.)

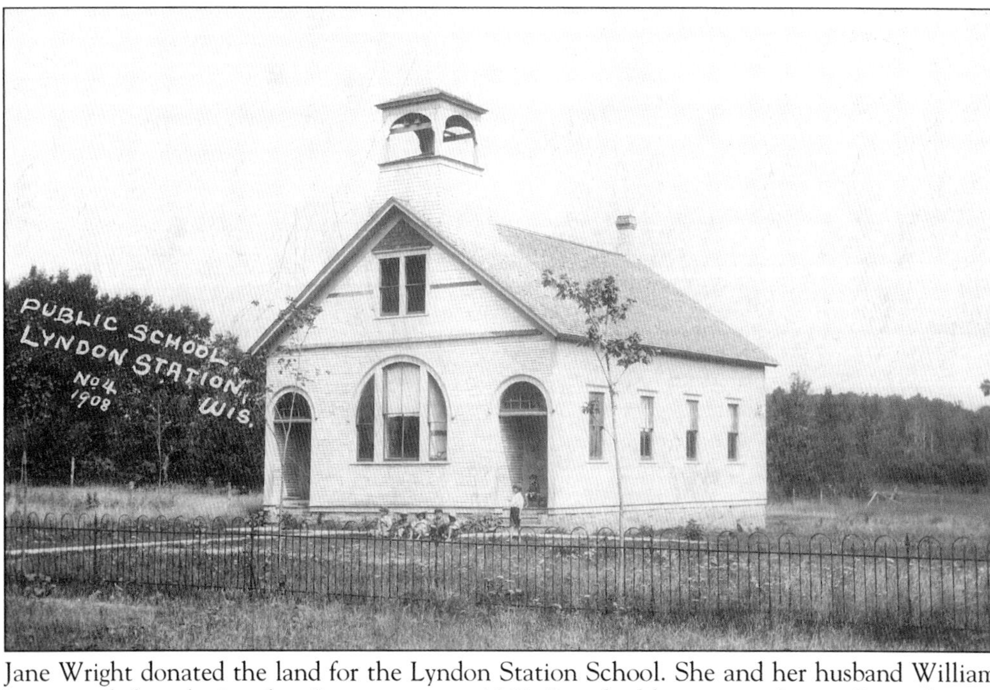

Jane Wright donated the land for the Lyndon Station School. She and her husband William homesteaded in the Lyndon Station area in 1852. Jane had been a teacher in Pennsylvania. Vernon Wright, Jane's son, taught at the Lyndon School. (1908, Mary Jean Cauley.)

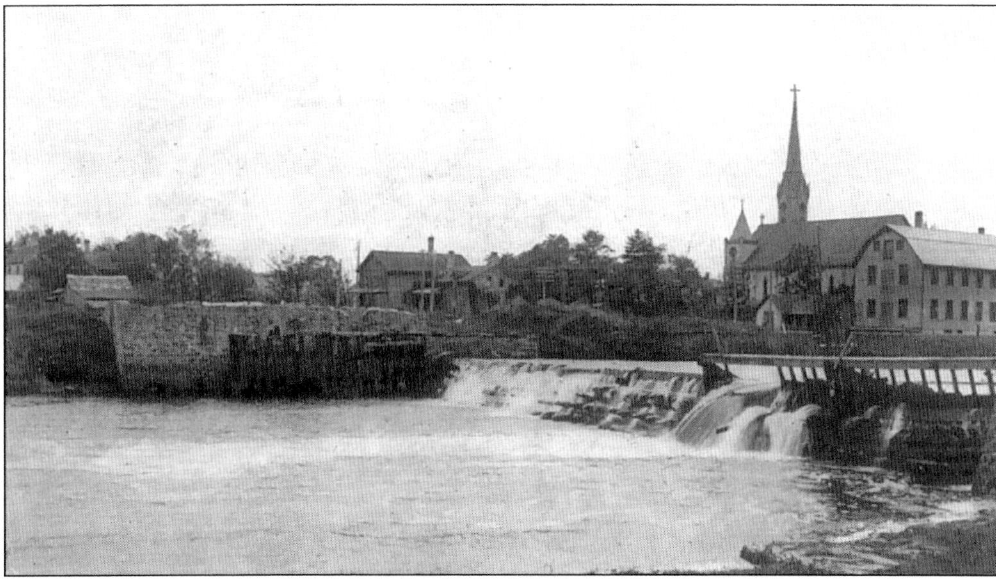

Mauston was given its name by Milton Maughs, who filed the original plat for the village that became Juneau's County seat. Mauston began beside the Lemonweir River with a stone and timber dam and a sawmill. The mill also ground grain. After several owners, Milton Maughs purchased the mill. Mansion Street was parallel to the river and had the original businesses and industrial companies. As the village expanded, new sawmills located up-river, and businesses moved south on Union Street and west on State Street. State Street became the village's main street. (1914, Juneau County Historical Society.)

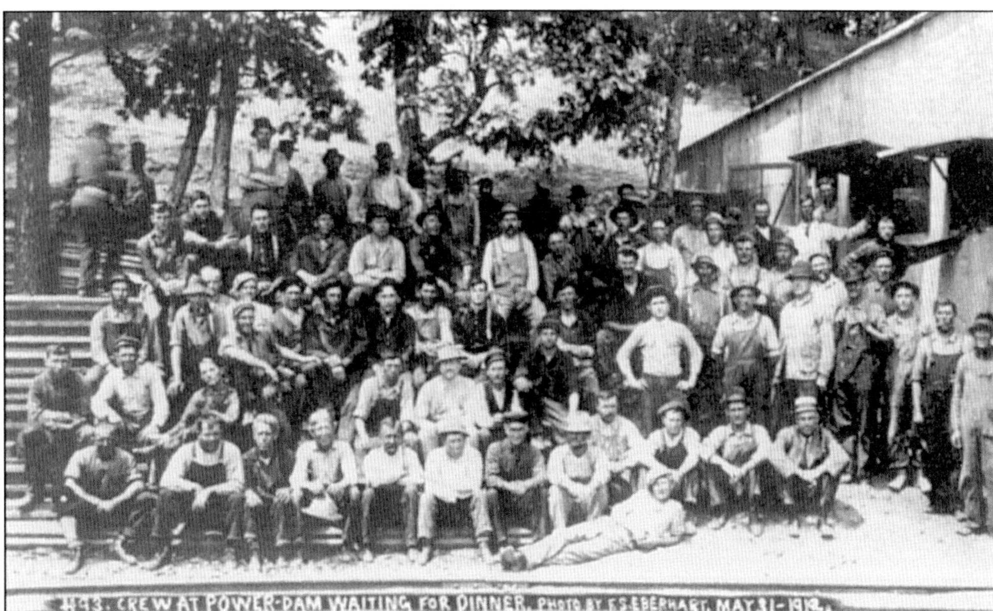

Dams were a necessity for early and continued electrical power in the villages and towns of Juneau and Sauk Counties. These workers are hungry and need dinner. They have been working at the Prairie du Sac hydroelectric project. In 1915, the dam was finished. The dam backed up the Wisconsin River and created Lake Wisconsin. (1912, Sauk County Historical Society.)

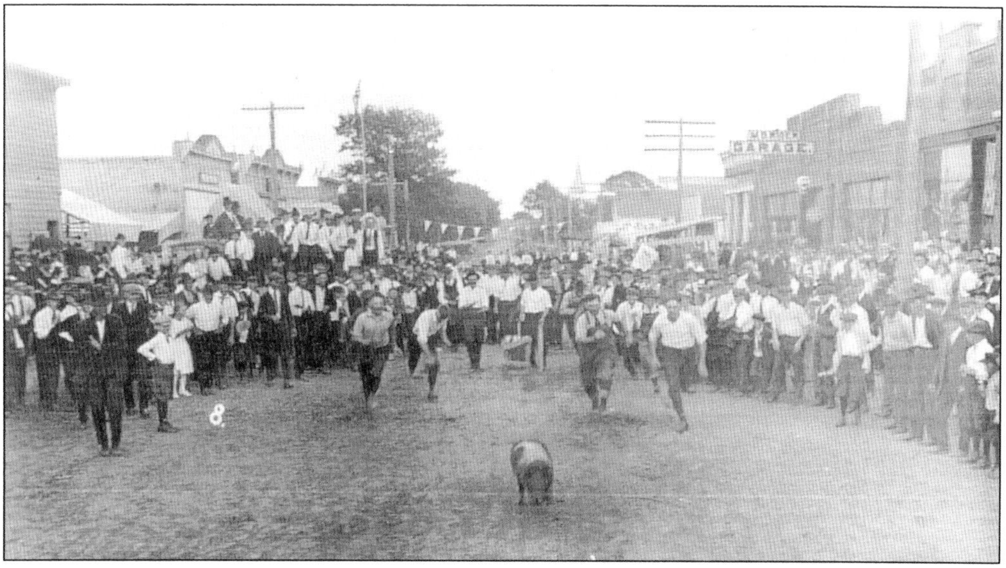

Hustler celebrates the opening of a new Ford garage. The race is on to catch the greased pig. (1926, Claire Ness.)

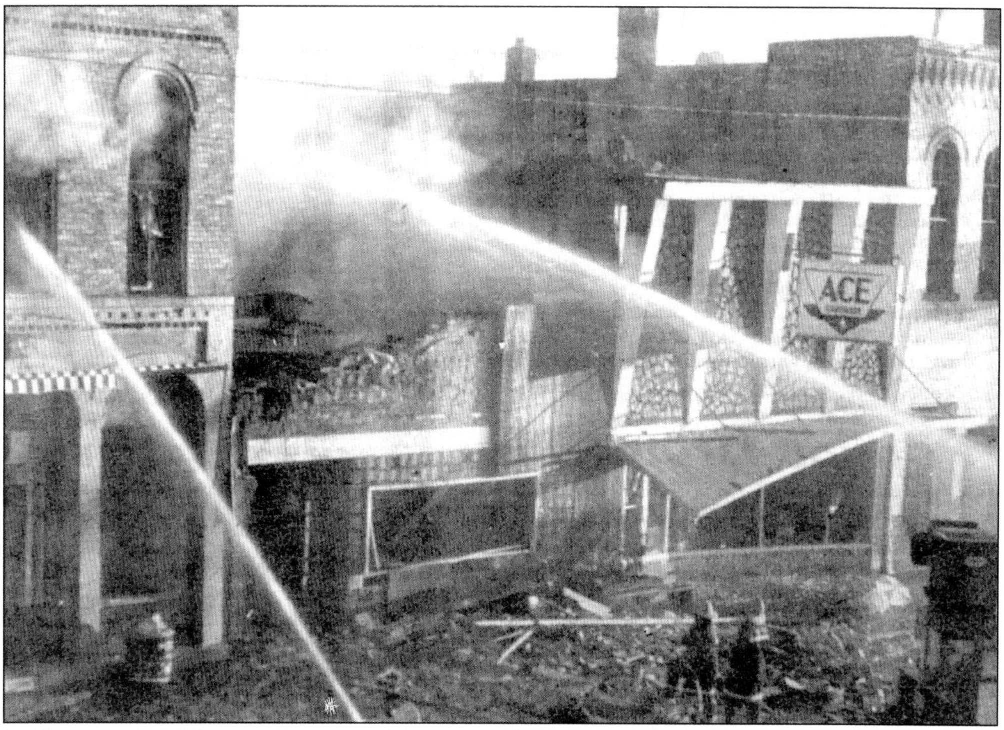

In October of 1985, an explosion and fire caused $500,000 in damages to New Lisbon's business district. The explosion and fire began in a building that housed a tavern and two apartments. That building and at least nine other buildings were destroyed due to gas problems. A woman, seriously injured in the front apartment, was either blown or crawled into the Ace Hardware Store next door to her apartment, where she was rescued and taken for medical treatment. (Juneau County Historical Society.)

Tommy Thompson practiced law on the lower floor of this white, two-story building from the mid 1970s to mid 1980s. The building faces State Street in Mauston, Wisconsin. Behind the building is the Riverside Park on the banks of the Lemonweir River. (Sheila Z.)

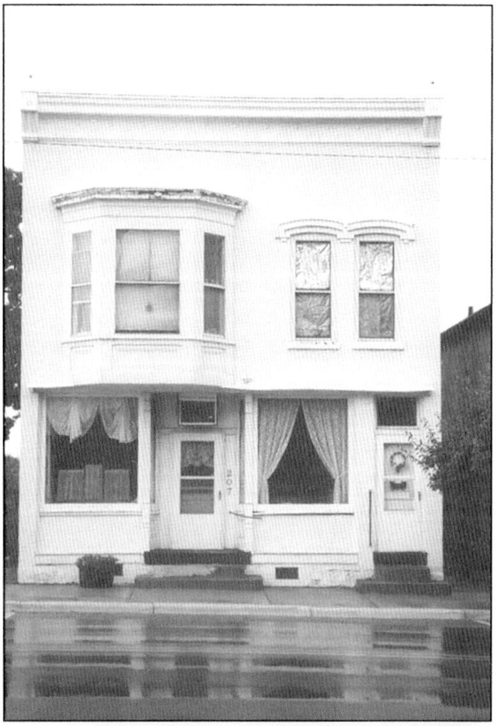

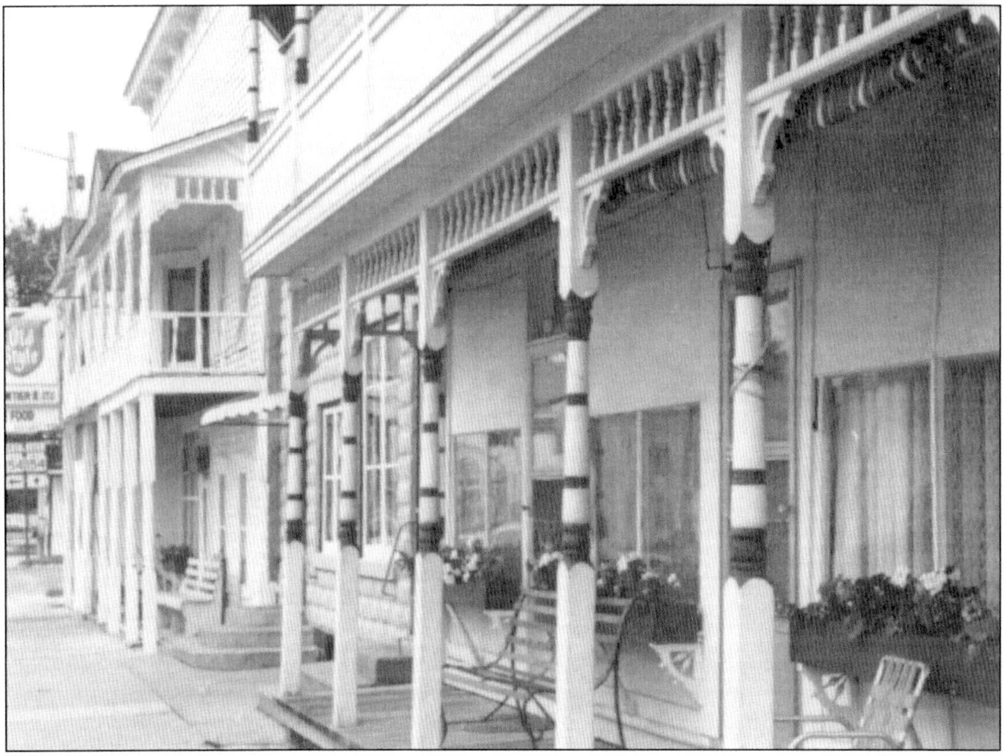

This is Loganville's attractive main street in 1975. Many buildings have false fronts and two-story porches. The porches are supported by turned posts. (Sauk County Historical Society.)

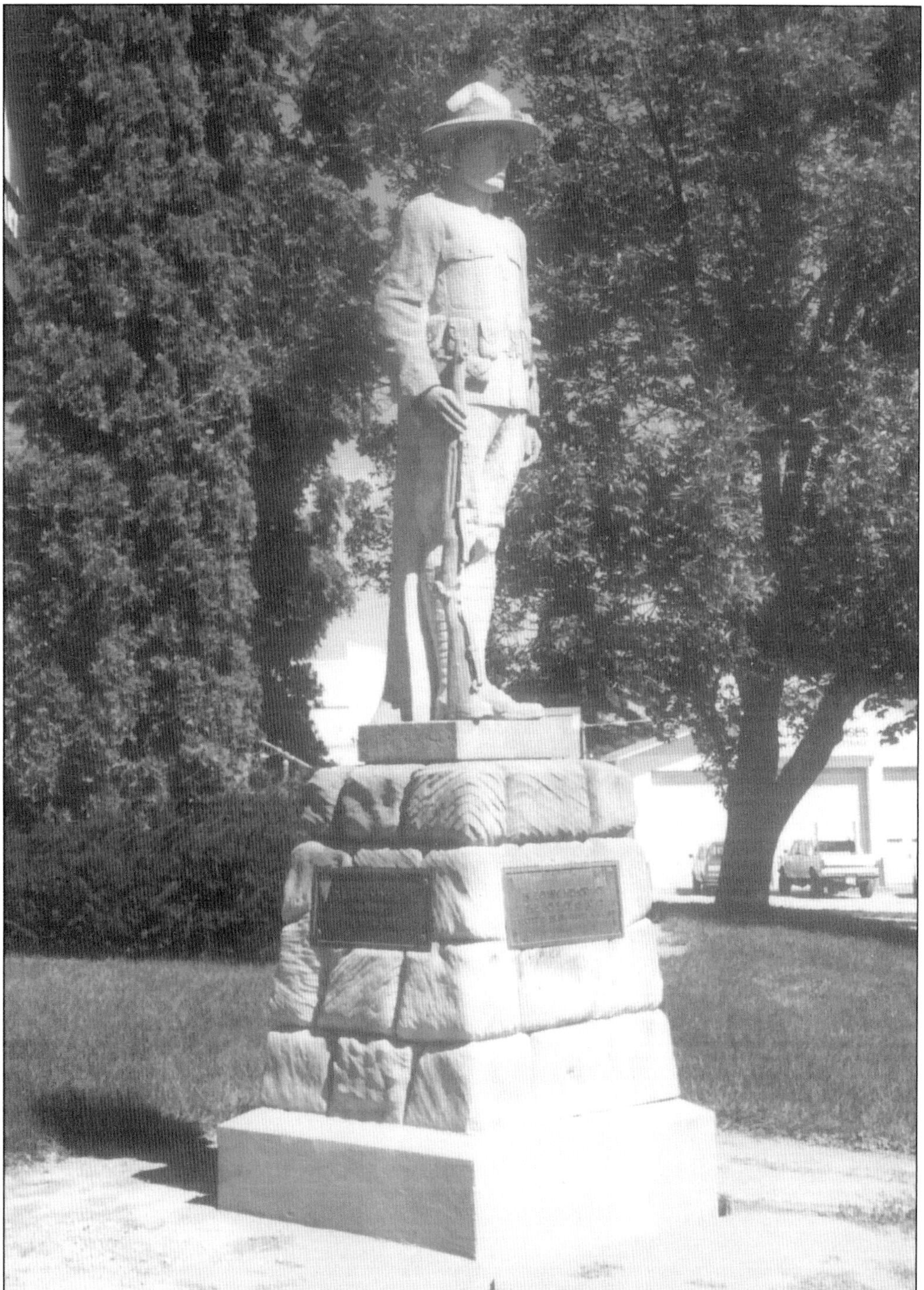

This World War I memorial stands in front of the library in Elroy. The words on the plaque read, "In loving memory of the boys of the World War." During World War I, people waited for the newspaper to check the casualty list. Eighty-nine graves in Elroy and the surrounding countryside are the graves of young men who died either in battle or from the effects of battle. (Sheila Z.)

Three

Rivers, Railroads, and Roads

Your rivers flow, your rails sing,
Your country roads go on and on.

Logging was an important industry for the early settlers. Rivers furnished the transportation for the logs, and power for mills was available by damming the rivers. Most settlements grew around mills and millponds. Sauk City and Prairie du Sac were on the Wisconsin River; Baraboo and Reedsburg were on the Baraboo River; Mauston and New Lisbon were on the Lemonweir; and Necedah was on the Yellow River. The logging industry ended, but the mills were still needed. Now most of the dams have been removed from the rivers. However, two important dams, Petenwell and Castle Rock in Juneau County, contribute thousands of dollars to the county's economy by furnishing electric power, creating desirable building sites around their lakes, and furnishing tourist attractions such as campsites, fishing, and boating.

Railroads caused some communities to grow and destroyed others. Passengers, mail, and freight could be moved more quickly and efficiently on the railroad. One of the important reasons Stewart's Settlement in Juneau County never developed as a community was because the railroad did not go there but went through Lyndon Station, Mauston, and New Lisbon instead. In Sauk County, the village of Newport, with a population of about 2,000 people, collapsed when the railroad went through the Wisconsin Dells instead of Newport. Roads grew from Indian trails into corduroy and macadam roads. Then they developed into black top and concrete highways. In the 1960s, Interstate 90-94 came through Sauk and Juneau Counties. Our roads have come a long way since there were about 30 stagecoach routes made of dirt roads in Sauk County.

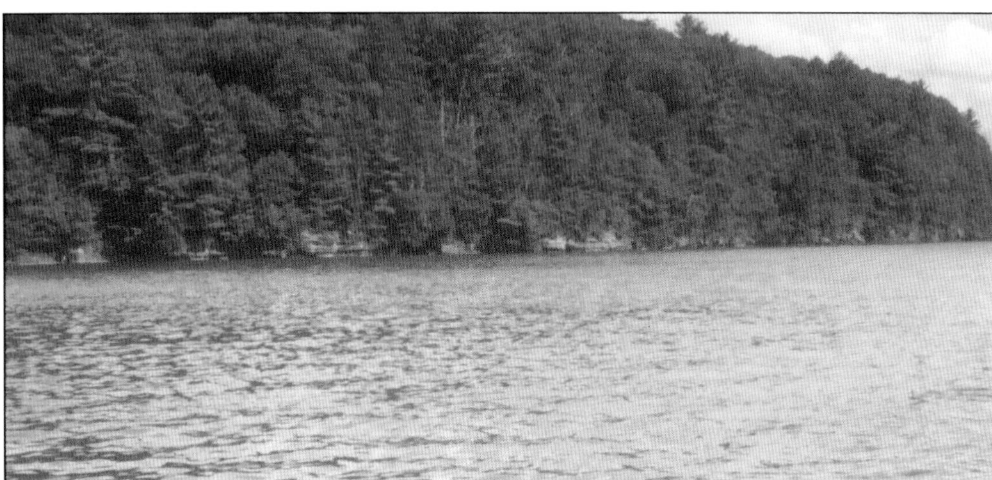

The Wisconsin River sparkles in the sunlight. (2000, Kathryn Wu.)

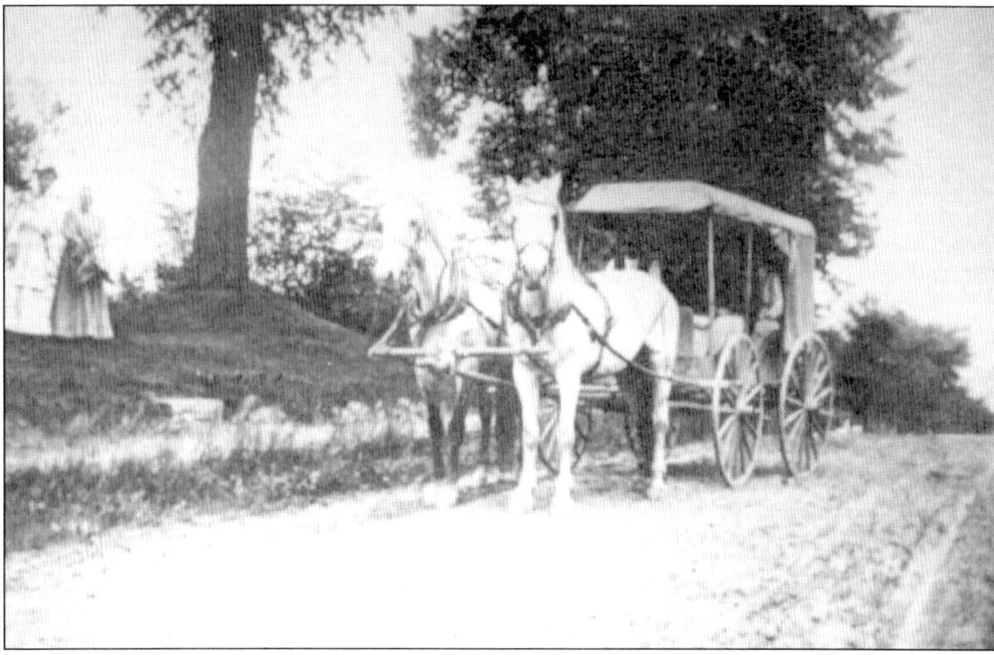

Railroads gradually replaced stagecoach lines. At one time, there were about 30 stagecoach lines in Sauk County. The coach in the picture was the Cazenovia, Ironton, and LaValle stage. (Mid-1800s, Sauk County Historical Society.)

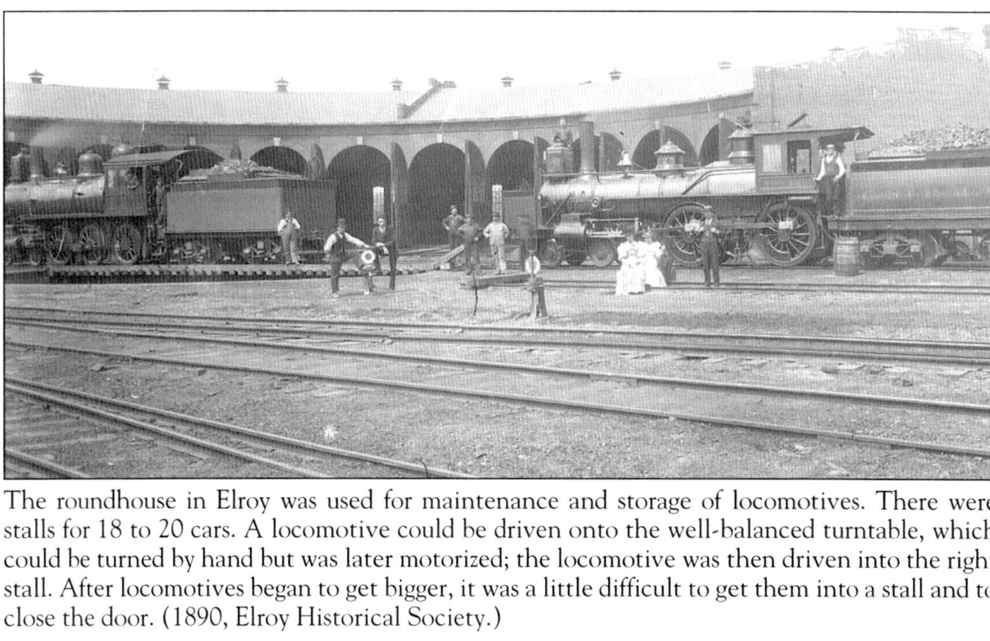

The roundhouse in Elroy was used for maintenance and storage of locomotives. There were stalls for 18 to 20 cars. A locomotive could be driven onto the well-balanced turntable, which could be turned by hand but was later motorized; the locomotive was then driven into the right stall. After locomotives began to get bigger, it was a little difficult to get them into a stall and to close the door. (1890, Elroy Historical Society.)

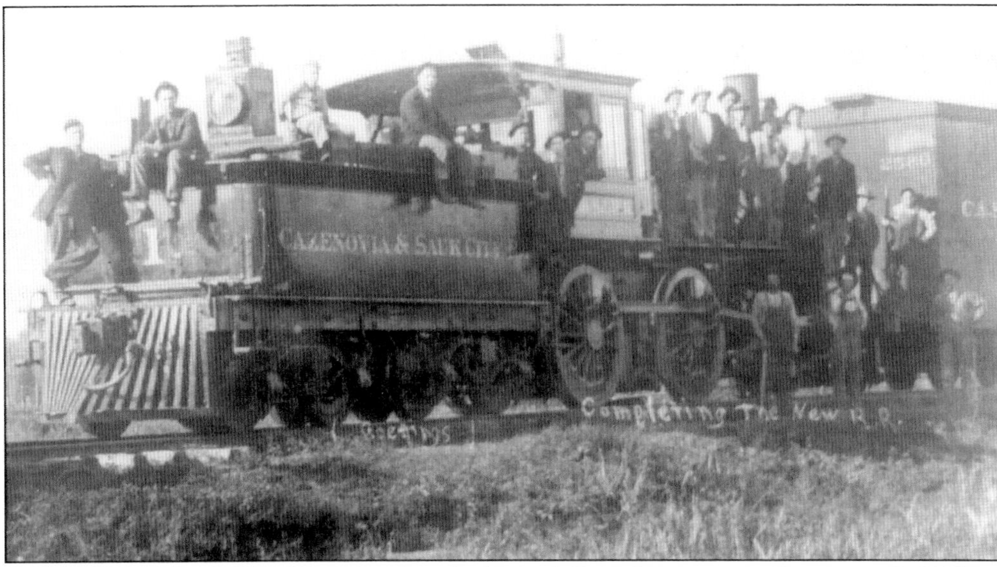

The Puckety Chute (Cazenovia Southern) chugged from Cazenovia to Ironton to LaValle, a distance of 7 miles. Sometimes Puckety jumped the track, but her crew could get her back on. One time a team of horses beat the slow Puckety Chute from LaValle to Cazenovia. The engineer accused the team driver of animal abuse. Sour grapes! When James Hill, president of Great Northern Railway, asked Joseph Duren, one of Puckety's owners, about the Cazenovia Southern, Duren replied, that the line wasn't very long but it was just as wide. (Late 1800s, Sheila Z.)

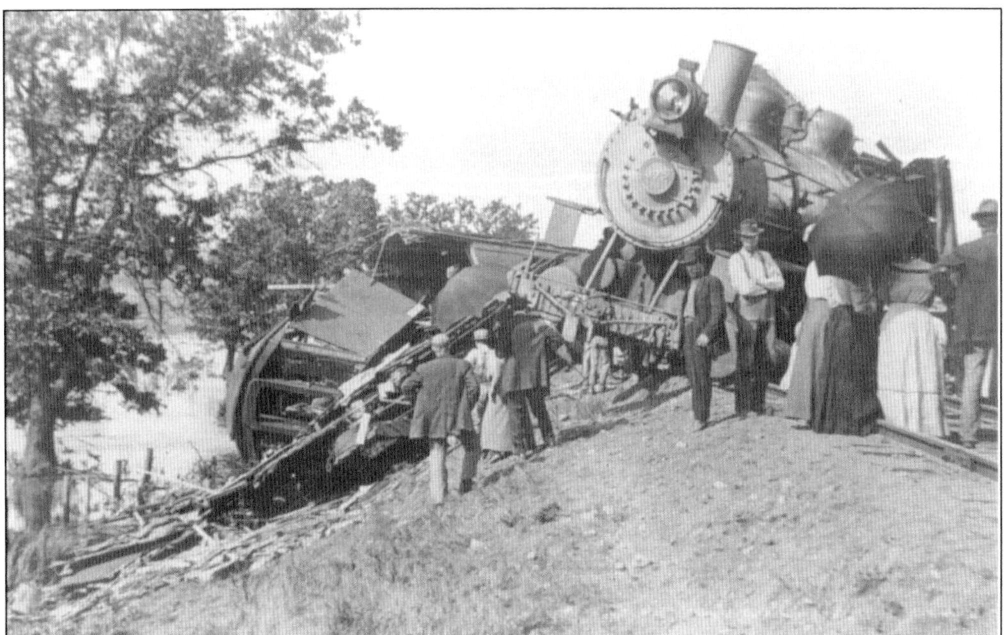

Tragedy struck on the Chicago, St. Paul, Minneapolis, and Omaha railroad when a train was flagged down at a tunnel as it headed toward Elroy from Camp Douglas. There had been a washout just west of Elroy. The train was ordered to back up to Camp Douglas for breakfast. (1912, Claire Ness.)

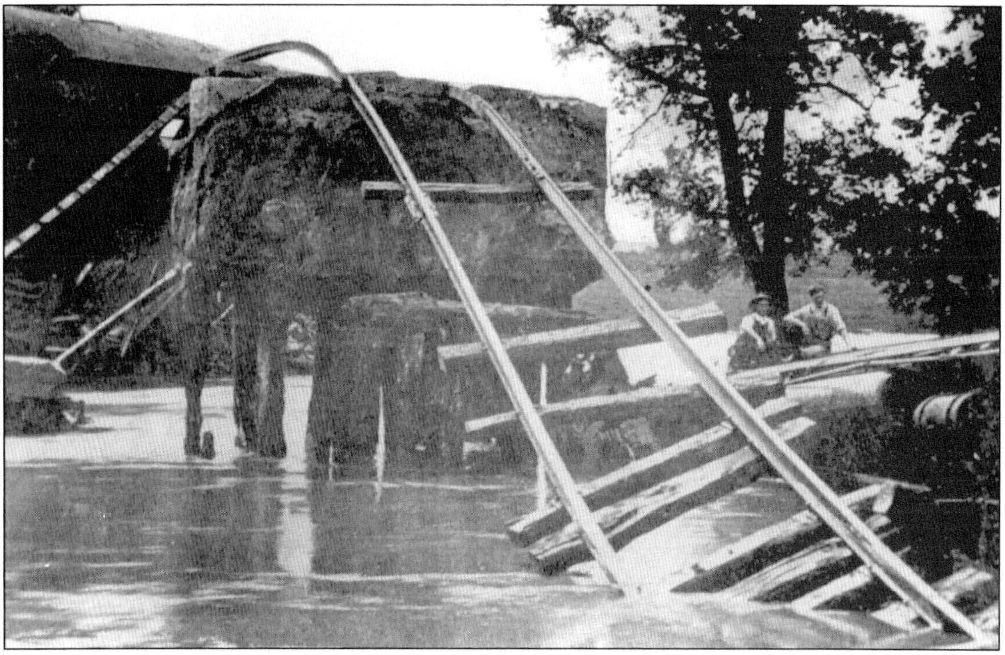

The bridge, 2 to 3-miles south of Camp Douglas, was washed out by a flood caused by a cloud burst farther up the valley. (1912, Claire Ness.)

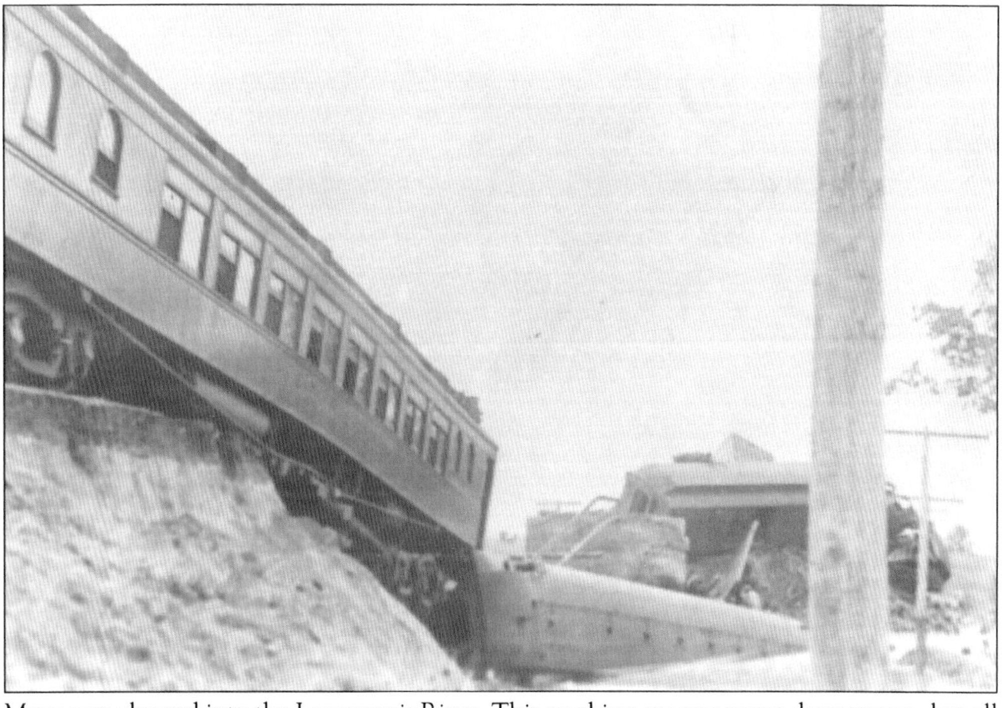

Many cars plunged into the Lemonweir River. This smoking car was swept downstream, but all occupants escaped. Passengers in the sleeping car got out in their nightclothes. Six people were seriously injured. Four people lost their lives: Thompson, the engineer; Abraham, the fireman; an unidentified mail clerk, and Lee, the baggage-man. (1912, Claire Ness.)

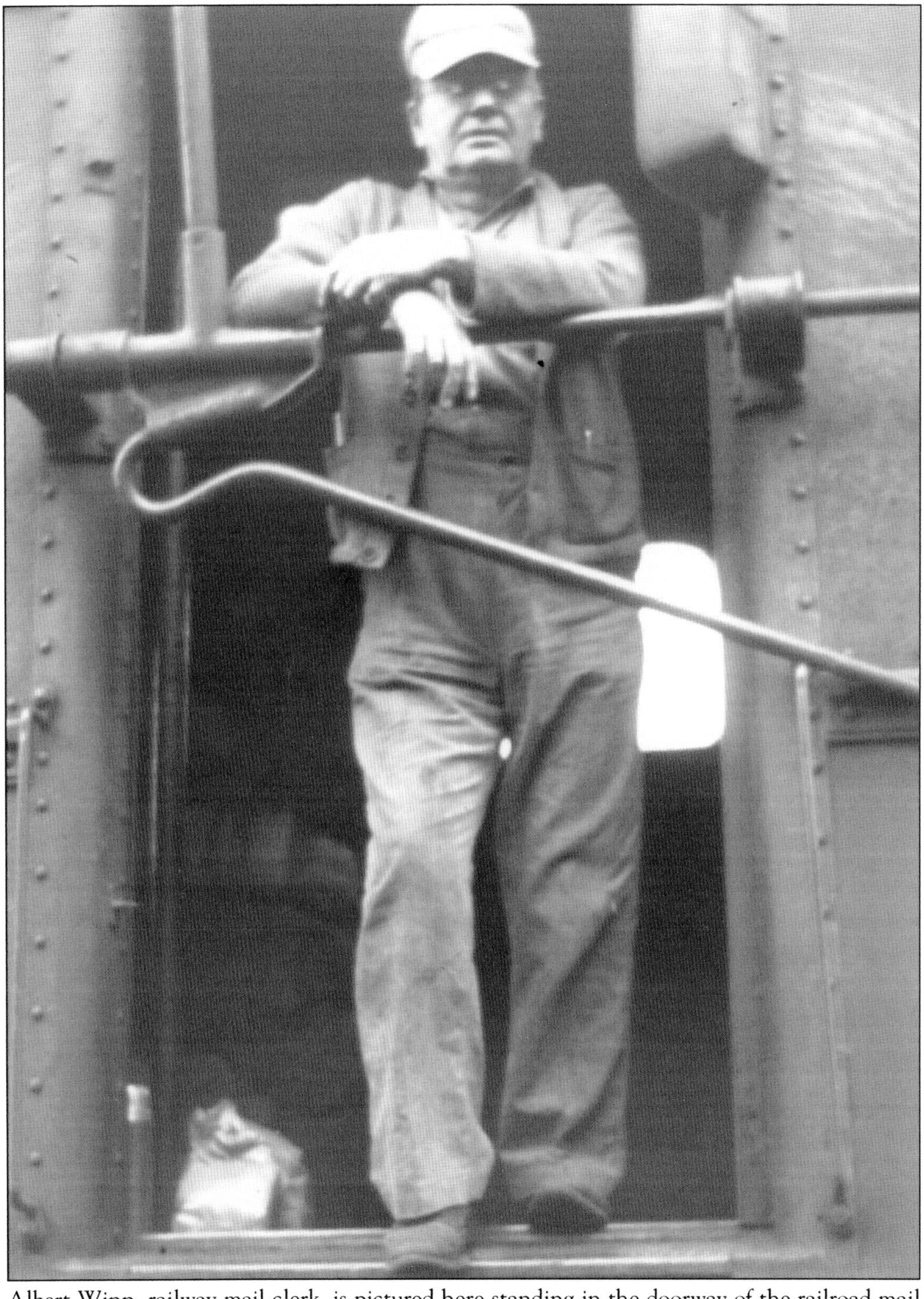

Albert Winn, railway mail clerk, is pictured here standing in the doorway of the railroad mail car. He pulled the perpendicular bar to his right down to cause the diagonal bar to extend away from the mail car. Fast mail trains would not stop in most communities, so the extended bar would catch the communities' pouch of outgoing mail. Three to six men would be sorting mail in the mail car while the train was moving. (1940, Elroy Historical Society.)

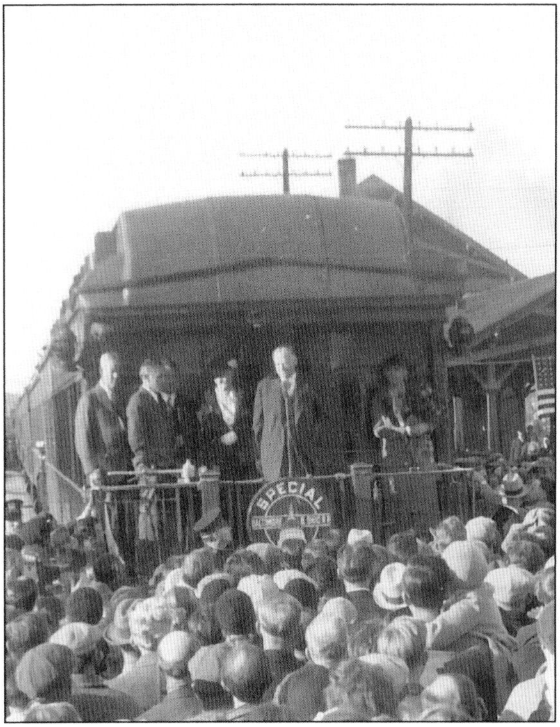

The trains made it possible for many national political figures to come to Juneau and Sauk Counties during their campaigns. Nixon came in 1953, Truman in 1948, and Hoover in 1932. (1948, Elroy Historical Society.)

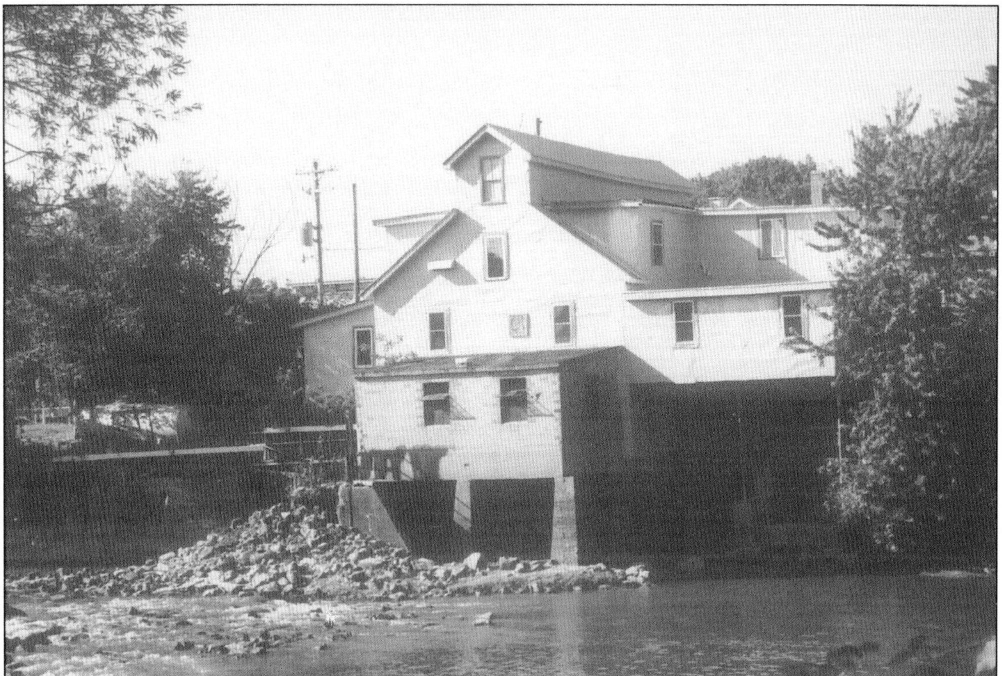

The Baraboo River had many dams. Today, all the dams except one have been removed. This dam at LaValle has been removed. In 1864, the LaValle Mill was built. The Duddleston family owned the mill for many years. Oats were fanned for the farmers' seeds. Oats and corn were ground into animal food at the mill. (Sheila Z.)

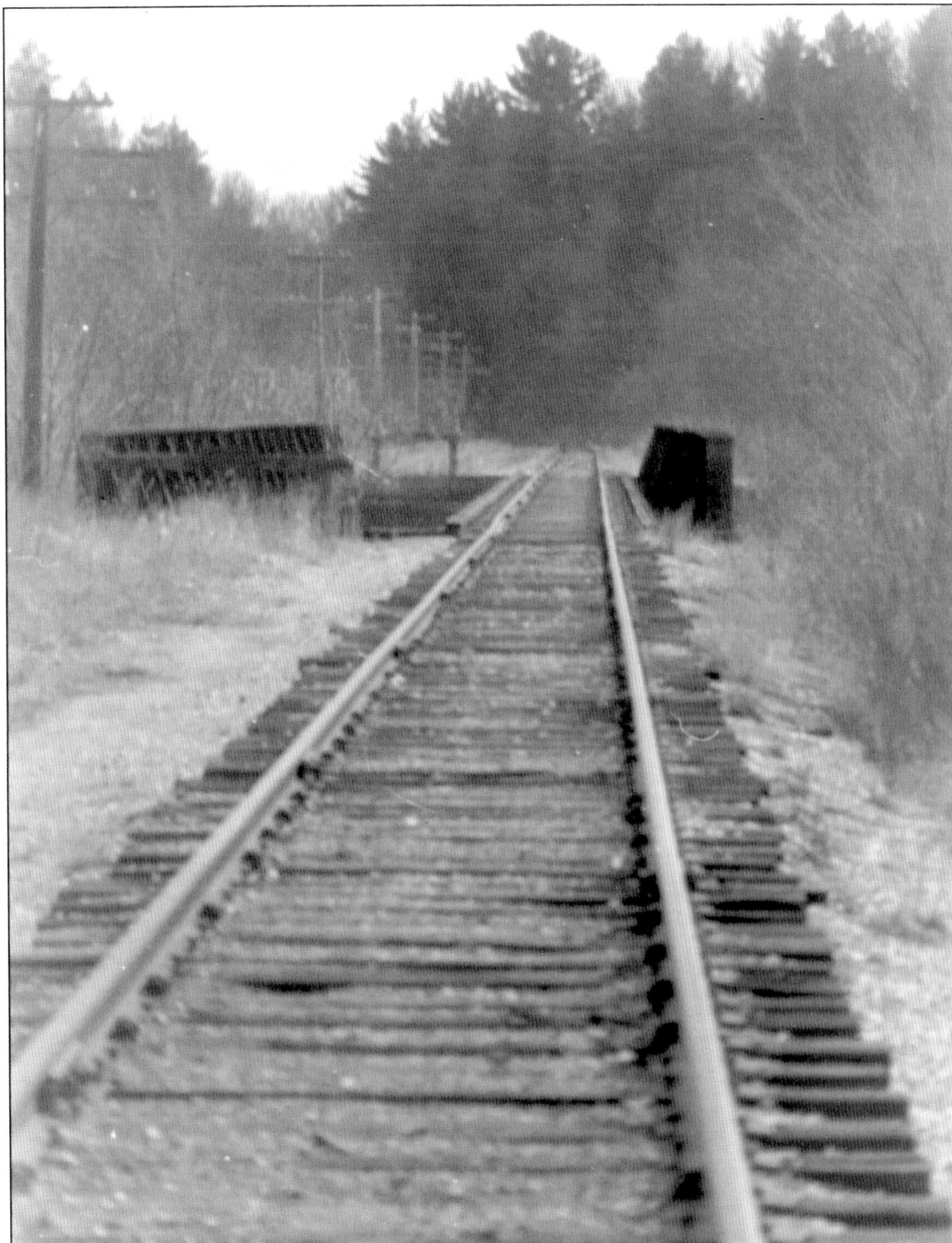

Farmers and industries, desperate to get their products to market, encouraged the Cazenovia and Southern Railroad by buying stock to help finance bringing the railroad to the LaValle, Reedsburg, and Elroy area in 1906. After selling the stock, the Cazenovia and Southern Railroad agents disappeared with the money; neither agents nor money were seen again. The Chicago Northwestern Railroad Company laid these tracks, completing the job in 1910. The train, the 400, streaked through this countryside from Chicago to Minneapolis, transporting passengers and freight from 1910 to about 1945. (Sheila Z.)

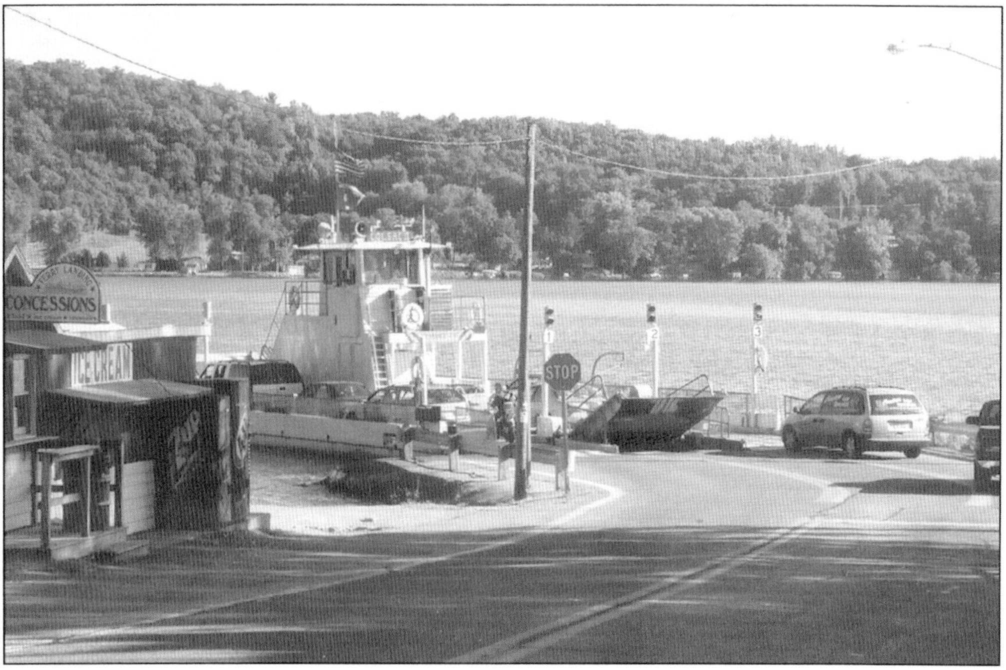

The state-operated Merrimac Ferry is part of Highway 113. The ferry connects Sauk and Columbia Counties and is a popular tourist attraction. On busy days, tourists may need to wait up to an hour to ride the ferry. They picnic, fish, and explore. The ferry was built across the river in the 1840s by Chester Mattson and George Grant. (2000, Sheila Z.)

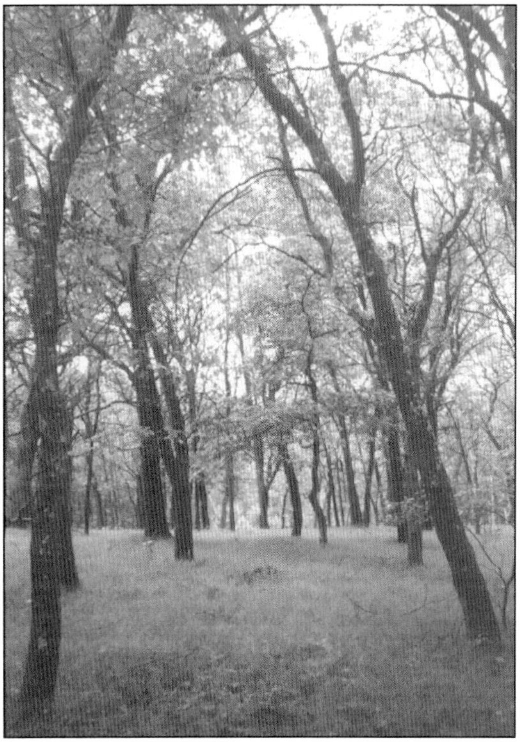

Before a road was built in Juneau County to connect Highway N to Highways 12 and 16, which were parallel to N just outside of Lyndon, people drove through the woods and around trees to get from one road to the other. Early pioneer roads in both counties were trails through the grass. Later the first roads were built using wooden planks (corduroy roads) or layers of crushed rock (macadam roads). To make a road, the settlers often followed Indian trails. (1860s–early 1900s, Henry Hajek.)

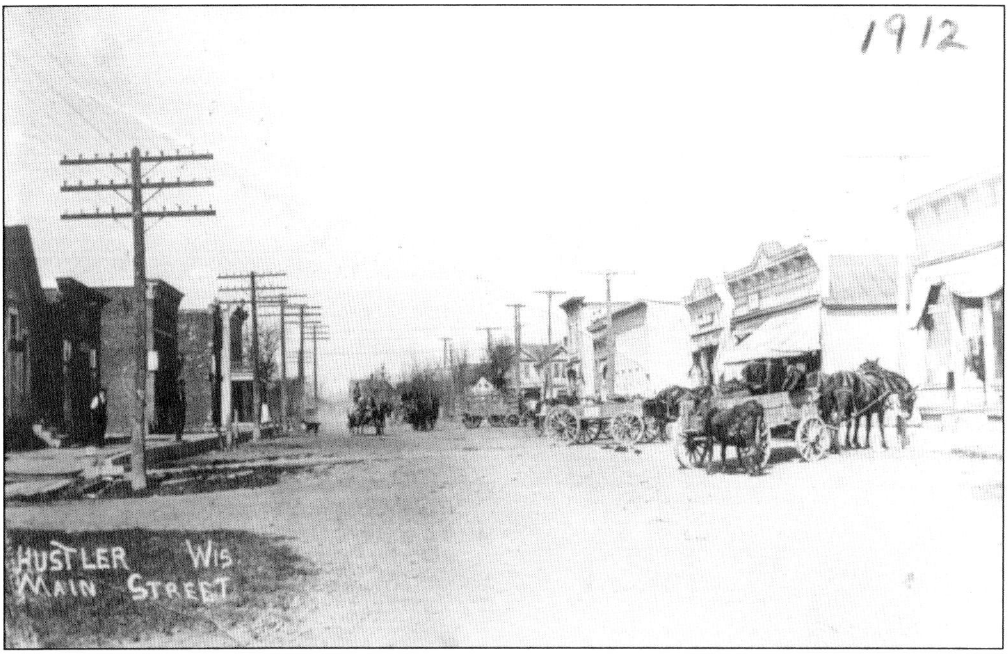

At first, Hustler's main street had no name. If people came from Mauston and wanted to go to Minnesota, they had to follow the correct paint color on the telephone poles. One direction had red paint, the other direction had blue. Hustler's main street became County Highway A. (1912, Claire Ness.)

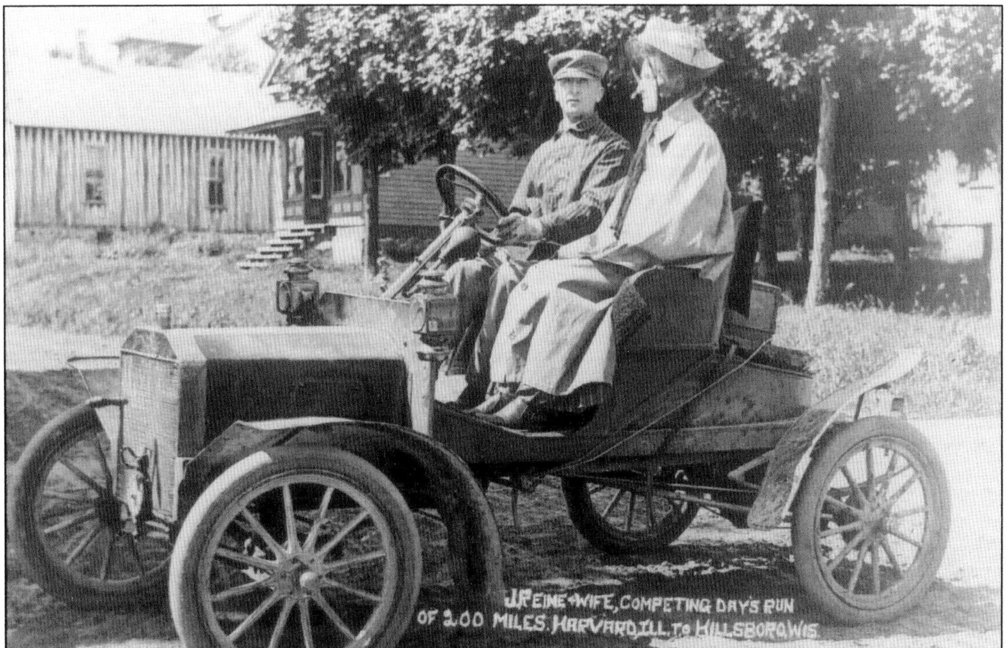

This couple is enjoying an exciting ride. The lady's hat and veil and cover-all outer garment offer her some protection from the sandy dirt roads. The fenders also help to shield the couple from the dust of the road. (Early 1900s, Hazel Owen.)

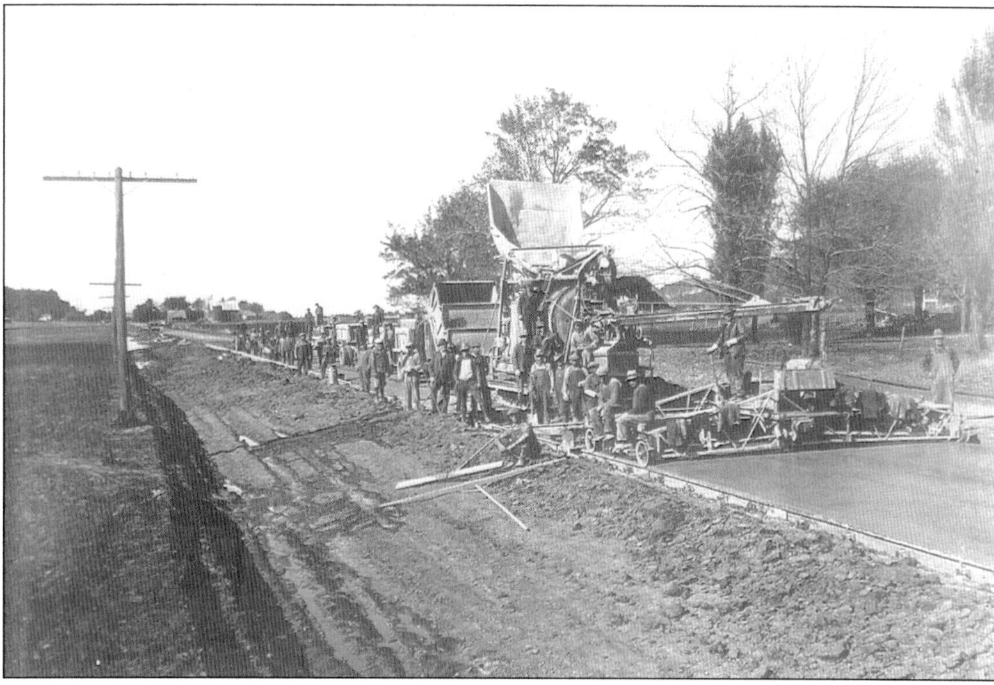

The road crew is putting in Highway 12 and 16 between Lyndon Station and Mauston. Thomas Cavenough, who lived on a farm the road was passing, was working on the new highway. He was 18 at the time. After the road was complete, he had to take his cows across the highway to get them from barn to pasture in the morning and from the pasture to the barn at night. (*c.* 1921, Mary Jean Cauley.)

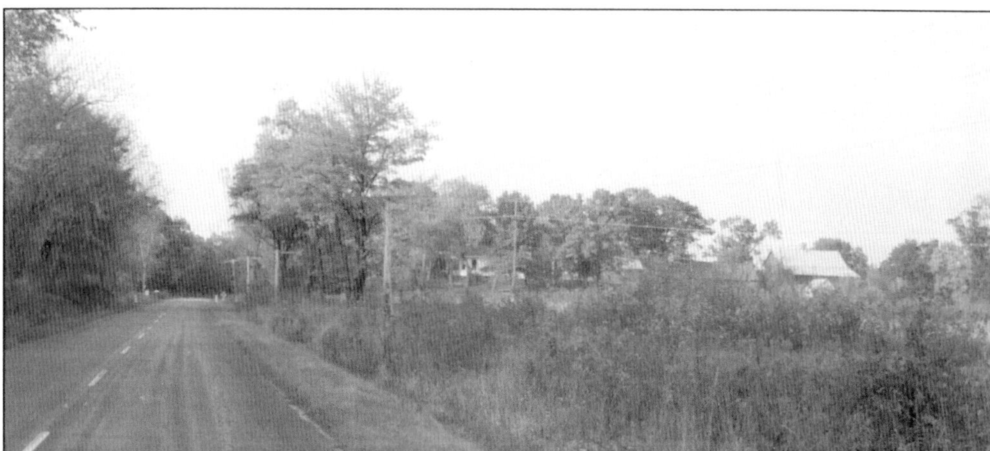

In 1960, traveling north on County Highway HH from Lyndon Station to Highway 82, a person would pass the Wright farm on the right. The cloverleaf for I 90-94 just outside of Lyndon Station was to be built on the site of the house and buildings. The highway commission took the site, and arranged an auction for the real estate. There was a good turnout of people from Lyndon Station and the surrounding area, but no one would bid on the house. Lyall Wright bought his house back for $1,000. He moved it through the field you see in the picture to the site by the Lyndon Creek where his grandfather had built a log cabin. People bid on the other buildings because they knew Lyall didn't want them. (1960, Jacqueline Ann.)

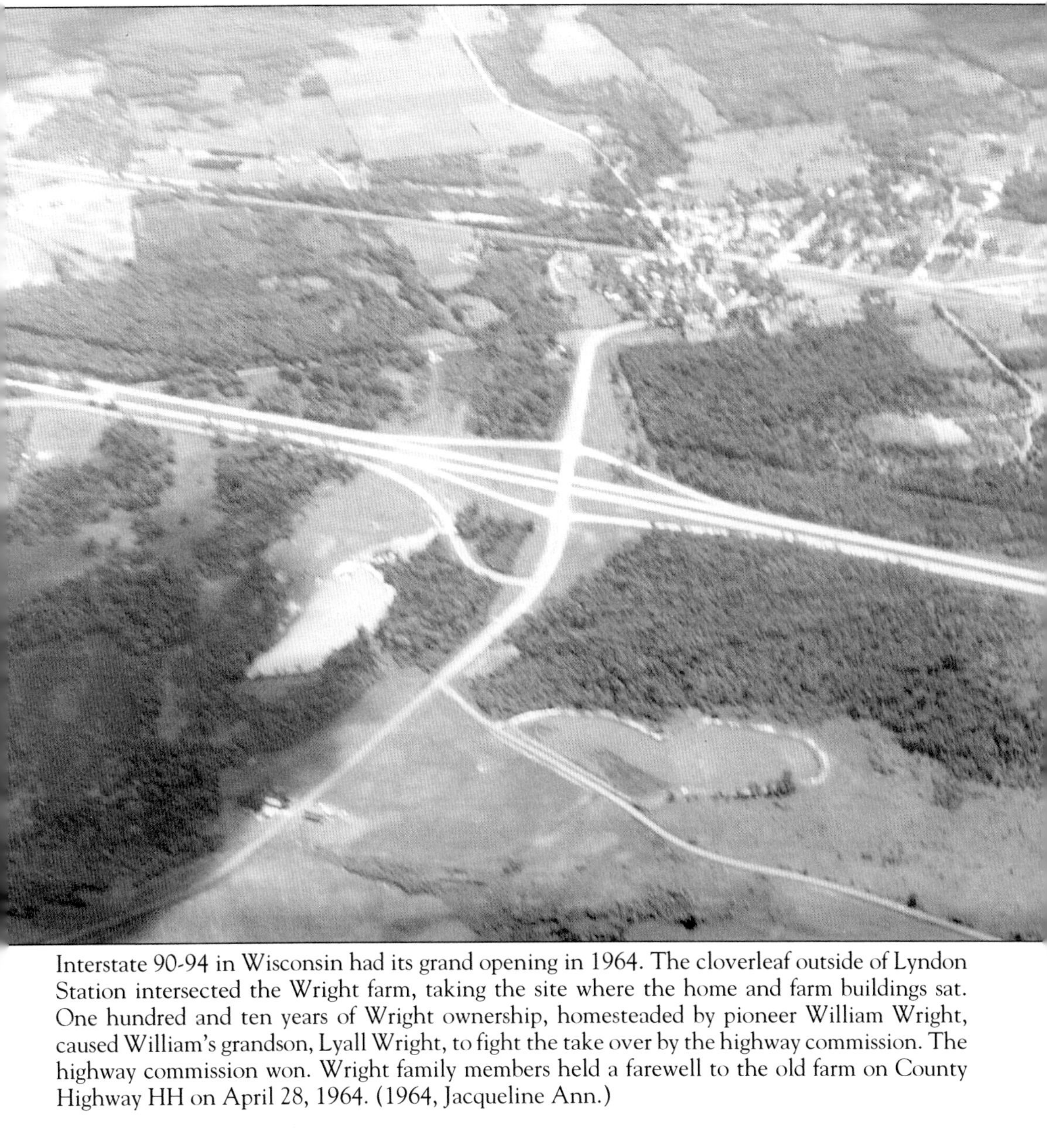

Interstate 90-94 in Wisconsin had its grand opening in 1964. The cloverleaf outside of Lyndon Station intersected the Wright farm, taking the site where the home and farm buildings sat. One hundred and ten years of Wright ownership, homesteaded by pioneer William Wright, caused William's grandson, Lyall Wright, to fight the take over by the highway commission. The highway commission won. Wright family members held a farewell to the old farm on County Highway HH on April 28, 1964. (1964, Jacqueline Ann.)

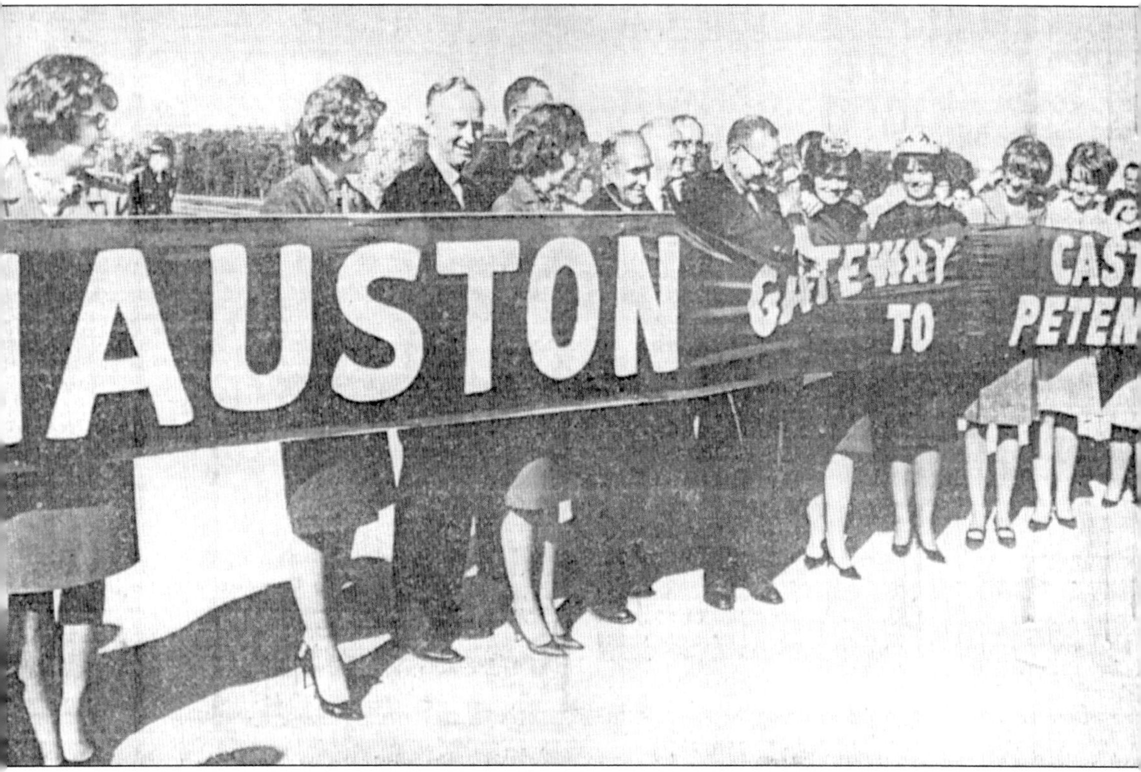

The people cheered. The motorcade started at Wisconsin Dells with a few official cars and swelled to more than 200 cars as it approached its destination. All scheduled stops, including Rocky Arbor, Lyndon Station, Mauston-New Lisbon, Camp Douglas, Juneau-Monroe Countyline, Oakdale, Tomah, Wyeville, and Camp McCoy, had huge crowds of people. Farmers watched from their fields, and fishermen waved from their boats. Governor Reynolds cut the ribbons and spoke to the people. I 90-94 was open in Juneau County. (1964, Elroy Historical Society.)

Four

BUSINESS AND INDUSTRY

Early settlers found lumbering to be a good industry because the woods supplied raw material and the rivers supplied transportation to markets. Communities grew up around mills and millponds. Sawmills supplied lumber. Flourmills were needed for food. Mills were used to grind grain for animal food.

Many farmers came from New England where wheat was being raised, so wheat was their first crop. They learned to diversify their crops and to raise animals for their own use and for sales. Needed businesses, such as hotels, to accommodate train passengers and employees, sprang up in the community. The general store supplied an outlet for farmers' products and sold needed supplies. The railroads took their goods to other markets. Liveries tended to shoeing horses and fixing wagon wheels.

Today in both counties, health care and tourism bring a substantial amount of money into the local economy and often many jobs to the residents. A few of Juneau's current businesses are Walker Stainless Equipment, Farnam, Meillor Sealing Systems, and Brenner Tank. Some of Sauk County's manufacturers are Land's End, Grede Foundries, Sysco Foods, Flambeau Plastics, Gerber, and Seats, Inc. Both counties want to encourage growth in the businesses already operating in the counties.

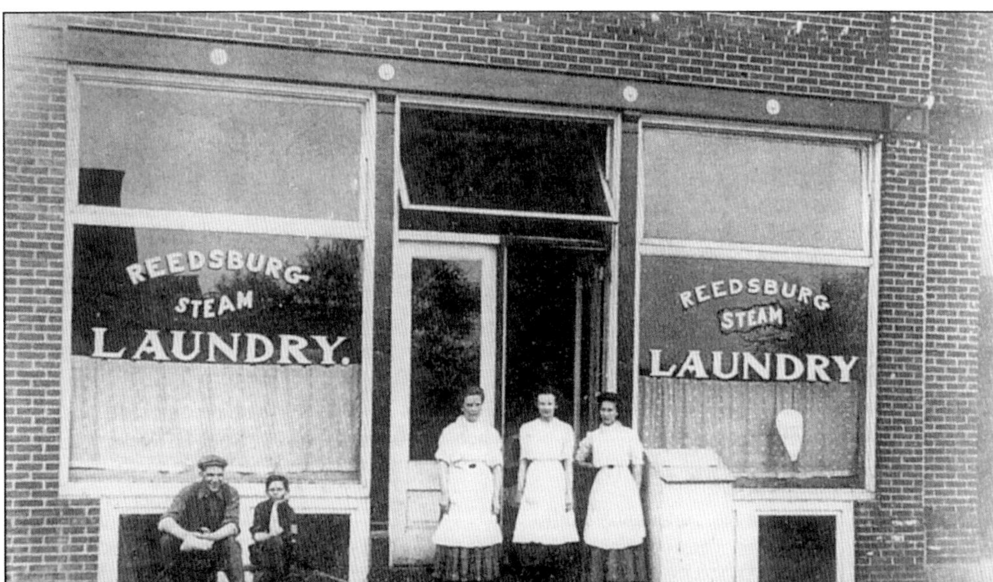

The steam laundry in Reedsburg was a busy place. Pictured here, from left to right, are as follows: George Strampe, Walter Schultze, Alma Tewes, Alta Rosenthal, and Edna Meyer. (Reedsburg History Committee.)

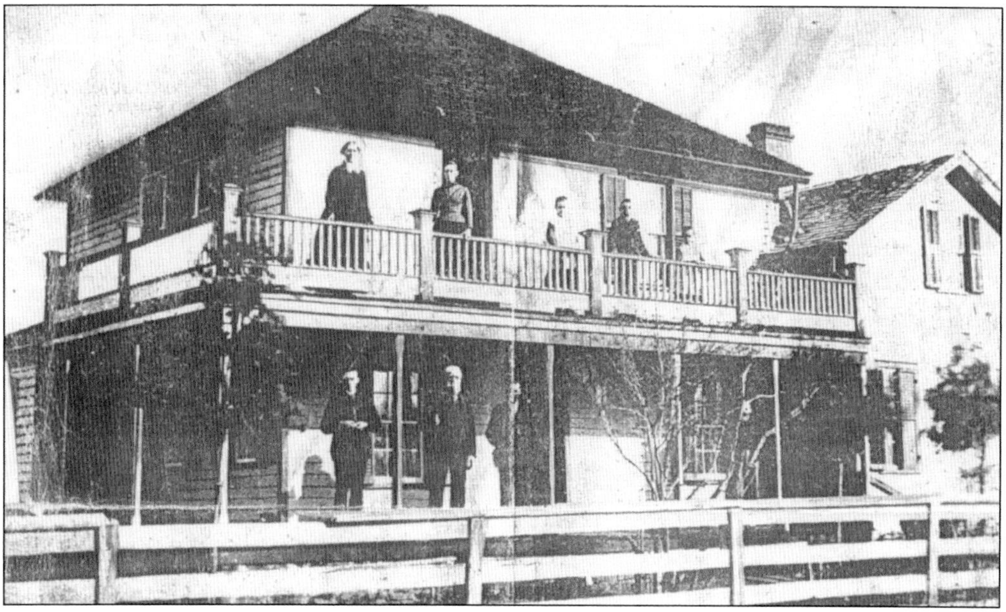

William and Jane Wright bought this home in 1868. The building, in Lyndon Station, had five rooms and was enlarged to twelve rooms so they could use it as a hotel and boarding house. Imagine how delighted these entrepreneurs were to learn the first railroad to come through Juneau County would run right beside their house. They made a deal with the construction crew to sell them timber for railroad ties. (Jacqueline Ann.)

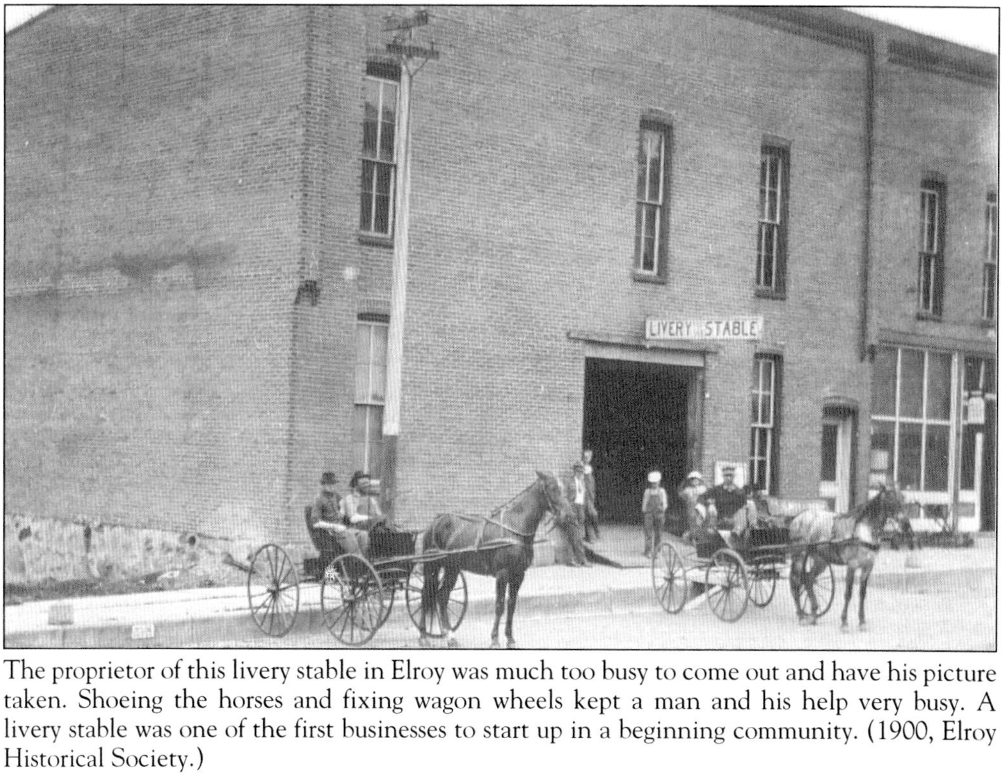

The proprietor of this livery stable in Elroy was much too busy to come out and have his picture taken. Shoeing the horses and fixing wagon wheels kept a man and his help very busy. A livery stable was one of the first businesses to start up in a beginning community. (1900, Elroy Historical Society.)

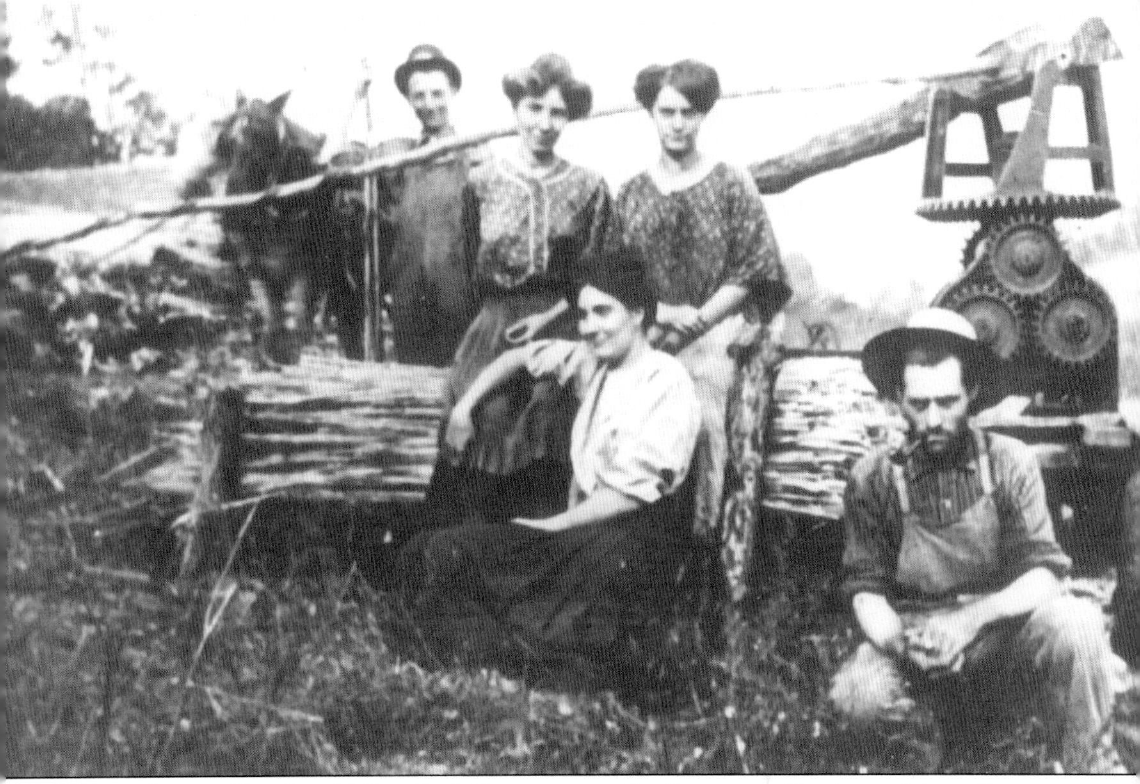

This sorghum mill in Carr Valley, Sauk County, was a family-operated business. A large fire was built to cook the syrup. Horses were hooked up to the crusher. As the horses walked in a circle, the cranks turned. The cane was fed in and crushed. Crushed cane slid down a trough into the vat and boiled all night until it reached its desired consistency. Pictured here, from left to right, are Frank, Atsy, Mary, and Jim Dietzman. The young girl kneeling is Mary Viette (niece). (1905, Hazel Owen.)

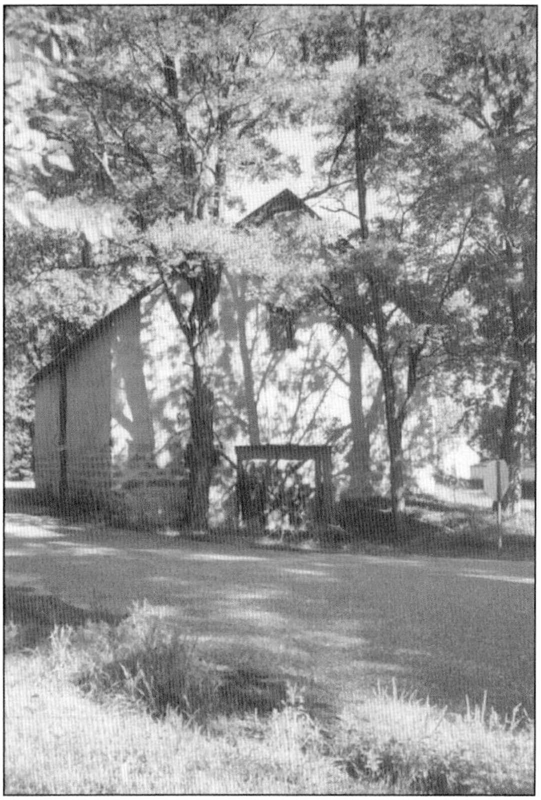

This old potato barn in Lyndon Station is located close to the tracks. Farmers would bring their potatoes there to be stored and then shipped to markets on the train. (Early 1900s, Sheila Z.)

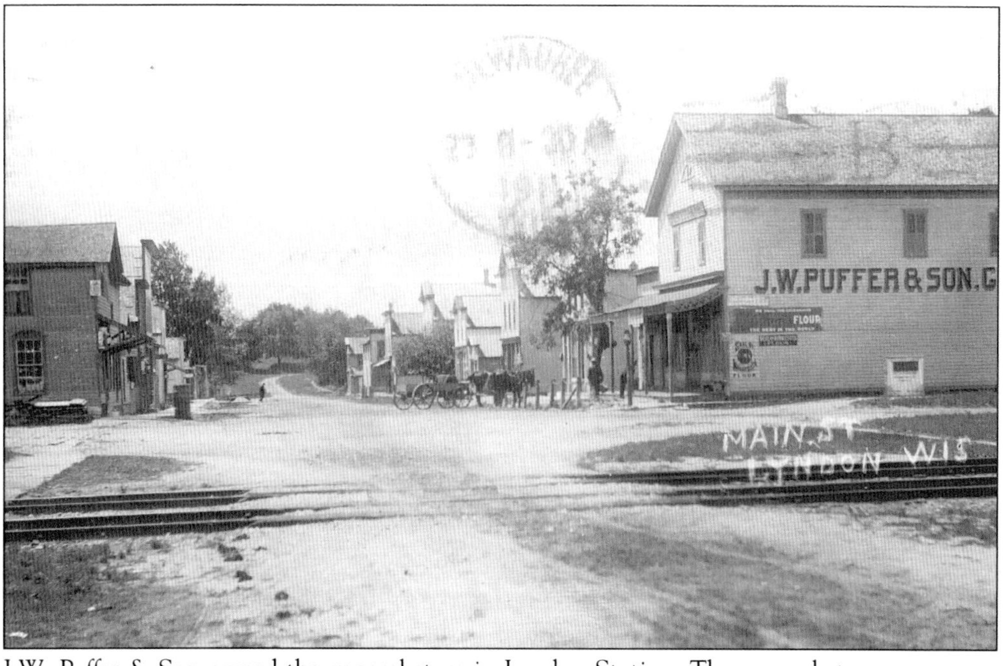

J.W. Puffer & Son owned the general store in Lyndon Station. The general store was a very important business to farmers in this area. They sold goods and supplied their own needs through the store. (1900, Mary Jean Cauley.)

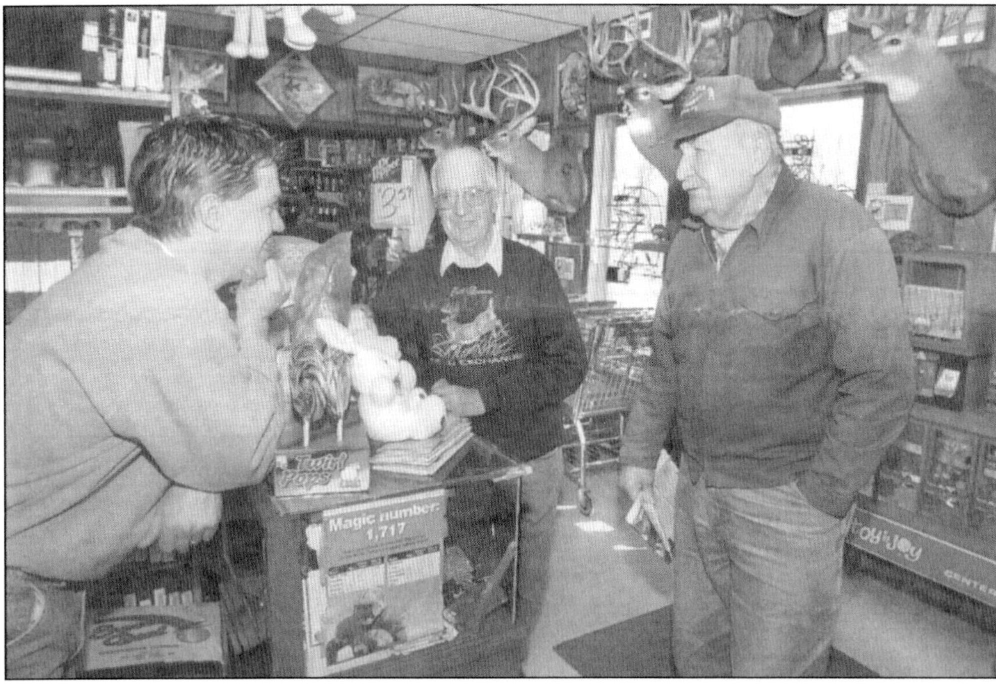

Bud and Francis Miller are semi-retired from owning and running the general store in Lyndon Station. One of their sons, Mark, now manages the store. This store was once owned and managed by J.W. Puffer & Son. It opened in 1857 and nine families have owned it since then. It is still a general store, and shoppers can usually find what they want or something close to it. The Miller family is creative and sponsors different events and contests. One of these contests is the "Big Buck Contest" during deer season. (2000, Mark Miller.)

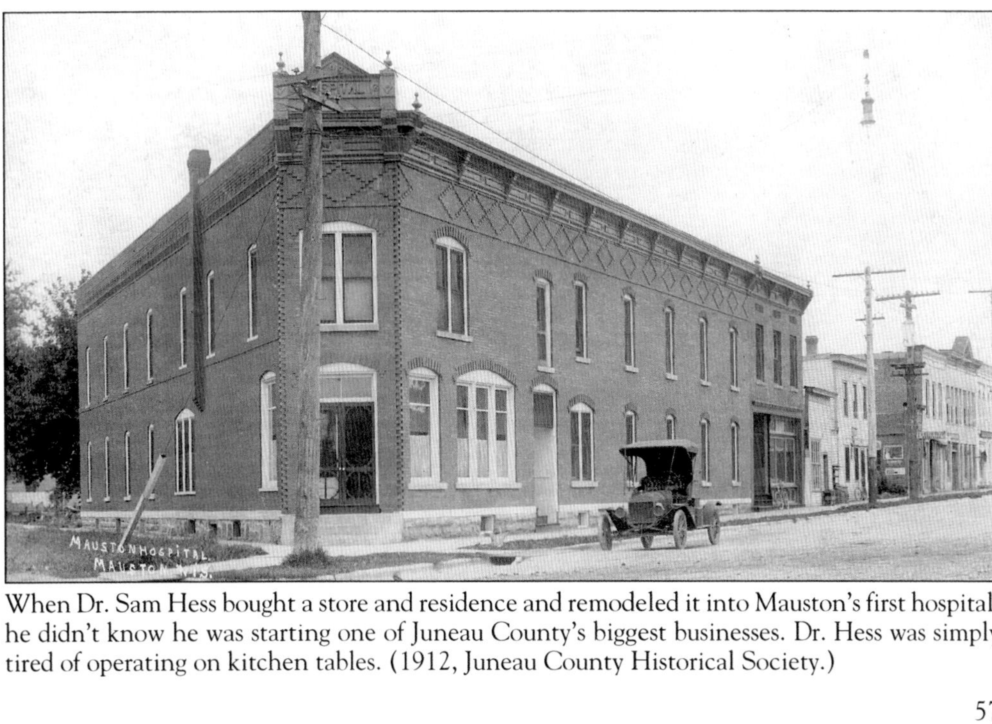

When Dr. Sam Hess bought a store and residence and remodeled it into Mauston's first hospital, he didn't know he was starting one of Juneau County's biggest businesses. Dr. Hess was simply tired of operating on kitchen tables. (1912, Juneau County Historical Society.)

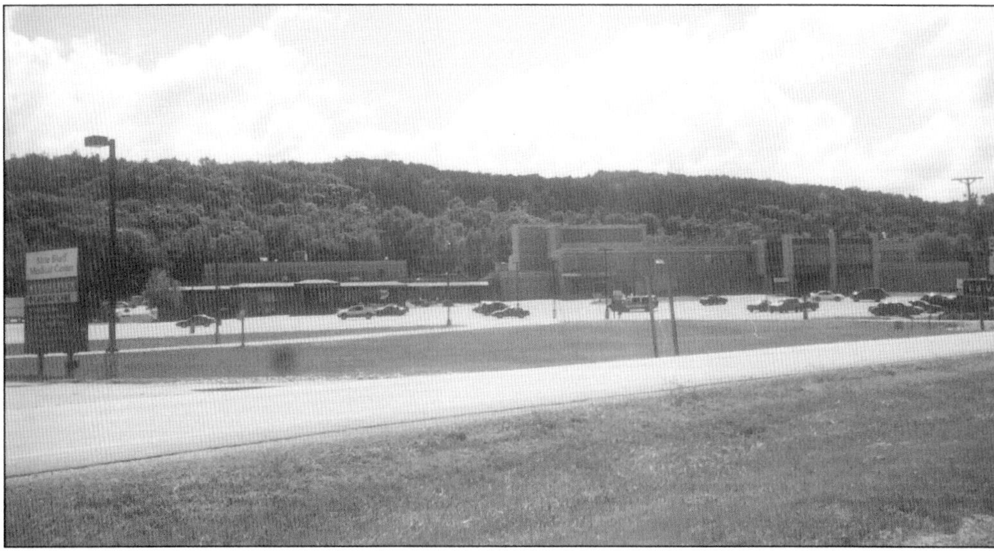

The Hess Memorial Hospital, completed *c.* 1981, is one of the four top employers in Juneau County. A lovely rural setting surrounds this hospital on the edge of Mauston. The hospital has 100 beds. In the acute care wing, there are 60 beds. A nursing home on the grounds also has 60 beds. In Sauk County in 1996—according to Karna O. Hanna, Executive Director of Sauk County—Development Corporation, health care provided 2,907 jobs, and health care plus linked services provided 4,376 jobs. The positive impact of health care into the economies of both counties is enormous. (2000, Sheila Z.)

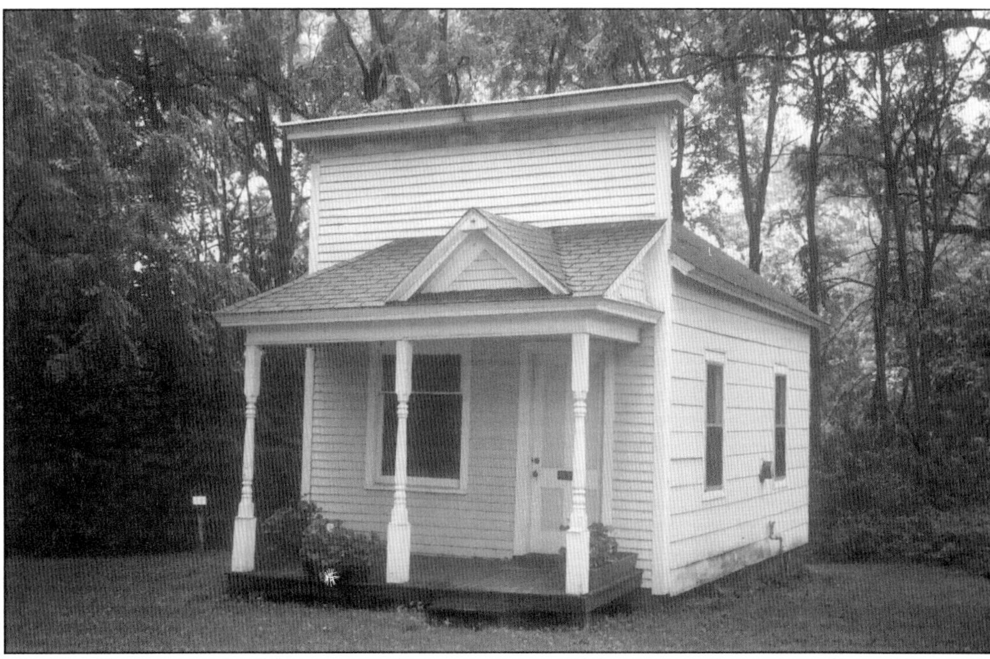

This small two-room building sat on the main street of Mauston and was the office of Dr. W.T. O'Brien. He practiced in Mauston for 41 years and delivered 2,000 babies in private homes and the Hess Memorial Hospital. Dr. O'Brien died August 3, 1943. The building is now part of the Juneau County Historical Society. (1900s, Sheila Z.)

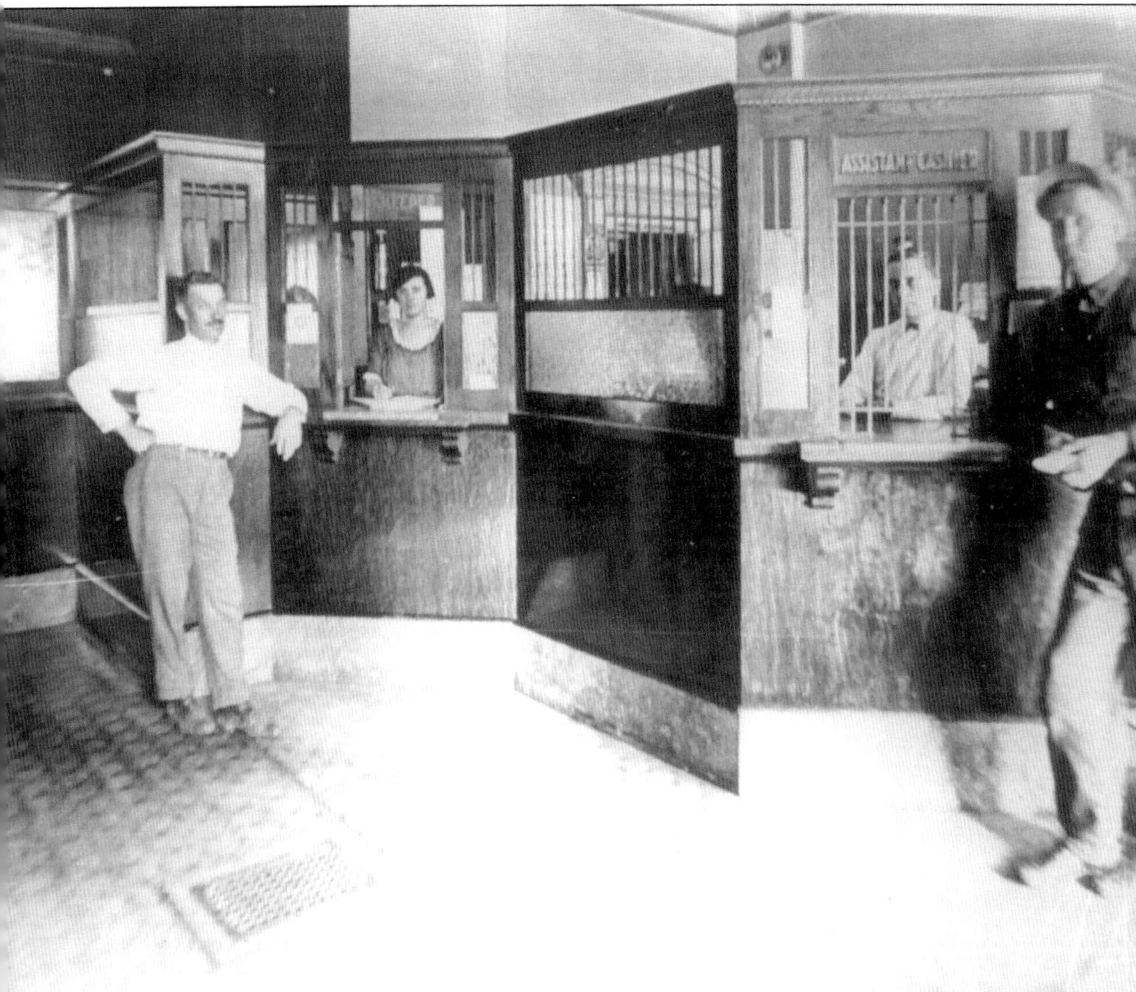

A bank business in Hustler is pictured here in 1924. Myrtle Adrian is at her window, ready to help customers. Myrtle became a 50-year employee. The biggest problem at the bank was the numerous false alarms. They caused quite a commotion. People always ran up to the bank, some carrying shotguns. (Claire Ness.)

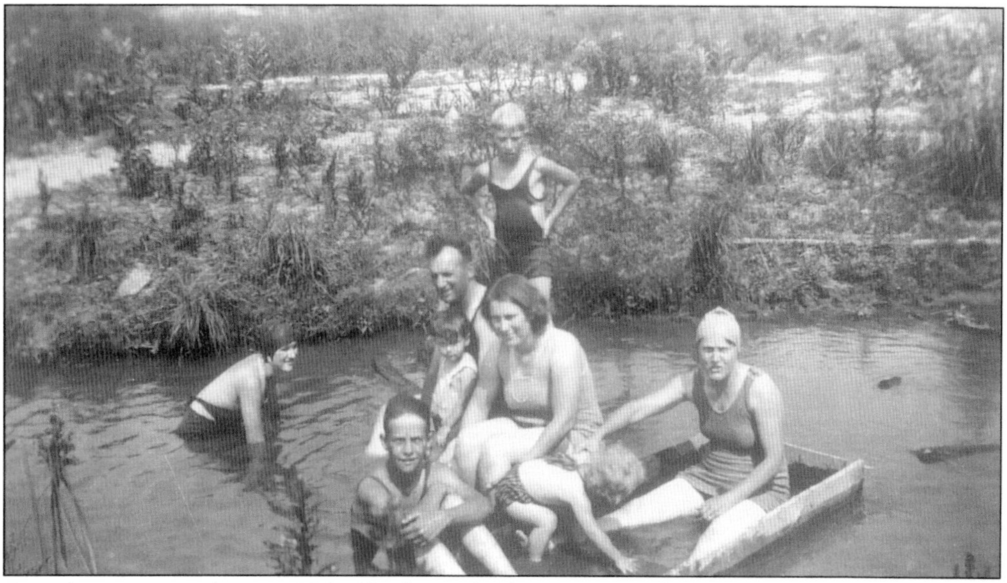

On a hot summer day in 1936, Charles and Clara Geitz took their little boy Lawrence and went with relatives and friends to paddle around in Big Creek on Douglas Road just outside of LaValle. It was fun splashing about; they never imagined a dam would turn Big Creek into Lake Redstone in the mid-1960s. It is a private lake now, but it does have public landings. There are 17 miles of shoreline on this lake. People can no longer purchase any 3 lots for $4,500. A lake front lot would be valued at about $100,000. Most of the homes on the lake would cost $300,000 to $800,000 today. Visitors and owners of property at Lake Redstone enjoy boating, swimming, and fishing there. (Marie Geitz.)

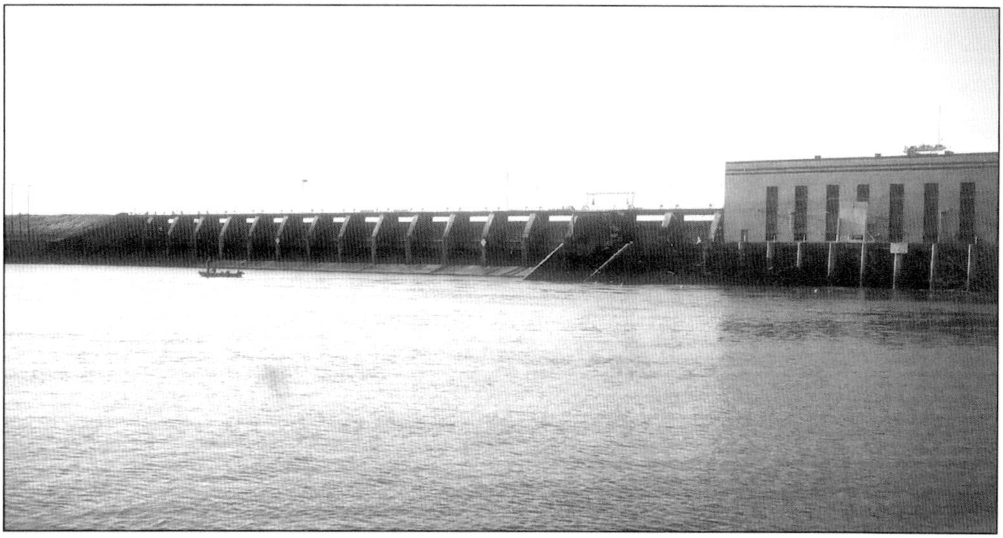

Castle Rock Lake covers 26 square miles. Castle Rock Dam is the fourth largest hydroplant on the Wisconsin River. Its five generating units generate 15,000 kilowatts of electricity. Many beautiful homes have been built on the lake. Castle Rock Park covers 160 acres and has 300 campsites. Buckhorn State Park (2,500 acres) is located on a peninsula in Castle Rock flowage. The Castle Rock Dam and Lake have contributed power and tourism to Juneau County. (1950, Jacqueline Ann)

The Petenwell Dam is the second largest hydropower development on the Wisconsin River. It develops 20,000 kilowatts of electricity from its four generating units on 15 miles of lake. Wilderness Park is on Petenwell Lake. The park has over 100 campsites for tents and trailers. Tourism is big business in Juneau County, bringing 83 million people into the county every year. Petenwell Dam and Lake contribute greatly to Juneau's tourist business. (1950, Jacqueline Ann.)

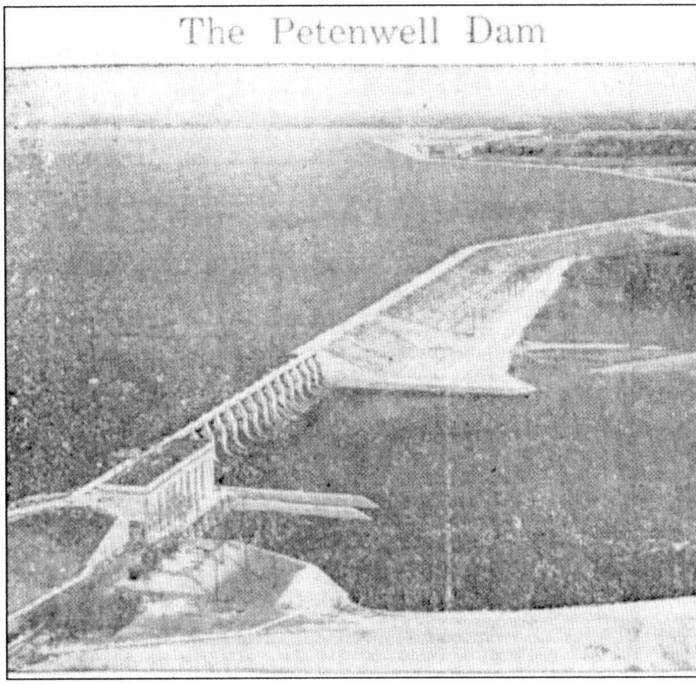

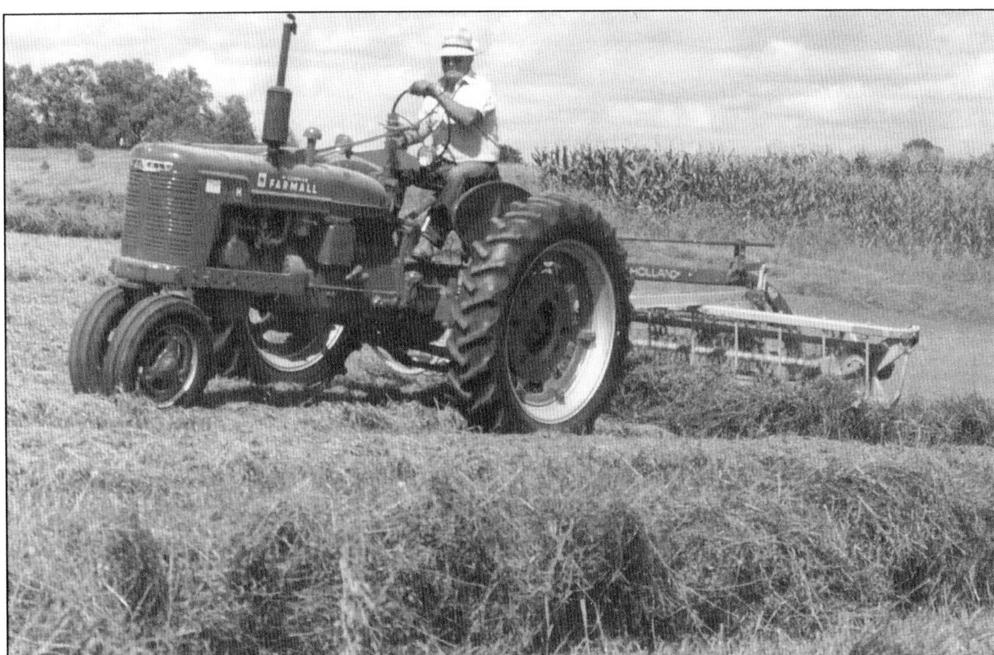

Farm equipment helps to cut a farmer's work hours on a particular task. In this picture, James Ott Senior is raking hay. Early settlers would have raked hay using their team of oxen or horses. The need and expense of more sophisticated equipment can push a small farmer out of business. Today we see many large farms in Juneau and Sauk counties as a result of consolidation. (1990s, Barb Ott)

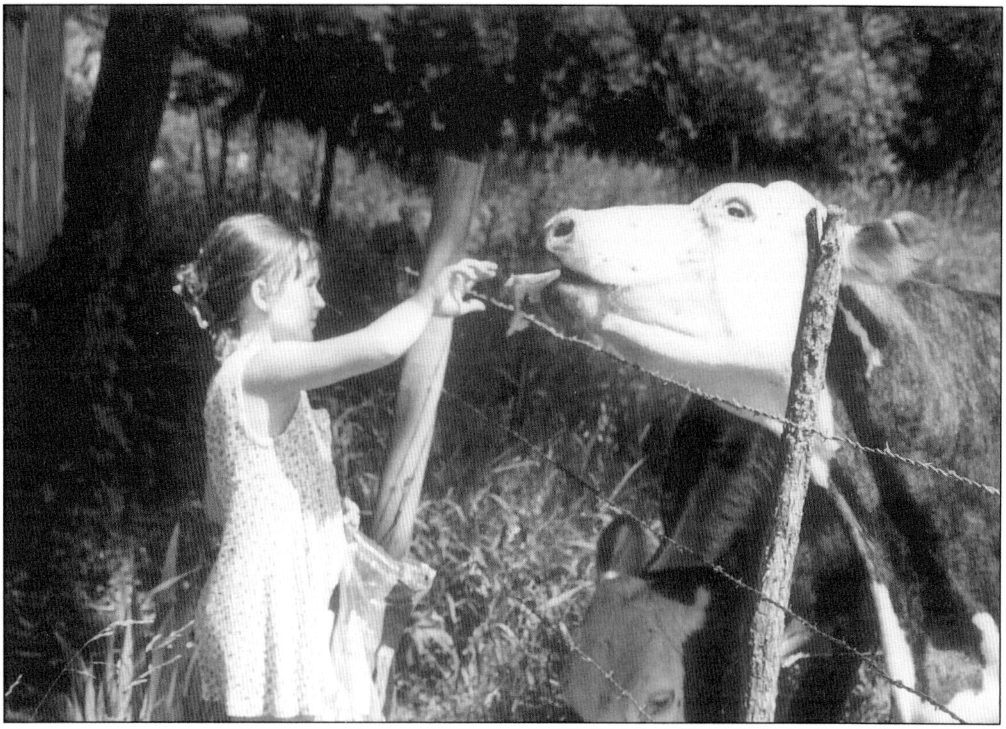

Kelly Herrewig knows farm fun. She rattles a bread bag and the Herefords come running. Kelly says, "These cows love eating my mom's bread and anything else she makes." (2000, Barb Ott.)

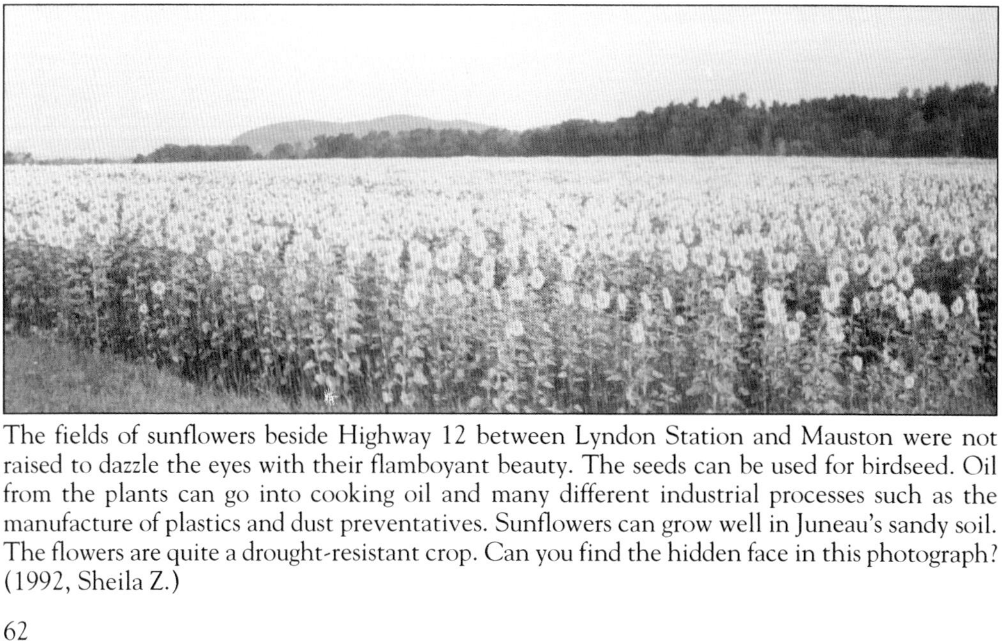

The fields of sunflowers beside Highway 12 between Lyndon Station and Mauston were not raised to dazzle the eyes with their flamboyant beauty. The seeds can be used for birdseed. Oil from the plants can go into cooking oil and many different industrial processes such as the manufacture of plastics and dust preventatives. Sunflowers can grow well in Juneau's sandy soil. The flowers are quite a drought-resistant crop. Can you find the hidden face in this photograph? (1992, Sheila Z.)

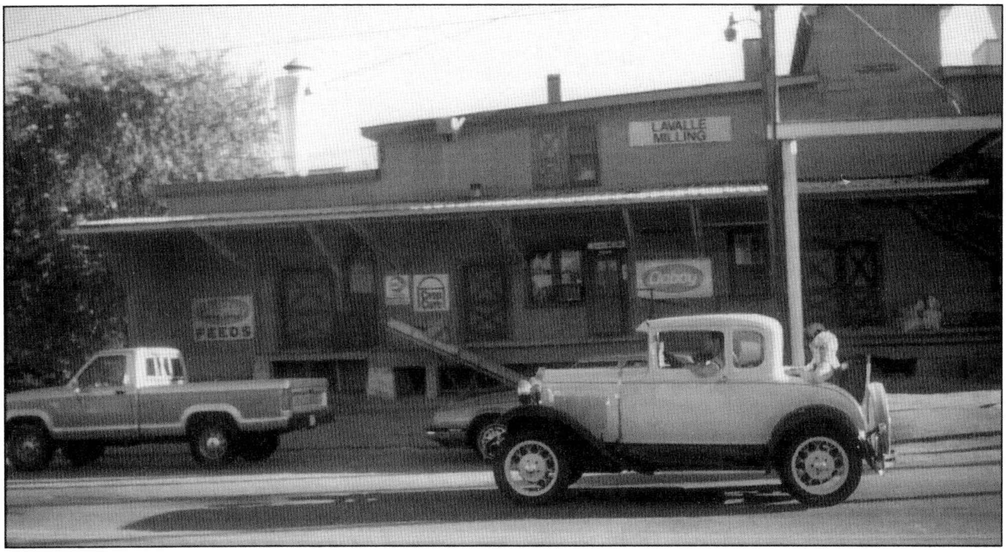

This is the Treasure Mill, formerly the LaValle Mill. In this picture, taken in 1992, Roy and Hazel Owen are touring past the LaValle Mill in a Model A to celebrate their 50th wedding anniversary. When they farmed, they used this roller mill to fan oats for their seeds. The LaValle Mill was built in 1864. The mill ground oats and corn into animal food. Today the Treasure Mill is owned by Mike and Judy Cummings, who keep the history of the mill alive through displays and by exposing some of the original structure. It is now a tourist attraction as well as a craft and antique mall. The Cummings lease sections to 10 to 12 other antique dealers. (1992, Marie Geitz.)

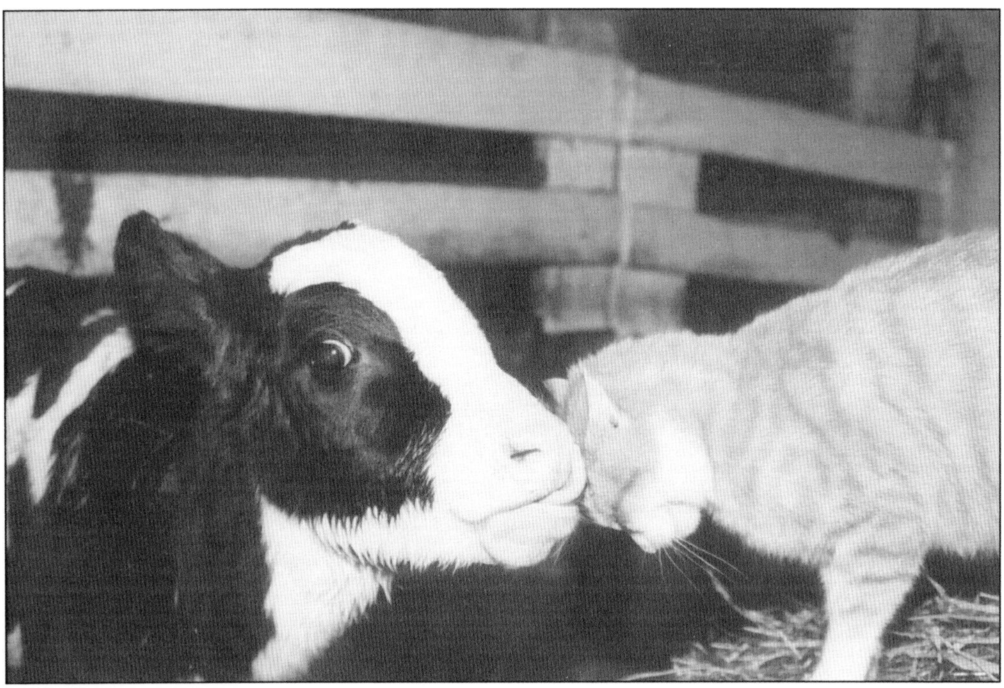

Dairy farming is big business in Juneau County. This playful Holstein calf will grow up to be a productive part of her dairy herd. (1990s, Barb Ott.)

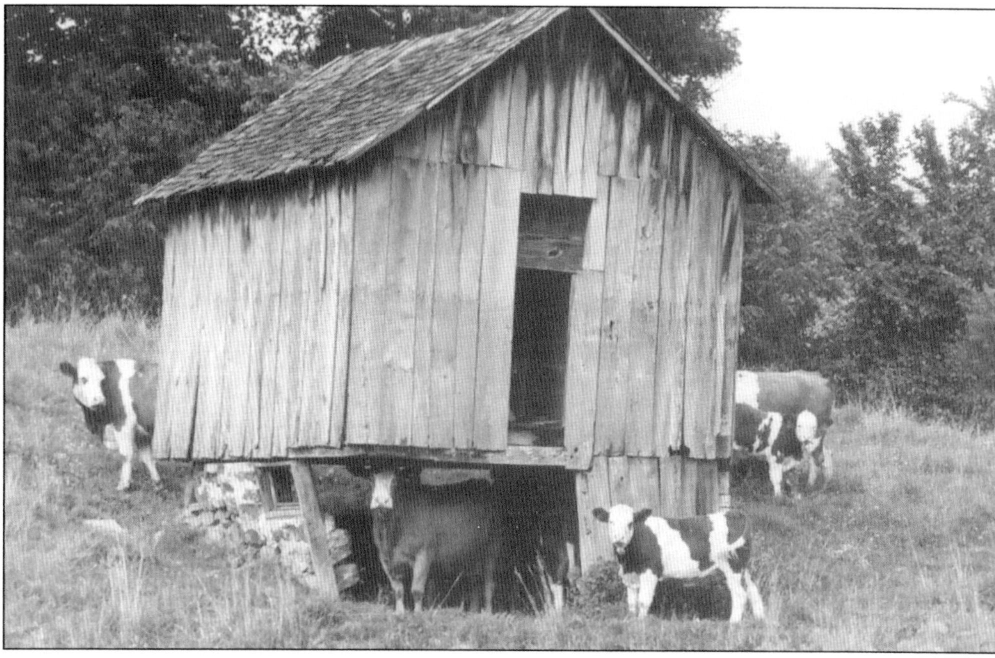

There is no end to the work these beef cattle in Sauk County have to do. The long Hereford is checking on the other Hereford who is holding up the shed. Since this picture was taken, the shed has fallen down. (1990s, Barb Ott.)

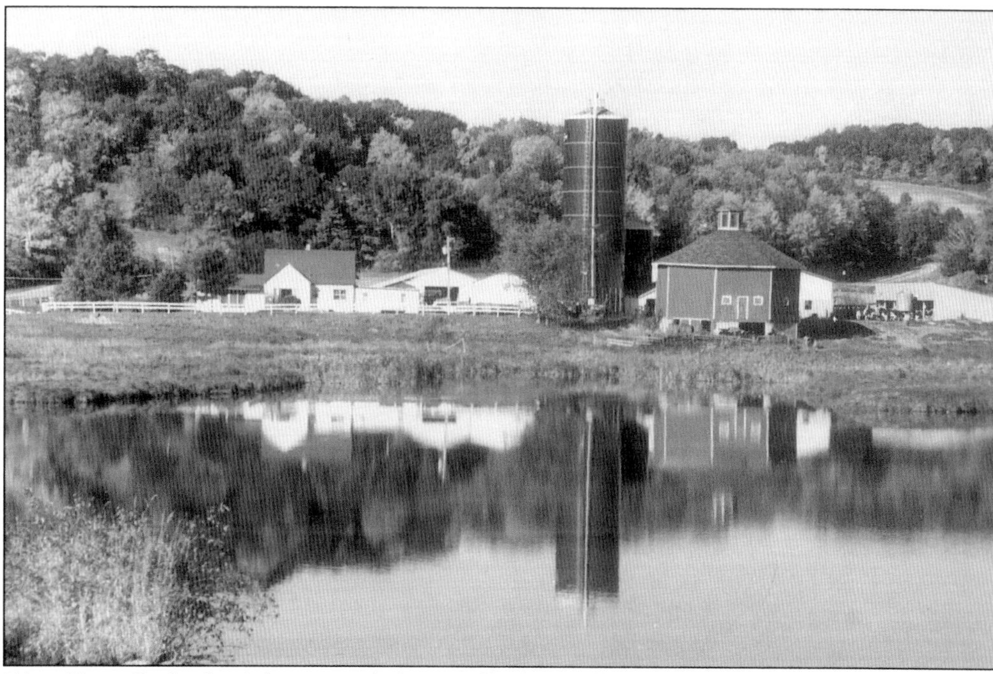

Ed and Joyce Bodendein's farm is nestled in a Valley by a millpond. Most early settlers began farming by raising wheat, then learned to diversify. Cattle, sheep, hogs, and chickens became a part of a farmer's business. The LaValle Dam was removed from the Baraboo River, so today this scene would not include the pond, another example that change is a constant. (1990s, Barb Ott.)

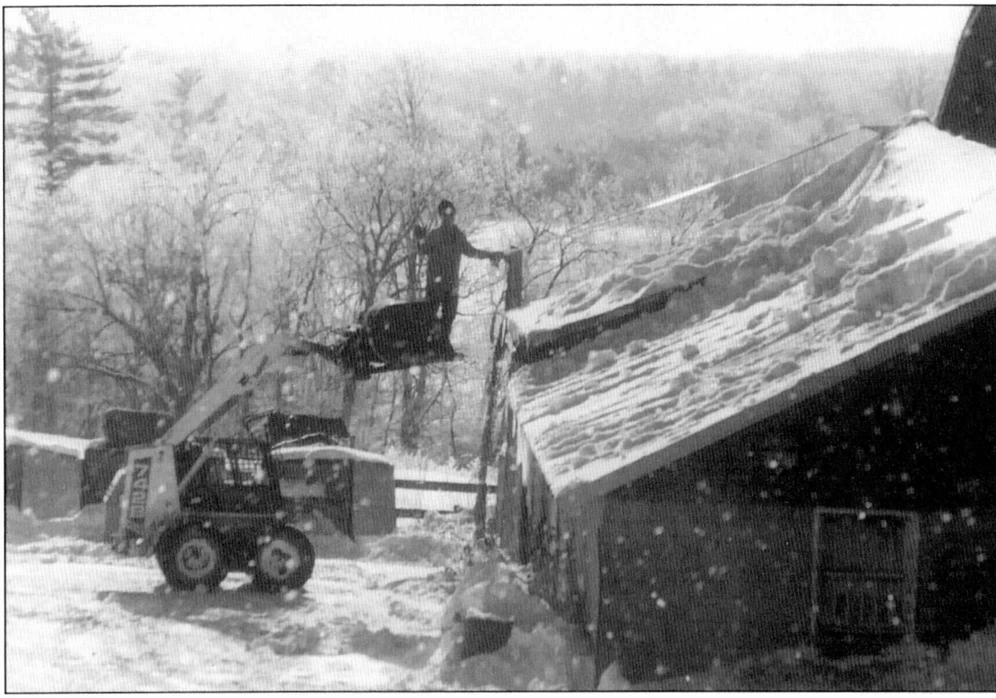

Lots of snow fell on this Juneau County farm during the night. This busy farmer is pictured cleaning snow off the barn roof with the help of a long metal rake and bobcat. (2000, Barb Ott.)

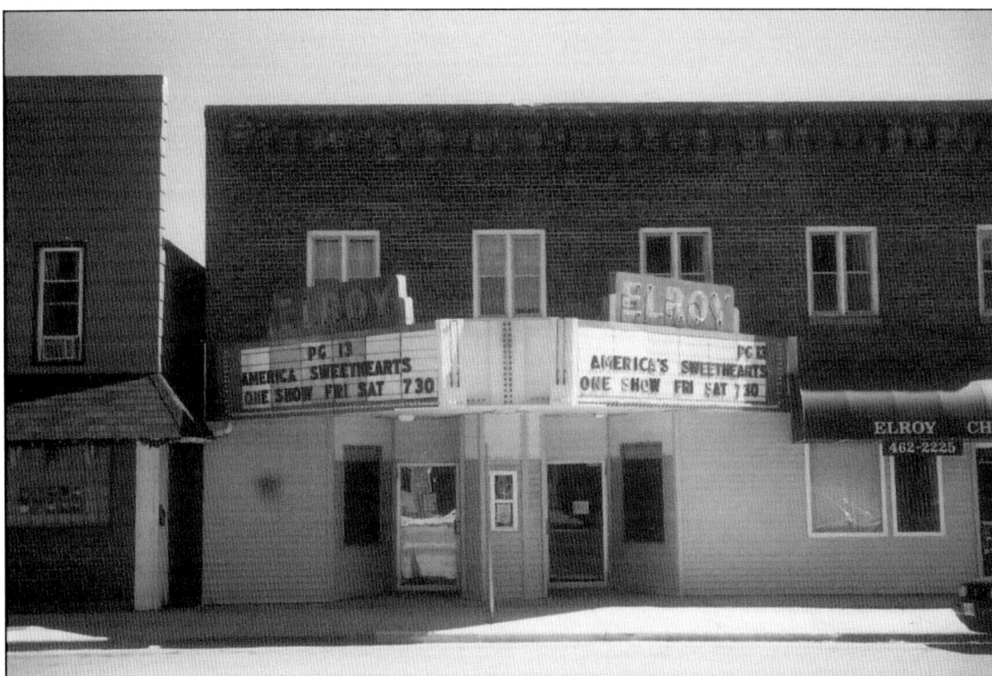

Today people go to multi-screen theaters if they want to see a movie, but not in Elroy. Elroy's old theater is the last of its kind operating in Juneau County. (2000, Sheila Z.)

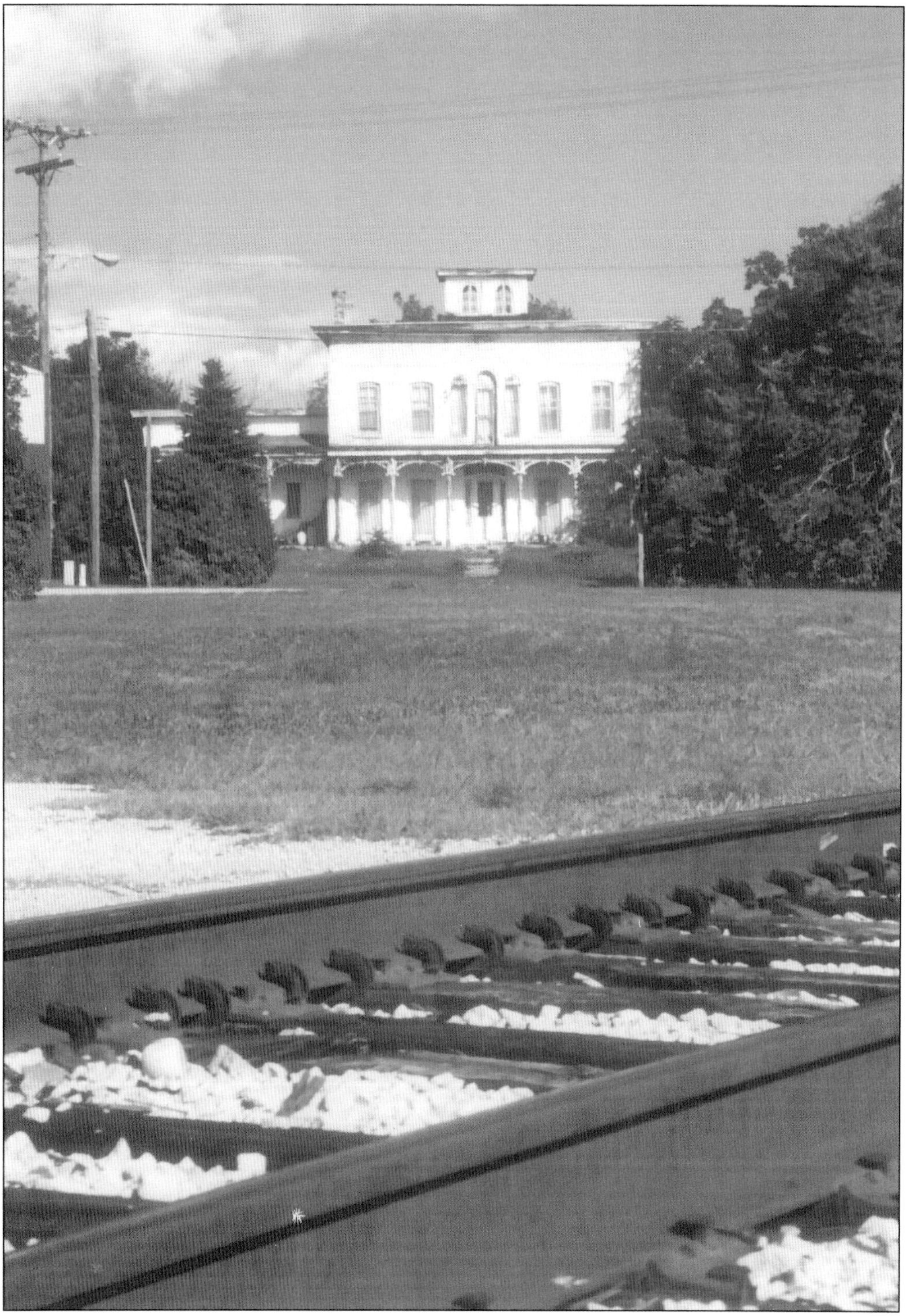

When the railroads were routed through villages, hotels would be built to accommodate the passengers. The Victorian Rooms was such a hotel in New Lisbon during the late 1800s and early 1900s. The hotel still rents rooms. (2000, Sheila Z.)

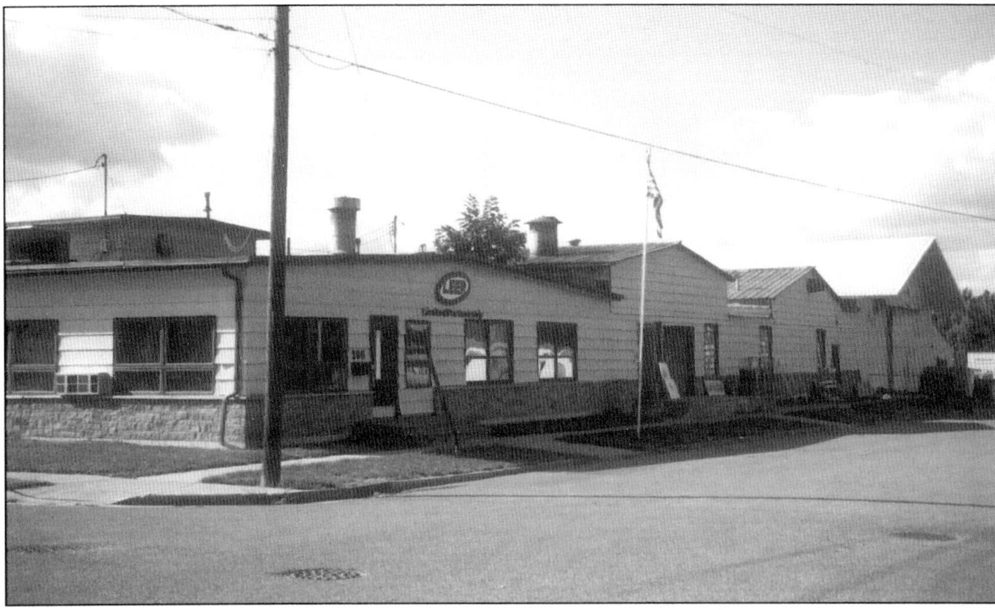

This is a picture of the Leer Company in New Lisbon. William Rothe came to this community when he was 23. He made the first ice-vending machine. This was the beginning of the Leer Company. (2000, Sheila Z.)

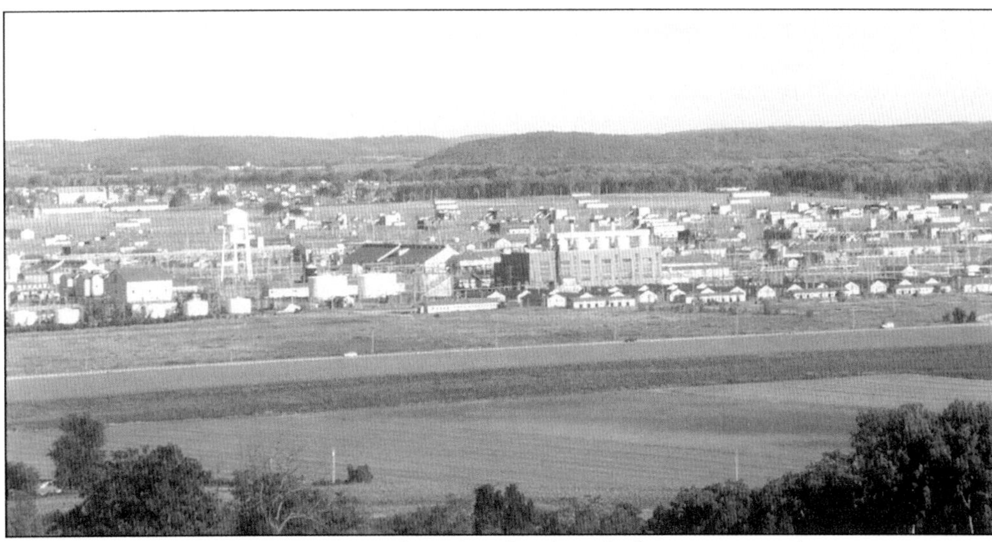

There were many unhappy farmers when they first heard of government plans to put an army ammunition plant on the fertile Sauk Prairie. Old Sauk Prairie had loam soil. After Pearl Harbor, the dissension ceased. All the farmers wanted were fair prices for their land. The plant was built in 1942 and 1943 for World War II and employed 13,000 to 14,000 people. After the war, the plant was deactivated. In 1951, the plant re-opened for the Korean War. Employees numbered 4,900 in 1953. The plant was deactivated until the Vietnam War, employing 5,200 people in 1969. After World War II, when employment declined because of the plant, a group of local people incorporated as the Baraboo Industrial Expansion Company. Due to this Corporation, Baraboo has a variety of businesses today. There is now a coalition of parties to return land such as Sauk Prairie to its former natural condition. (2000, Sheila Z.)

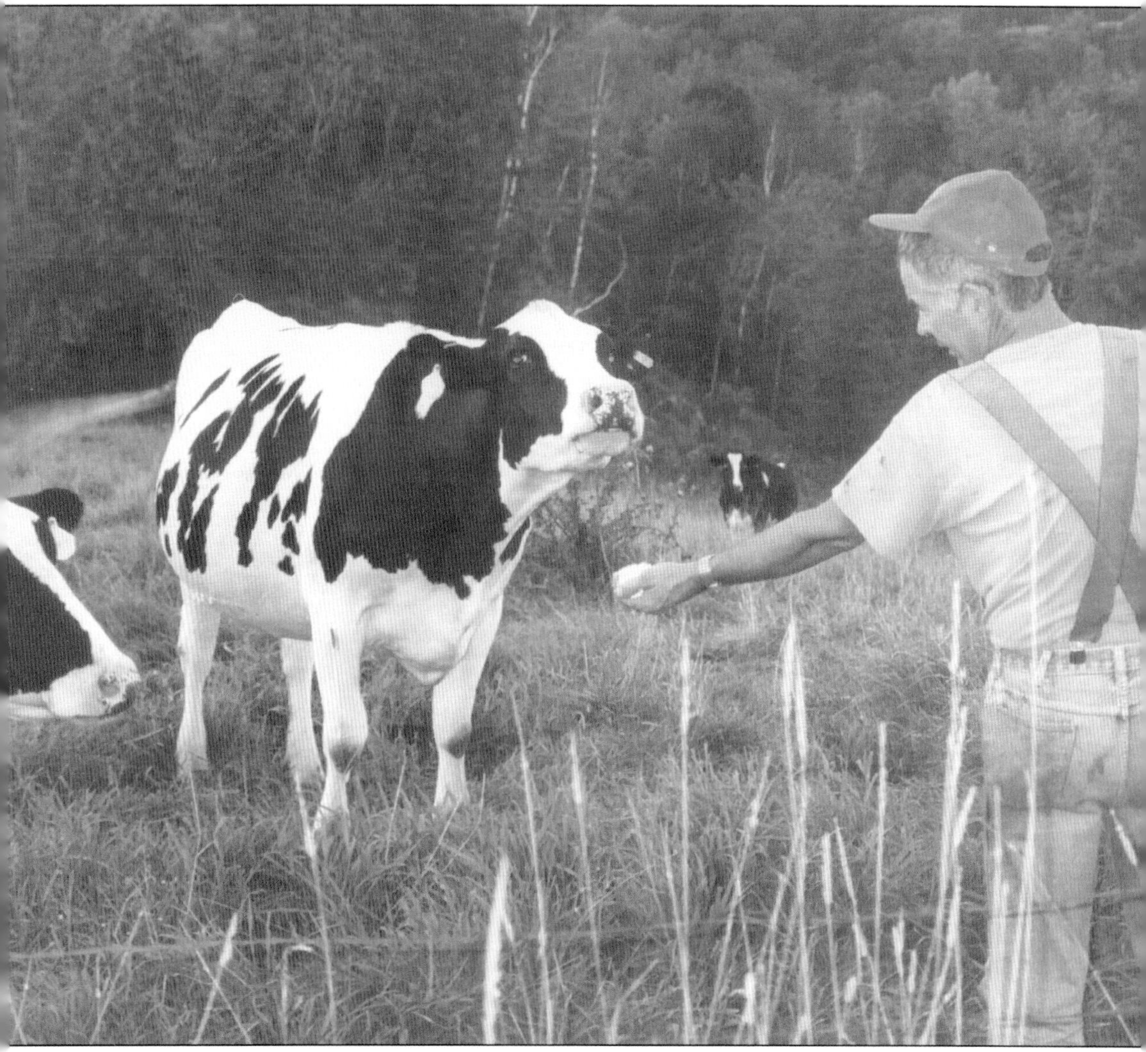

The Holstein Herefords are out in the pasture. When Jim goes to check on them once or twice a week, he takes a pail of grain. The Herefords come running when he calls. (1990s, Barb Ott.)

Five

TOURISM

Juneau and Sauk Counties are a tourist's paradise. These counties are home to the fantasy world of the Wisconsin Dells, the duck rides from Lake Delton, and numerous antique shops. The natural beauty of the unusual rock formations near Camp Douglas and New Lisbon draw both the tourist and geologist. Our abundant plant life is admired by tourist and studied by groups from the University. In addition, different types of Indian effigy mounds have been preserved in both counties. There are excellent historical museums in Mauston, Baraboo, and Elroy. Reedsburg is home to a pioneer village and the Norman Rockwell Museum. In Baraboo, we have the Circus World Museum, and North Freedom has a train museum.

The sportsman can hunt, fish, use all kinds of watercraft, camp, hike, bike, and ride horses. There are activities for all seasons. The animal life in our counties is excellent, from the Crane Foundation to the black bears in Buckhorn Park. Accommodations range from campgrounds to luxurious motels. Restaurants can be simple or elegant.

Juneau and Sauk Counties appreciate tourists.

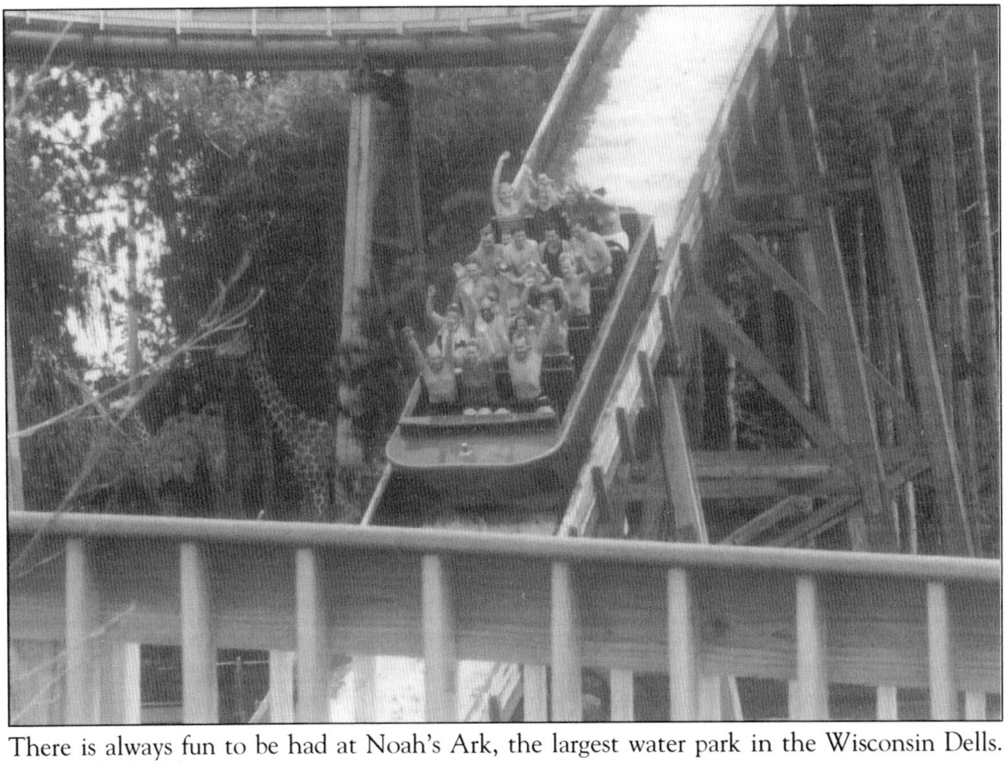

There is always fun to be had at Noah's Ark, the largest water park in the Wisconsin Dells. (1999, Sheila Z.)

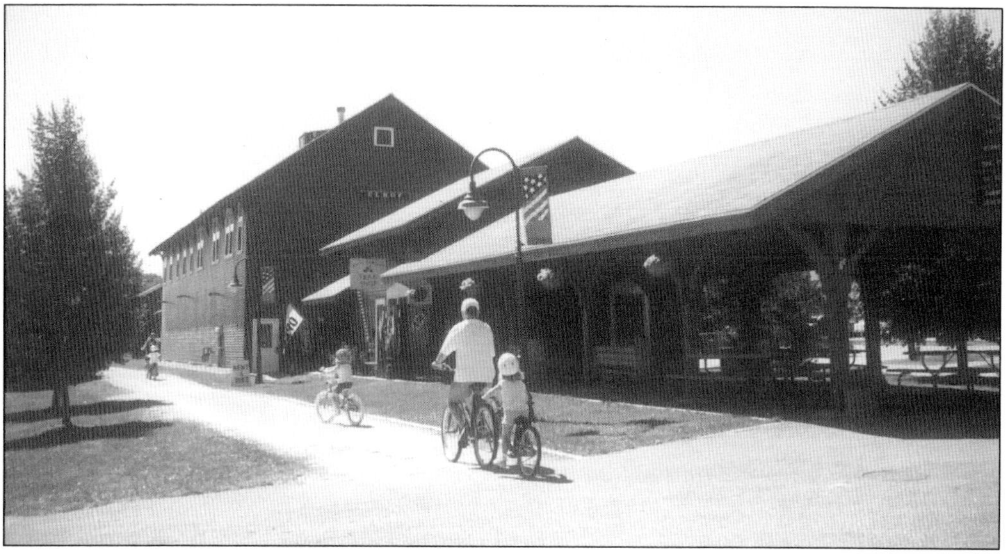

This family is biking in front of Elroy's Trail Shop on the Elroy-Sparta Bike Trail. When the Chicago & Northwestern Railroad discontinued its service to Elroy, the old rail bed was made into the Elroy-Sparta State Trail—the first of its kind in the U.S. Two other trails begin at Elroy. The seal-coated Omaha Trail goes from Elroy to Camp Douglas and is 12.5 miles. It travels through an 875-foot tunnel. The 22-mile 400 Trail runs from Elroy to Reedsburg, paralleling the Baraboo River. (2000, Sheila Z.)

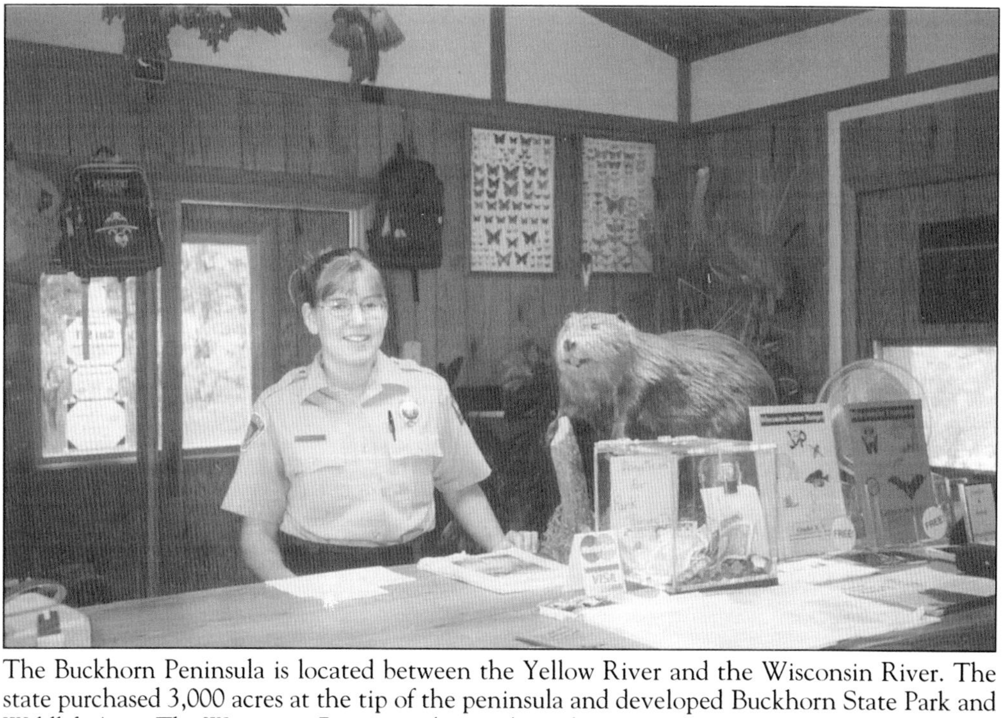

The Buckhorn Peninsula is located between the Yellow River and the Wisconsin River. The state purchased 3,000 acres at the tip of the peninsula and developed Buckhorn State Park and Wildlife Area. The Wisconsin River was dammed just downstream from where the Yellow River flows into the Wisconsin River, creating Castle Rock Lake, the fourth largest lake in Wisconsin. Heather McPherson is the Assistant Manager at Buckhorn. (2000, Sheila Z.)

Besides its natural wilderness beauty, Buckhorn State Park offers a smorgasbord of outdoor experiences. There are opportunities to use every kind of watercraft, daily encounters with the wild animals that live there, and the chance for each individual to follow his or her own interests. Some of the animals living at Buckhorn are Canadian geese, herons, sand hill cranes, ducks, muskrats, beavers, otters, minks, deer, coyotes, wild turkeys, and sometimes a black bear. There are a variety of different kinds of campsites, activities, and programs for all seasons. (2000, Sheila Z.)

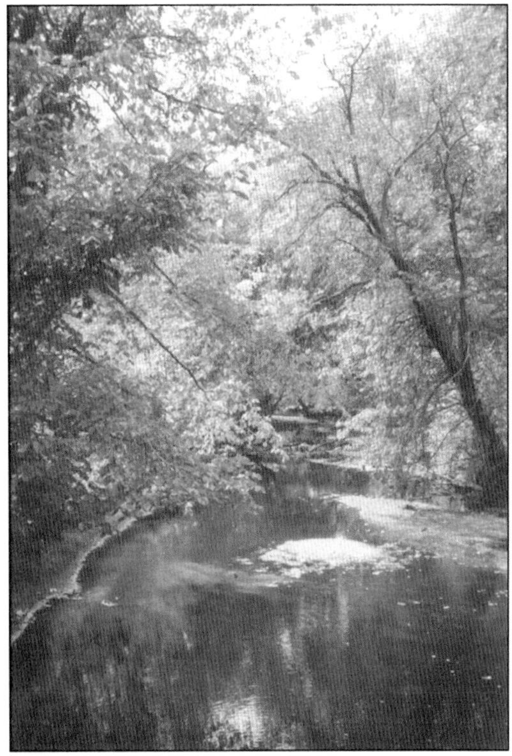

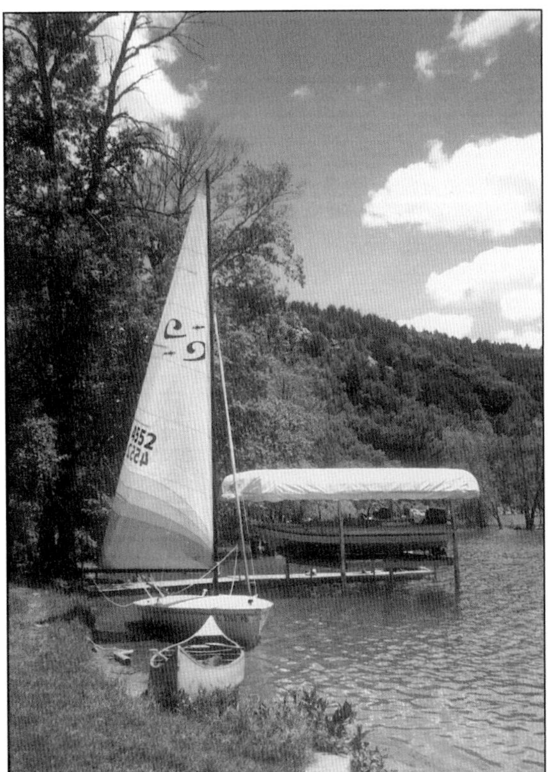

Devil's Lake is 3-miles south of Baraboo. The bluffs rise 500-feet above the water. There is camping, swimming, fishing, use of watercraft, and hiking, all in a beautiful setting. Millions of tourists visit Devil's Lake each year. (1998, Barb Ott.)

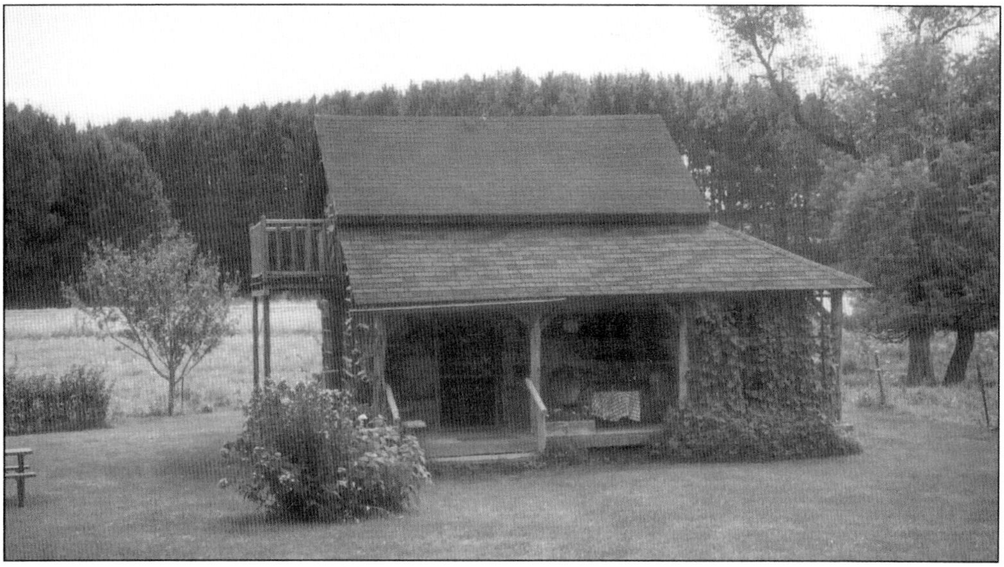

This is an authentic 140-year-old pioneer cabin known to tourists as the Waarvik's Century Farm Bed & Breakfast. A farmhouse on the property is also available for bed and breakfast. The property is 3-miles from Elroy. Osmund K. Ormson, called O.K. for short, lived in the cabin during the 1800s. For years it was used as a granary. In 1991, the cabin was moved 4-miles to the Waarvik farm. A sleeping loft, private bath, balcony, and porch contribute to its charm as it nestles on 110 acres of rolling farmland and woods. (2000, Sheila Z.)

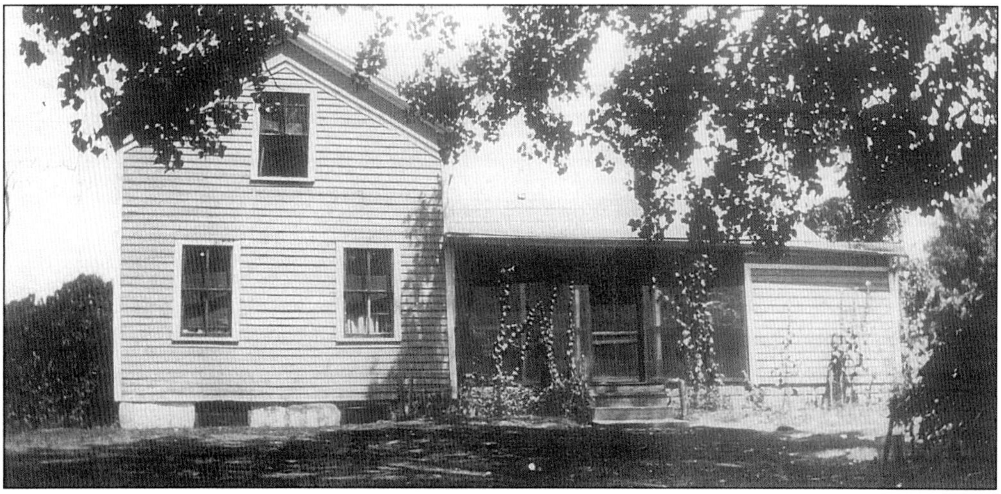

In 1913, William and Sophie Feldman and their children, Violet, Harold, Raymond, and Lucille, lived in this home about 5-miles from Mauston on Highway 82. Violet went to North Dakota to teach for a year. She came home and secured the job as teacher at the Lemonweir School where Lucille was a student. Lucille, who was eight, was so terrible that Violet locked her in the school. Lucille was very creative and crawled out a window. She did not return home until hours later; she was busy having fun in her farm neighborhood. Violet quit teaching and went to Chicago to get a job. Raymond went to North Dakota, then on to Chicago. His job brought him into contact with entertainers. Violet and Raymond began bringing home guests, many at a time. Sophie was hospitable, but one morning she looked around the breakfast table and saw 18 people. "I like you," she said, "But I can't afford to feed you." "We'll pay," the guests said. (Jacqueline Ann.)

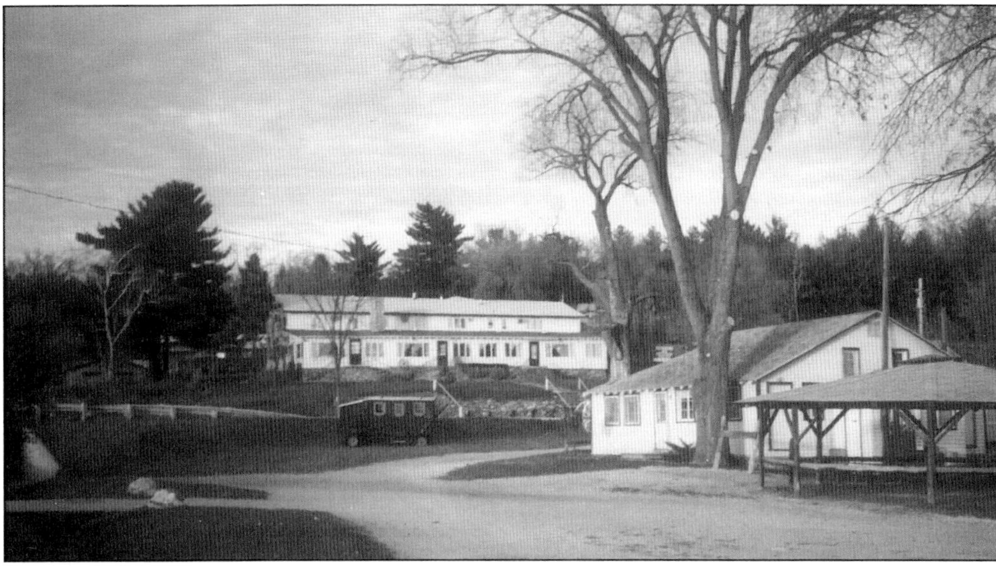

The Feldmans began charging $5 a week for room, board, and entertainment. Bob Temple, who published the *Star* (Mauston newspaper), sold the family some extra cardboard he had. They made 200 signs, started in Chicago and stapled a sign to every permanent post. "Two-hundred miles to Woodside Ranch where the fun begins." A steady procession of people began to come. (2000, Sheila Z.)

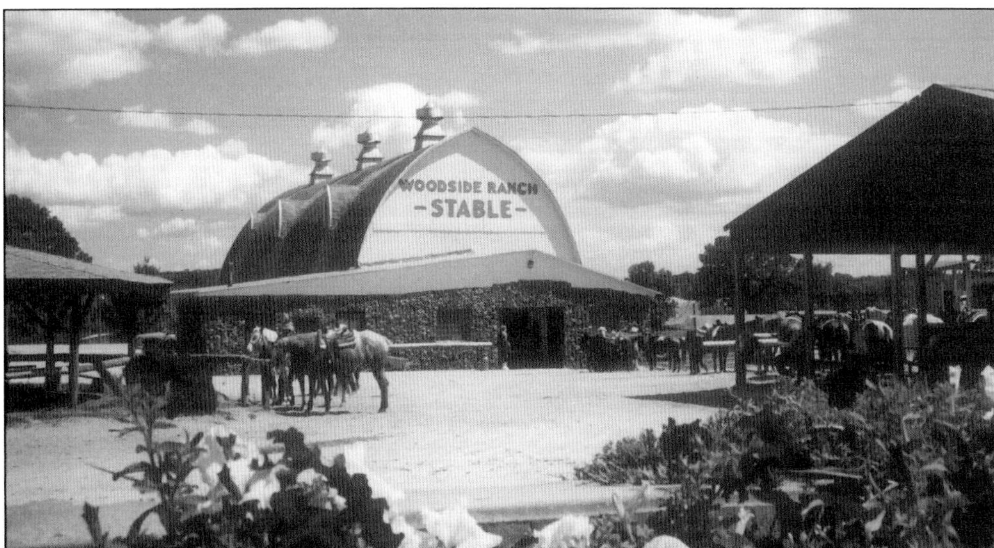

Lucille's uncle lived in Rock Springs. He bought a horse for his five daughters to share. None of the girls could ride the horse because he bucked. Uncle said to Lucille, "If you can ride that horse, I'll give him to you." Lucille rode the horse. She rode that horse from Rock Springs to Reedsburg to Lyndon Station to Woodside Ranch. Young people staying at Woodside wanted to ride her horse. Dad said, "Let them ride." Lucille didn't want to share, but there were no words to explain that to Dad. She put a pebble under the saddle and the horse bucked everyone off. So, William bought a horse or two, the herd grew, the guests grew, and William would build another cabin or two. (Jacqueline Ann.)

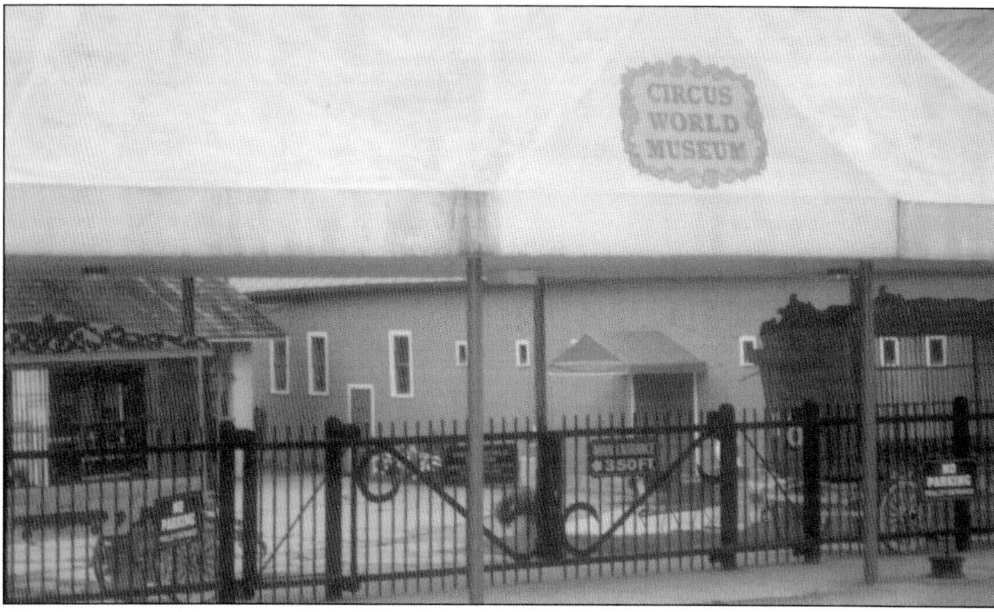

The Circus World Museum shares the history of the circus by preserving its past and sharing its excitement through circus performances. The Circus World Museum is owned by the State Historical Society of Wisconsin. The original Ringling Brothers Circus wintered at the site of the Circus World Museum. This museum is considered a National Historic Landmark. In 1918 Ringling Brothers circus wintered in Baraboo for the last time. The Ringling brothers were hop-pickers and began their circus careers by performing for other hop-pickers in the evenings. (2000, Kathryn Wu.)

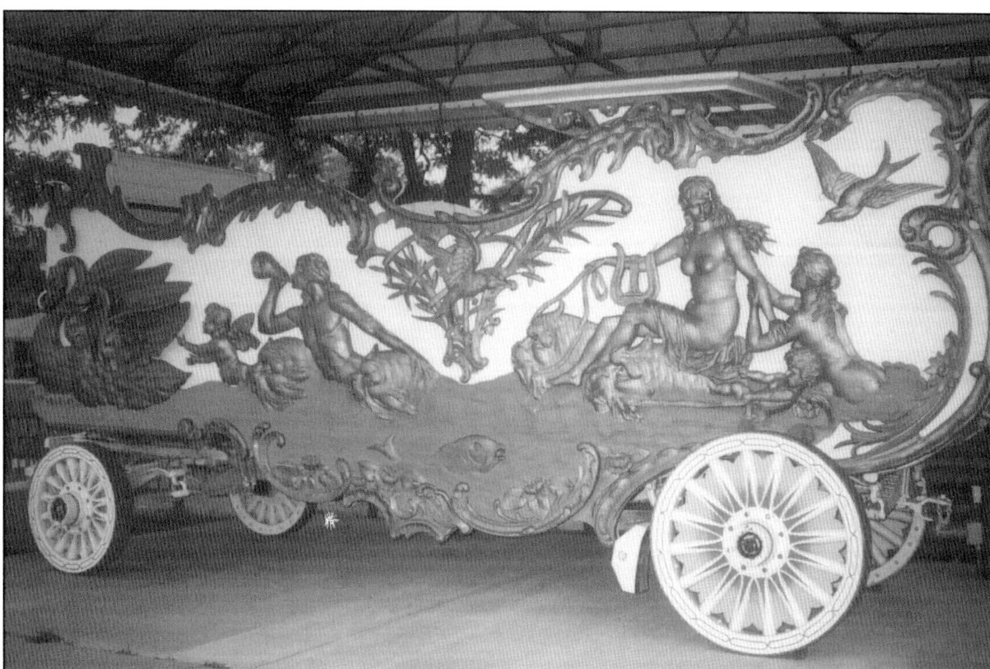

A circus wagon from the collection at the World Circus Museum. (2000, Kathryn Wu.)

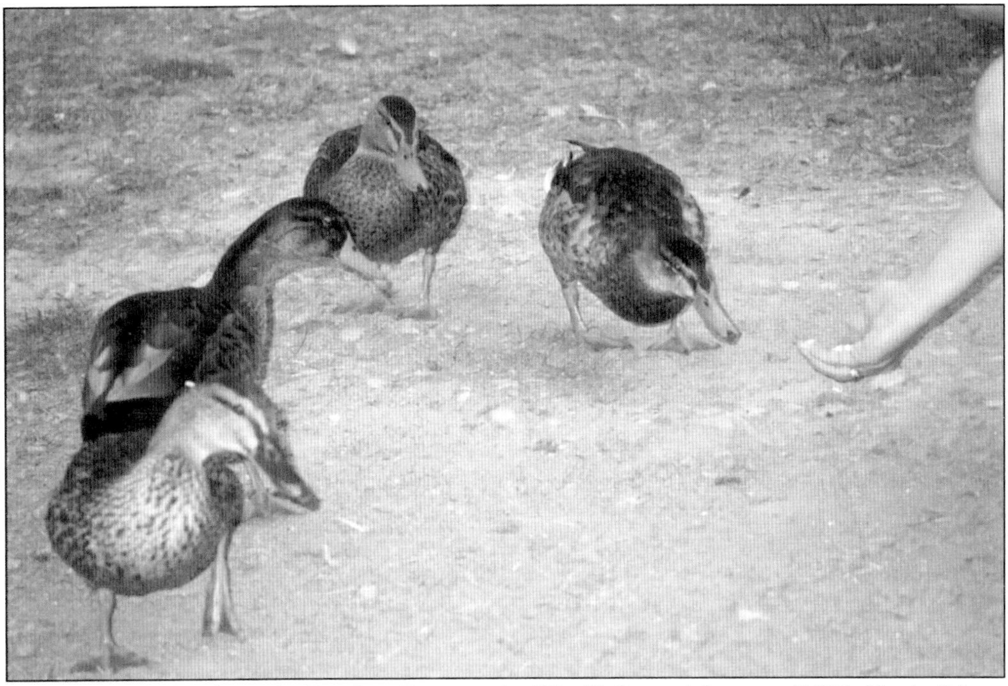

Feeding the ducks along the Baraboo River at the World Circus Museum. (2000, Sheila Z.)

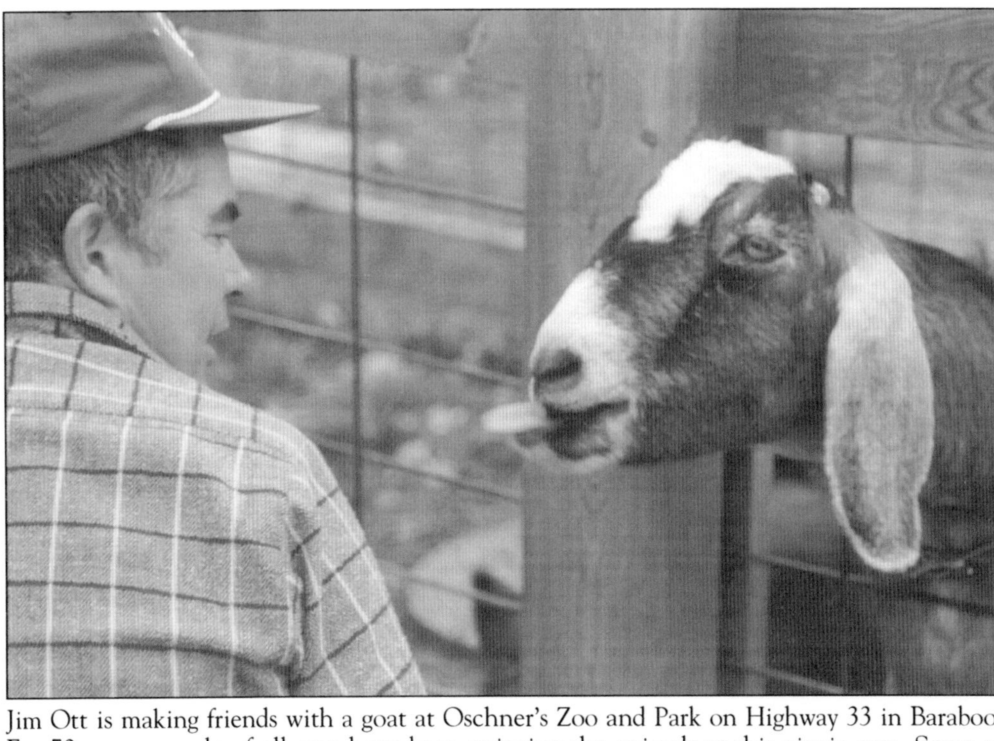

Jim Ott is making friends with a goat at Oschner's Zoo and Park on Highway 33 in Baraboo. For 70 years, people of all ages have been enjoying the animals at this picnic area. Some of the animals are timber wolves, black bears, capuchin monkeys, whitetail deer, llamas, bobcats, prairie dogs, and even a pot-bellied pig. (2000, Barb Ott.)

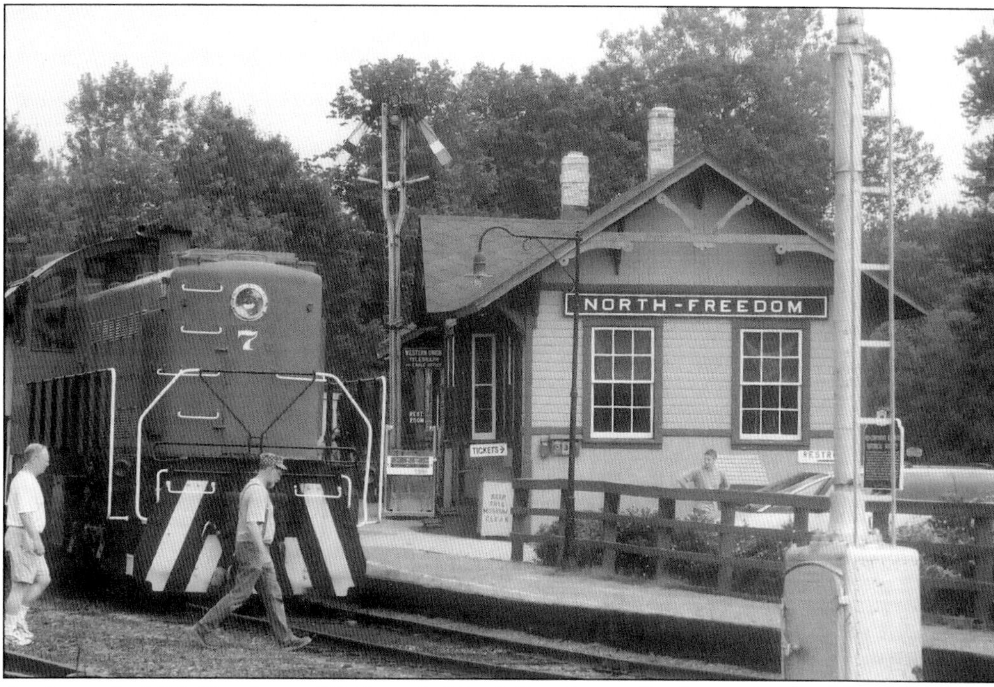

A trip on the Mid-Continental Railway in North Freedom will take you back to the early 1900s. The rides are offered daily during the summer, and on weekends until October 21. An ice cream shop, a depot, a conductor, and an engineer make for an enjoyable visit. (2000, Sheila Z.)

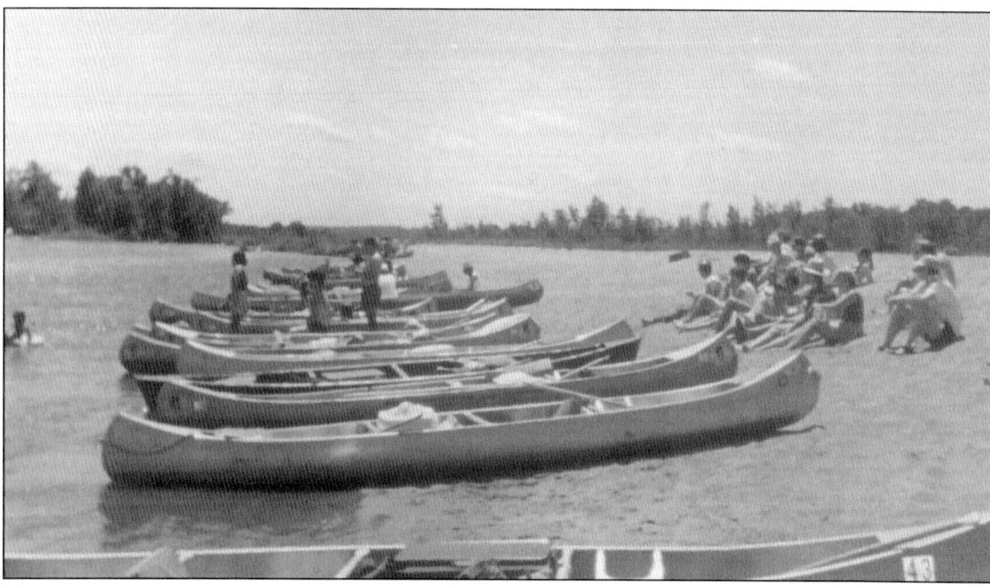

Many tourists enjoy renting canoes in Sauk City, canoeing on the Wisconsin River to Spring Green, and then returning by bus to Sauk City. The canoes can be rented for various amounts of time, as little as four hours and up to a weekend. Folks can camp out, eat, and sleep along the way. A brochure from the bus company in Sauk City lists times and pick up points. Occasionally travelers who have righted their overturned canoes can be seen diving for their possessions. (1989, Sheila Z.)

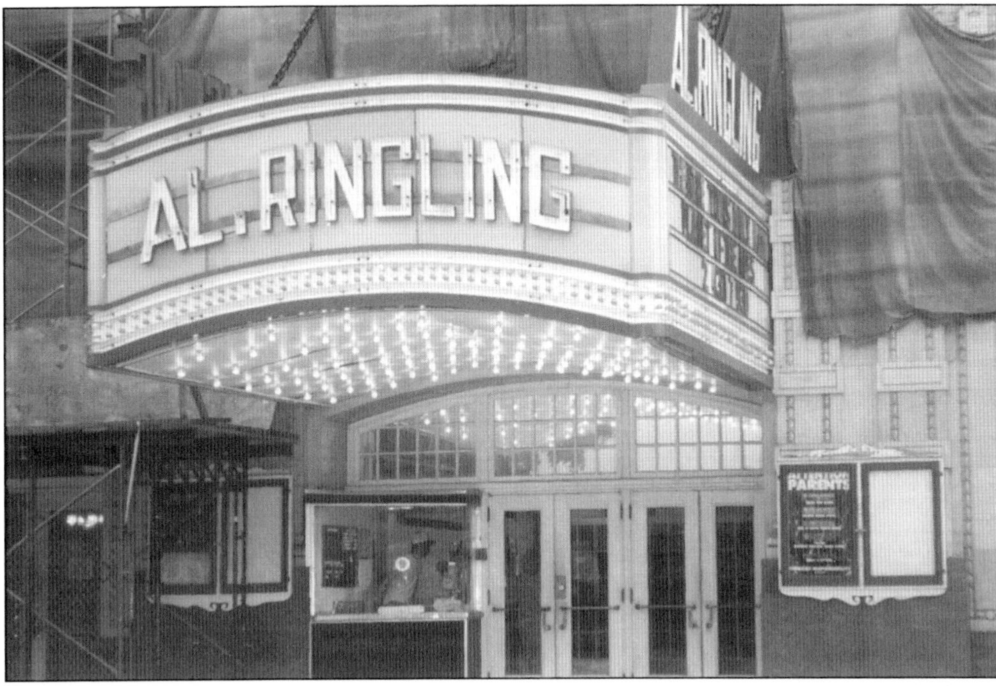

The face of the Al Ringling Theater is getting a touch up, but its beauty still causes a flicker of excitement. When visitors enter the lobby, they are tempted to lay on the floor and study the beautiful paintings covering the ceiling. (2000, Kathryn Wu.)

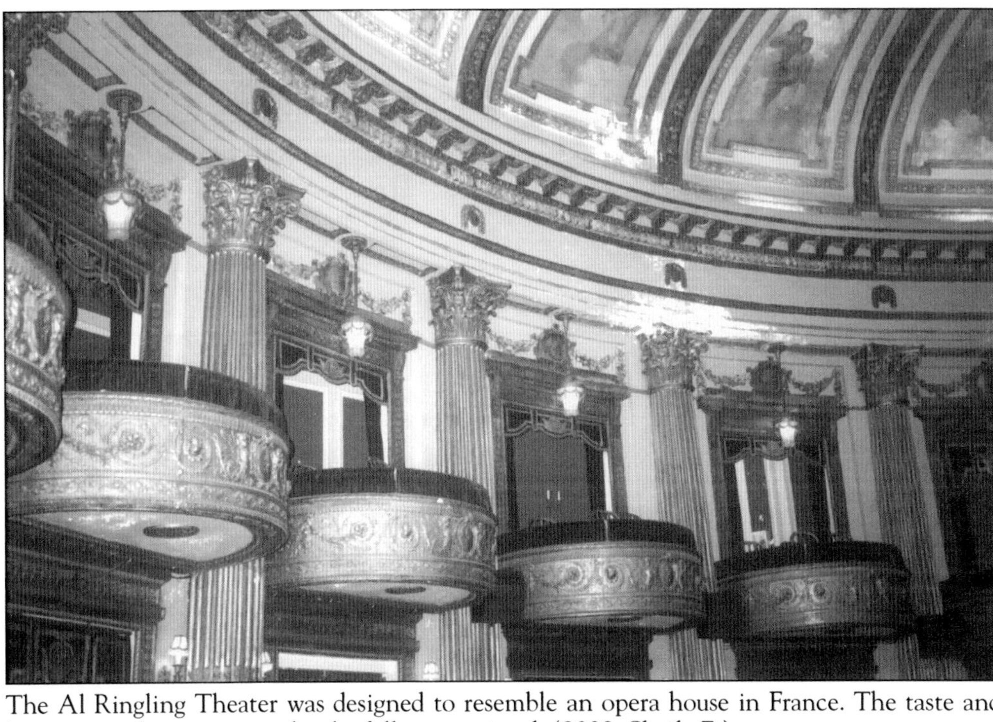

The Al Ringling Theater was designed to resemble an opera house in France. The taste and beauty must be experienced to be fully appreciated. (2000, Sheila Z.)

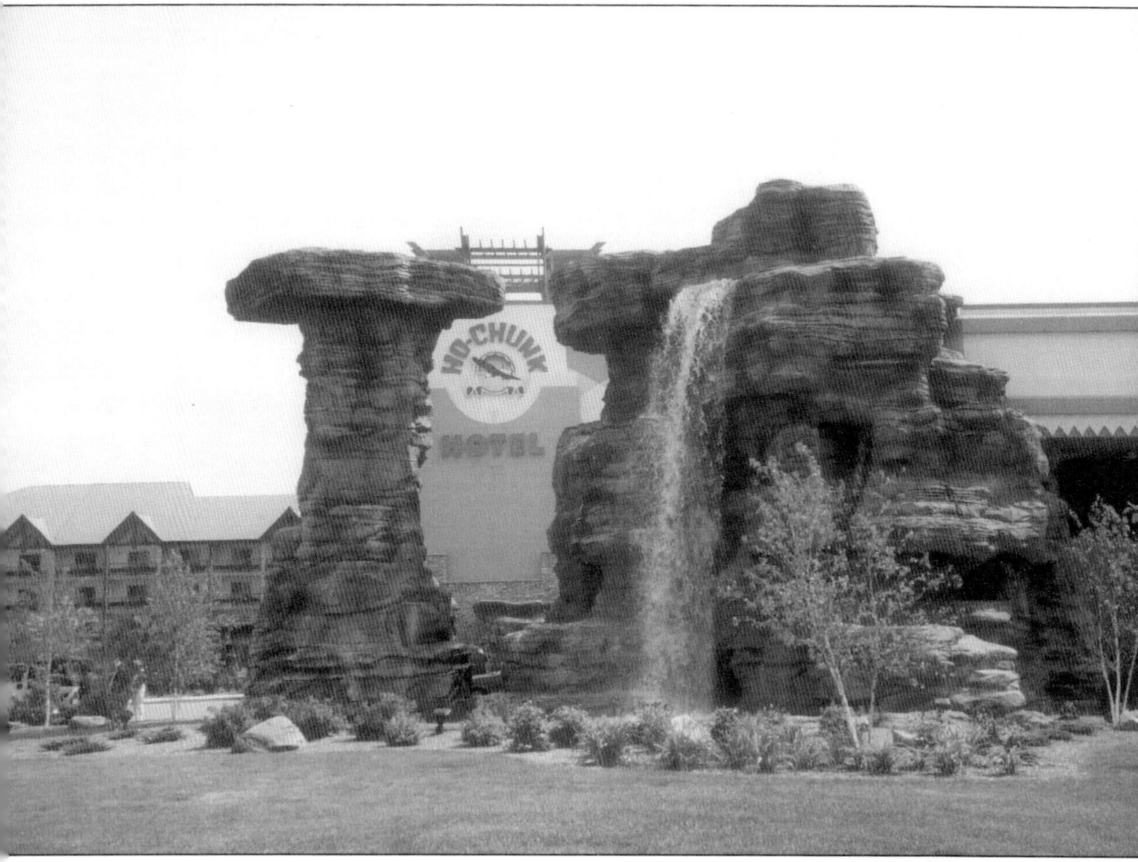

It is never easy to find a parking spot in the parking lot of the Ho-Chunk Casino. The restaurants are excellent, the hotel is beautiful, and people like to gamble. The casino offers employment to many residents of Sauk County and surrounding areas. (2001, Sheila Z.)

Six

Animals

Animals make up a wonderful part of our environment. The residents of Juneau and Sauk Counties appreciate them for their beauty and the contributions they make to keep balance in nature. The Necedah Wildlife Refuge has helped the gray wolves increase in number. The Karner Blue butterfly, as larvae, eats a plant found on the refuge, and the adult Karner butterfly eats nectar from wild flowers that grow on the refuge. Private individuals concerned about the welfare of endangered birds started the International Crane Foundation. Everyone needs to be concerned about educating themselves about animal welfare and preservation.

Your woods are still if we intrude,
But he who moves in harmony with you,
Meets hundreds of inhabitants.

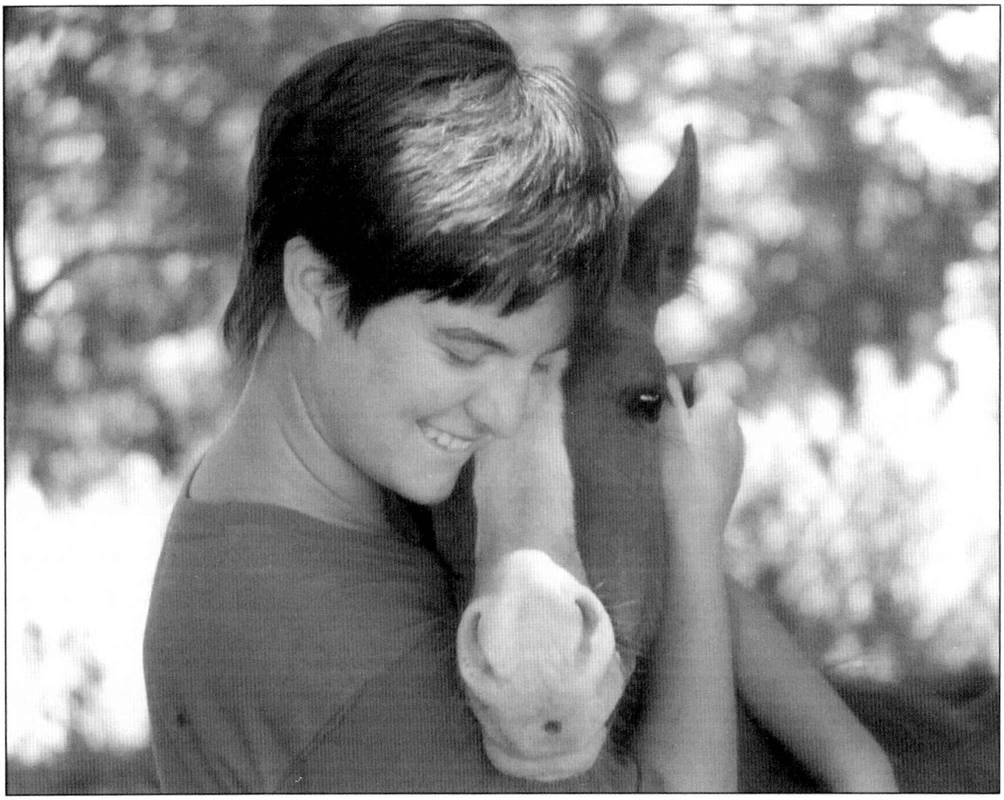

Amy hugs her colt, Smoky, nine months old. (1985, Barb Ott.)

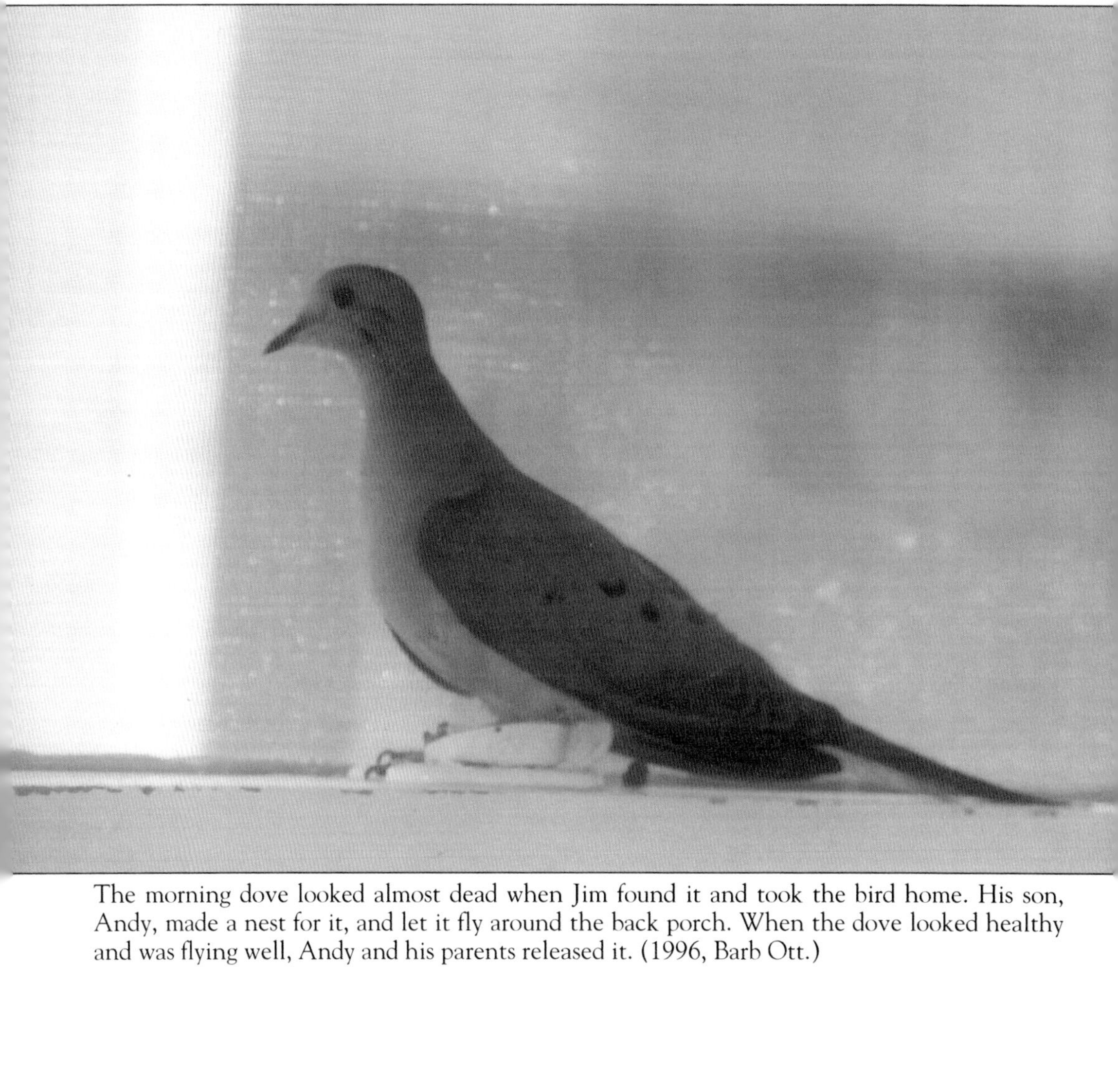

The morning dove looked almost dead when Jim found it and took the bird home. His son, Andy, made a nest for it, and let it fly around the back porch. When the dove looked healthy and was flying well, Andy and his parents released it. (1996, Barb Ott.)

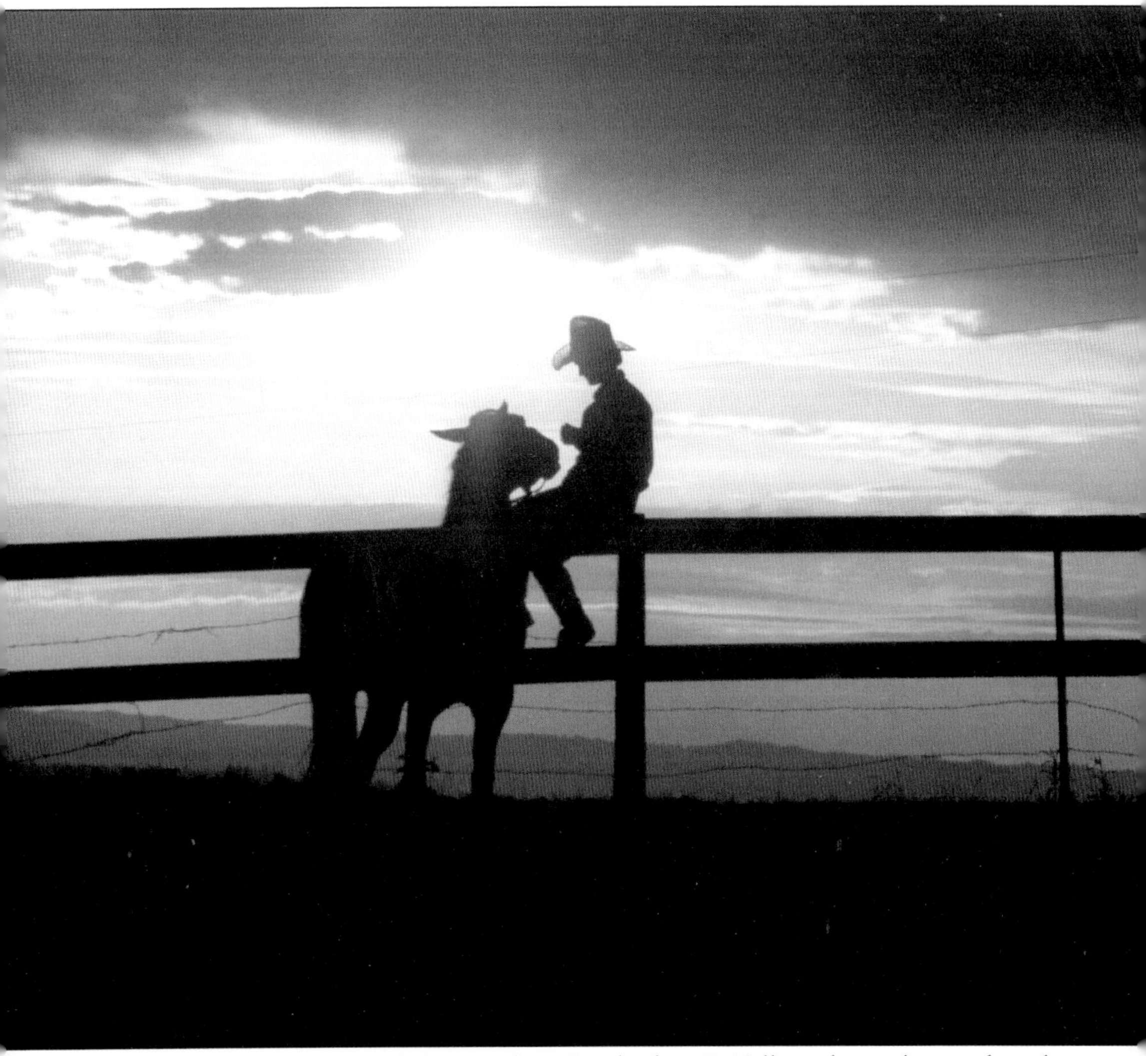

Amy, who lives on a farm in Sauk County about 5-miles from LaValle, is sharing her candy with her Arabian horse, Lucky. (1990, Barb Ott.)

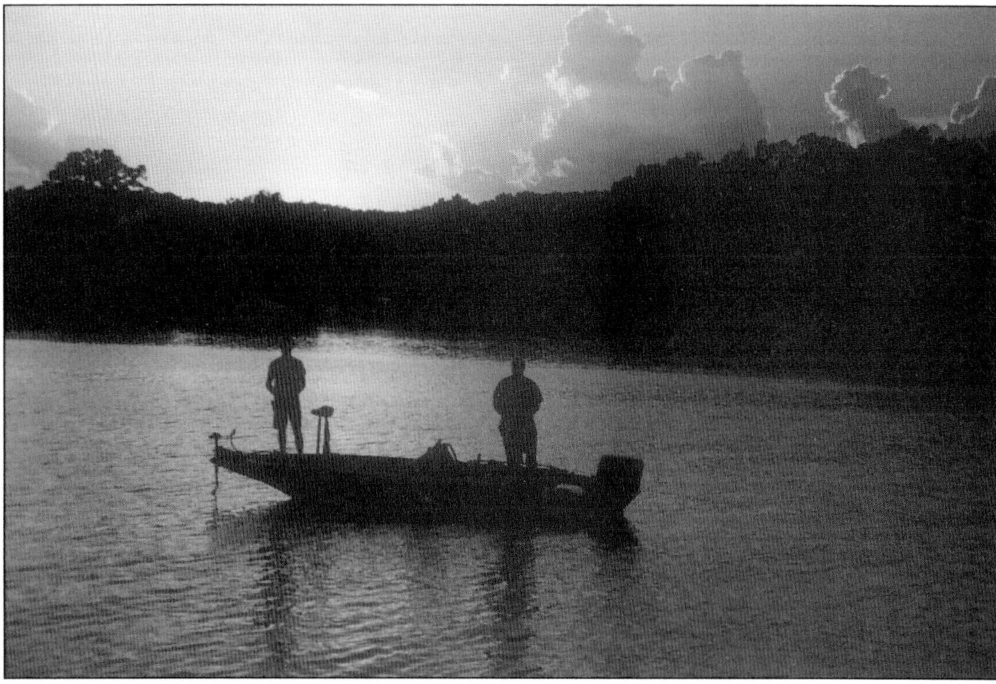

Two men are pictured here enjoying a fishing experience on Dutch Hollow Lake, near LaValle in Sauk County. (1998, Barb Ott.)

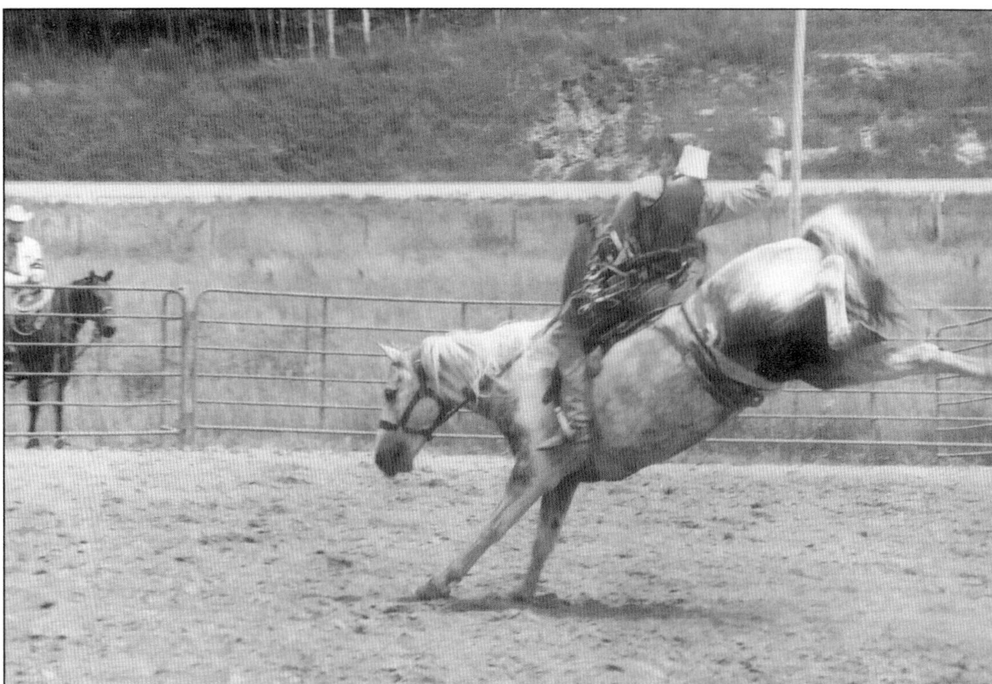

The "Little Britches Rodeo" is held on the Potter's farm between LaValle and Reedsburg. To enter, the children must be between eight and eighteen years old. They ride bucking horses and bulls in the contest. (1999, Barb Ott.)

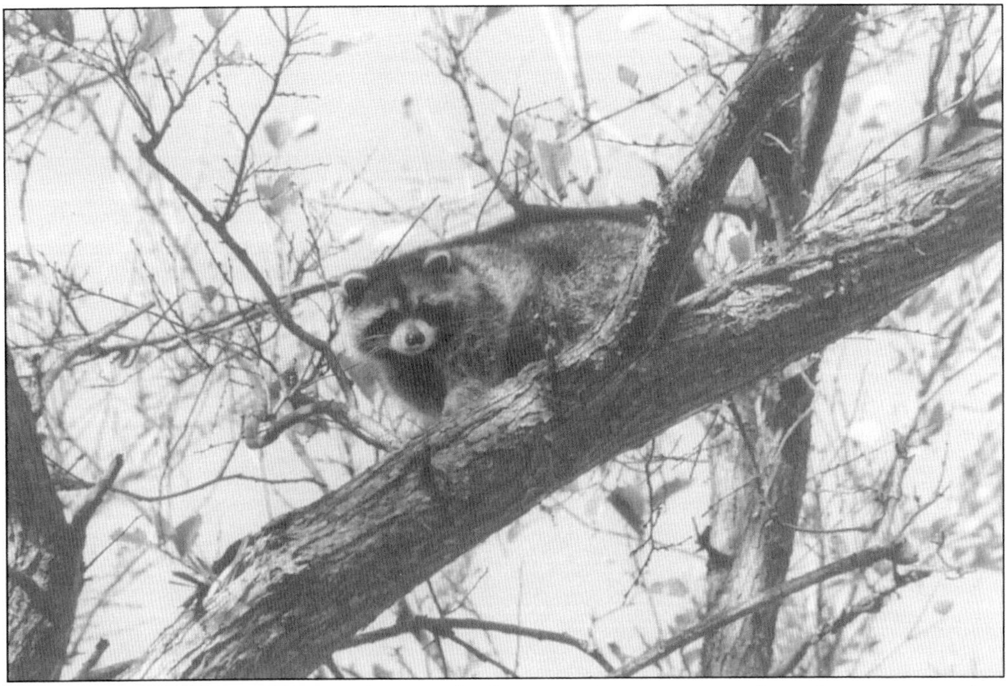

When Barb Ott was out hiking in her woods, she spotted a raccoon at about the same time that he spotted her. (1995, Barb Ott.)

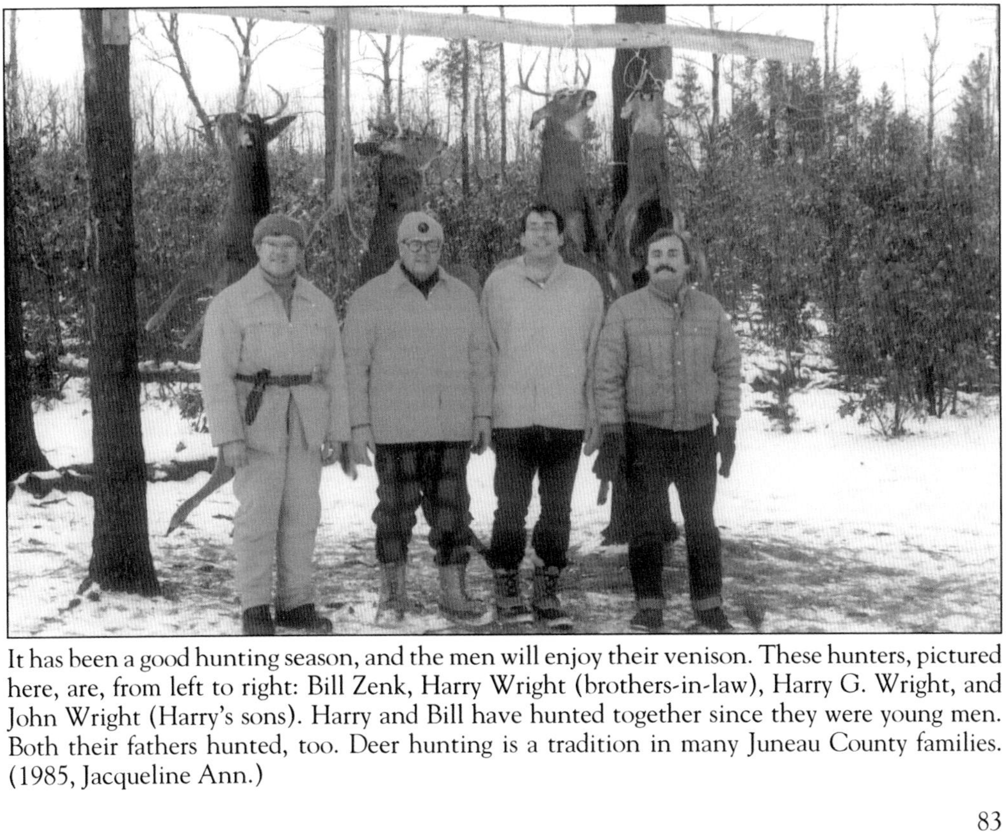

It has been a good hunting season, and the men will enjoy their venison. These hunters, pictured here, are, from left to right: Bill Zenk, Harry Wright (brothers-in-law), Harry G. Wright, and John Wright (Harry's sons). Harry and Bill have hunted together since they were young men. Both their fathers hunted, too. Deer hunting is a tradition in many Juneau County families. (1985, Jacqueline Ann.)

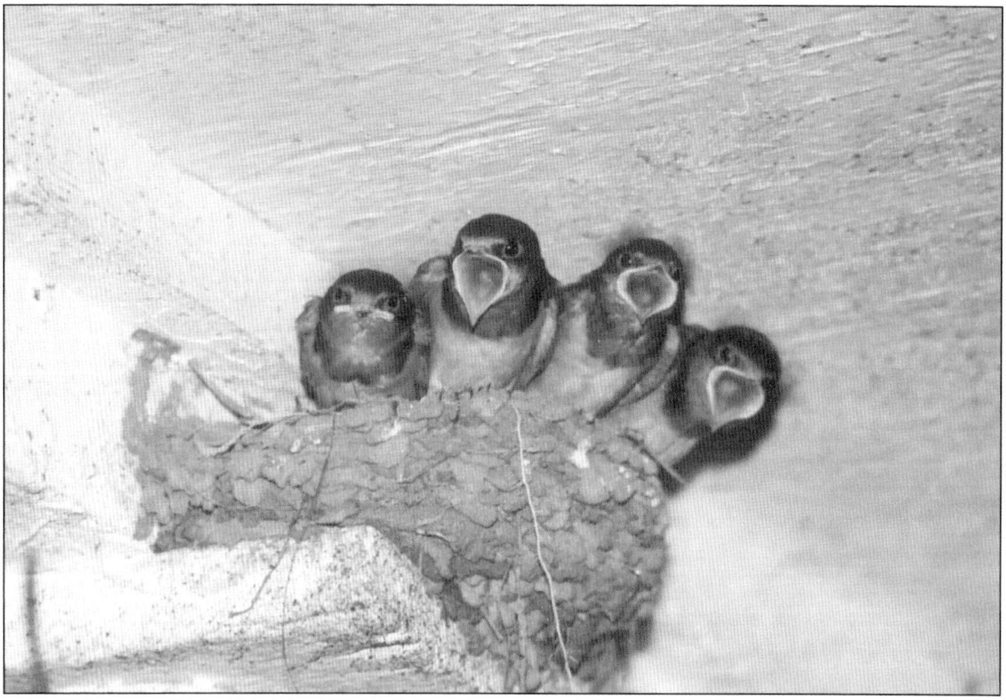

Except for the one bird fed by Mama Bird, these little barn swallows, in their home on the barn beam, are very hungry. (1992, Barb Ott.)

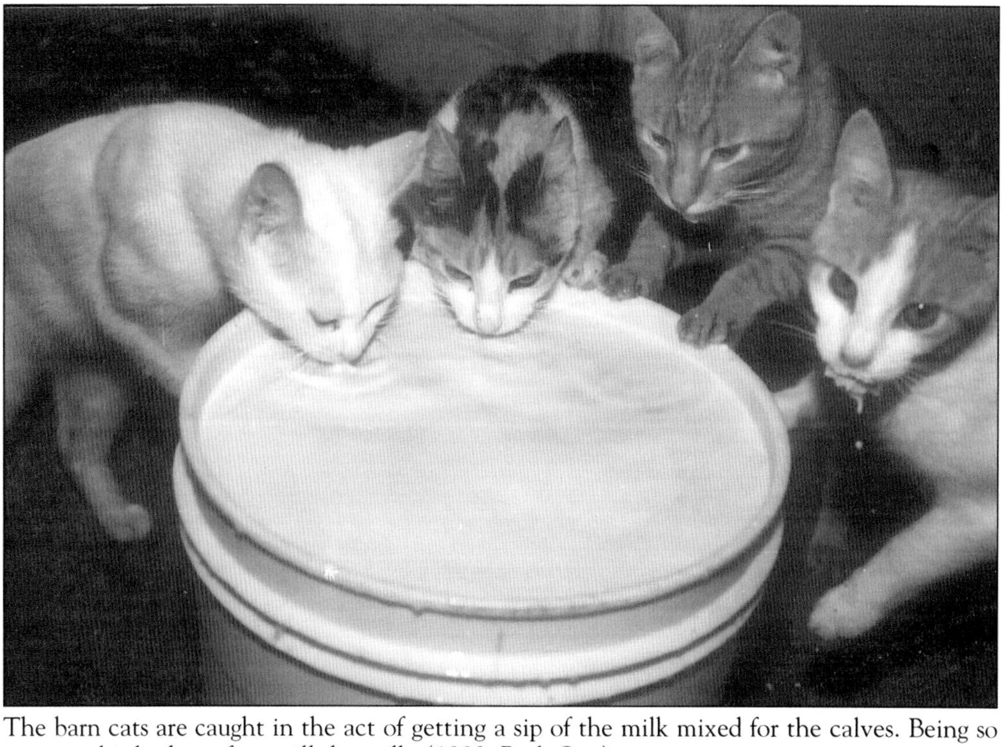

The barn cats are caught in the act of getting a sip of the milk mixed for the calves. Being so eager to drink, they often spill the milk. (1992, Barb Ott.)

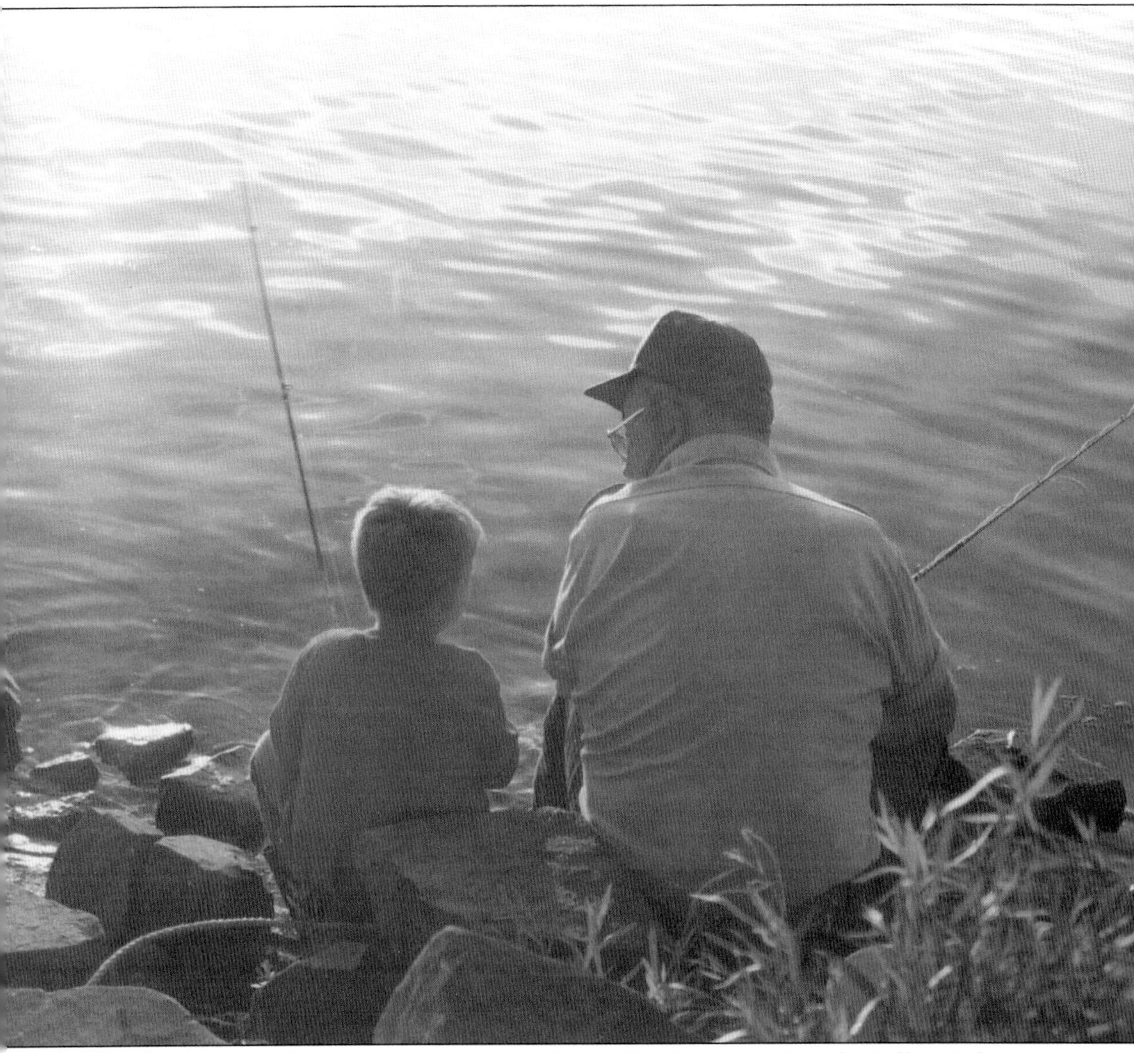

Bobby Kennedy is fishing with his grandpa, James Ott Senior, at Dutch Hollow Lake near LaValle. (1992, Barb Ott.)

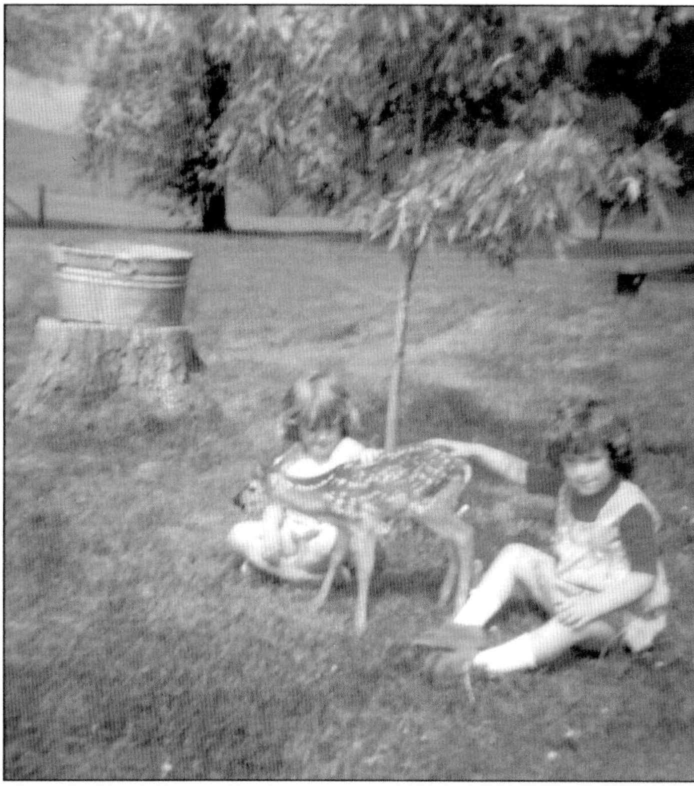

They named him Bambi. The Geitz family—including Mom, Dad, three little girls, and one little boy—loved the fawn. Dad's friend found him in the woods, not far from where its mother had been killed by a car. They fed Bambi, played with him, and sometimes even brought him in the house. During the hunting season, Bambi wore a large orange collar and no hunting was allowed on their land. In the spring, when Bambi was a year old, it was decided the best permanent home for him would be at the Wisconsin Dells Deer Park. (1978, John Geitz.)

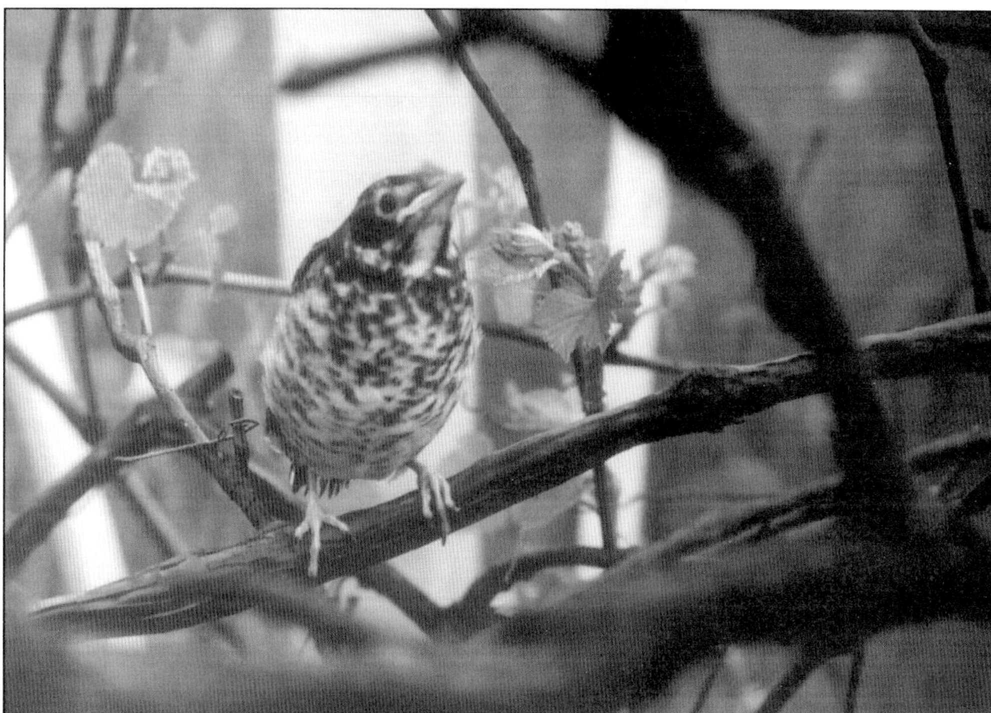

A young robin is pictured here enjoying the spring. (1993, Barb Ott.)

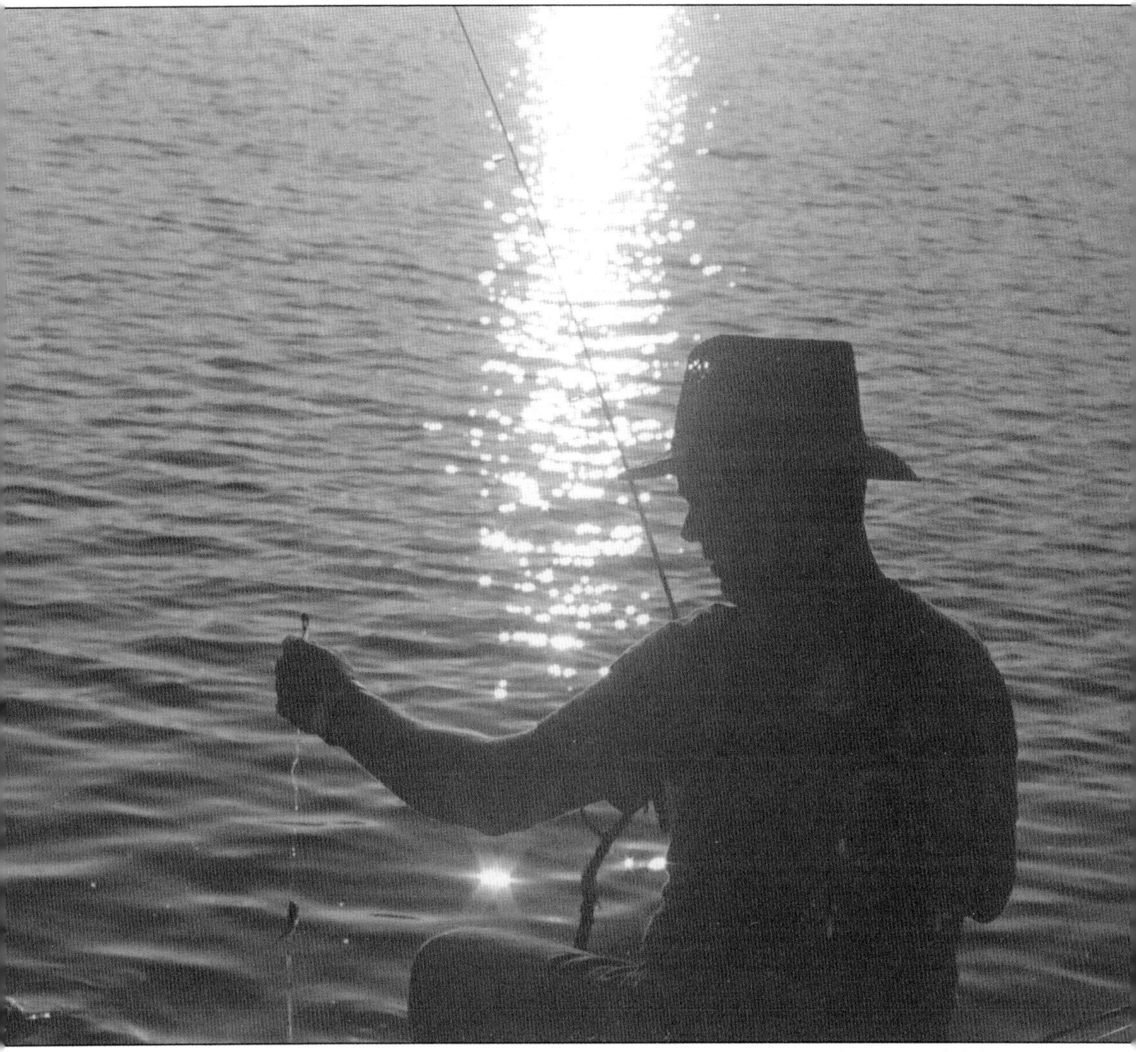

Jim Ott, a farmer on Highway G near Wonewoc in Juneau County, is relaxing and fishing at Hemlock Park in LaValle. Hemlock Park is located on some of the backwaters of the Baraboo River. (1997, Barb Ott.)

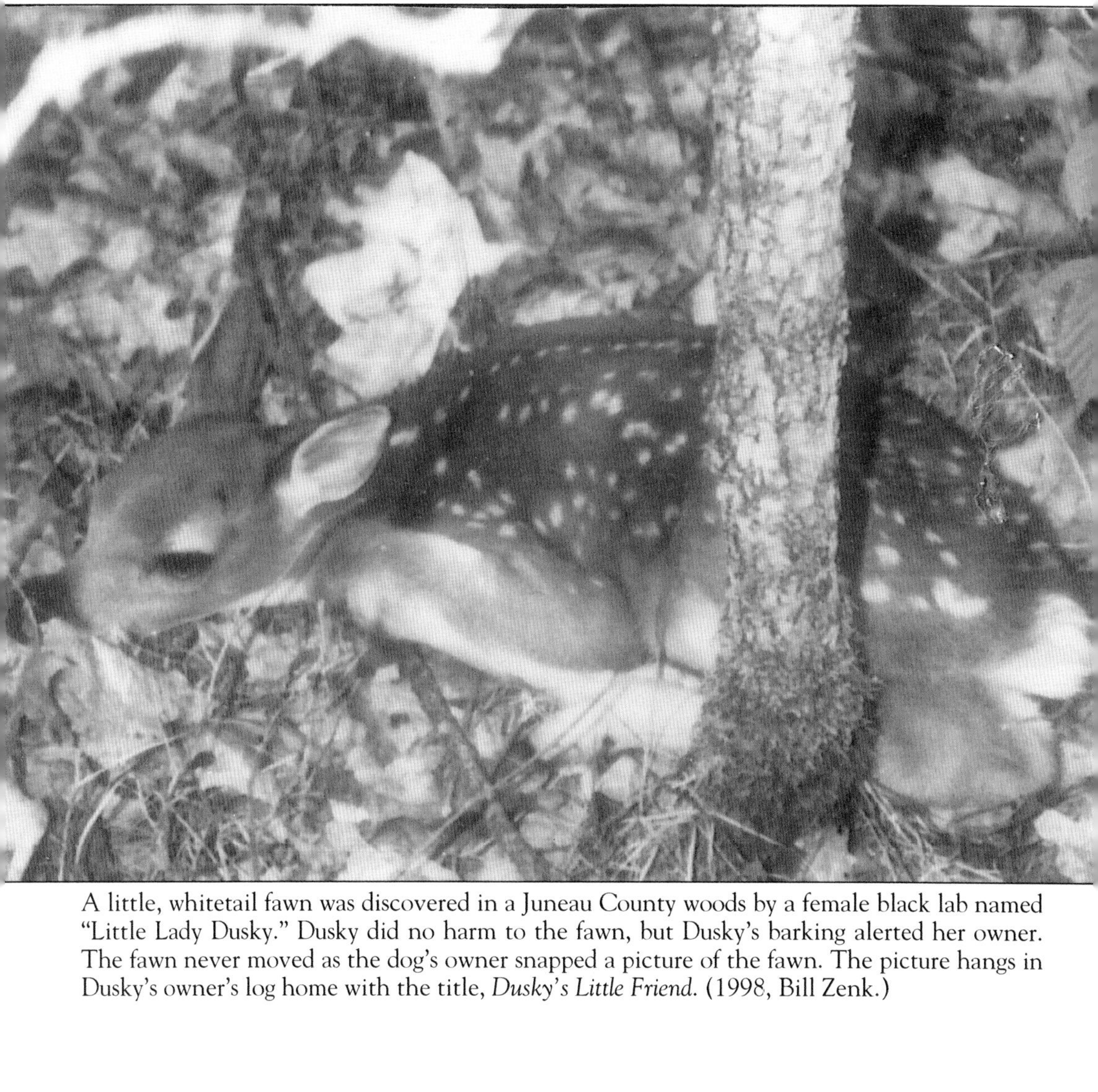

A little, whitetail fawn was discovered in a Juneau County woods by a female black lab named "Little Lady Dusky." Dusky did no harm to the fawn, but Dusky's barking alerted her owner. The fawn never moved as the dog's owner snapped a picture of the fawn. The picture hangs in Dusky's owner's log home with the title, *Dusky's Little Friend*. (1998, Bill Zenk.)

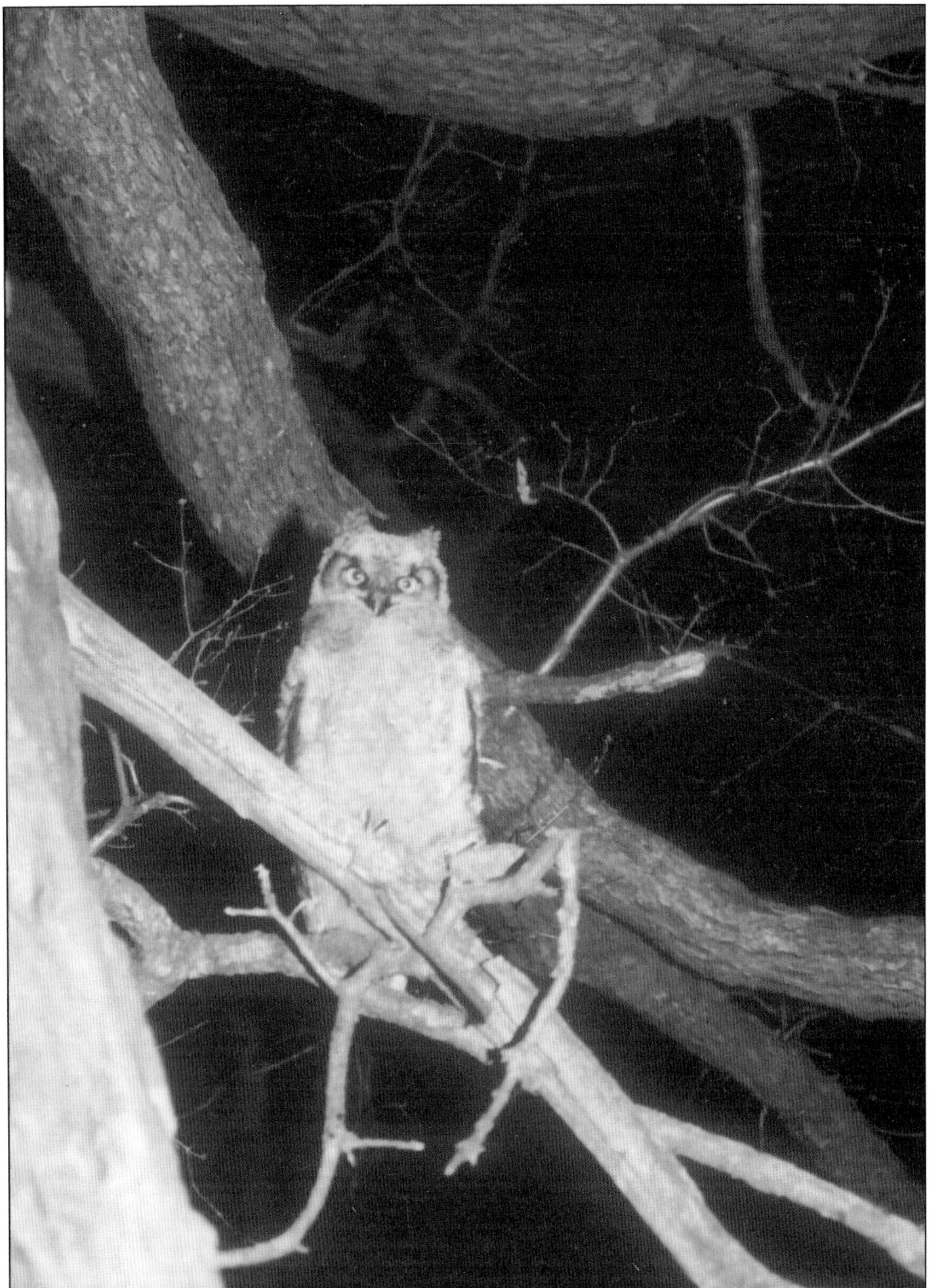

One night, Jim and Barb Ott were walking in the woods on their farm near Wonewoc when they noticed an owl roosting in a tree. They ran back to the house so that Jim could retrieve a flashlight and Barb could get a camera. Jim held the flashlight, and Barb captured the beauty of the bird. The owl stared at them. (1995, Barb Ott.)

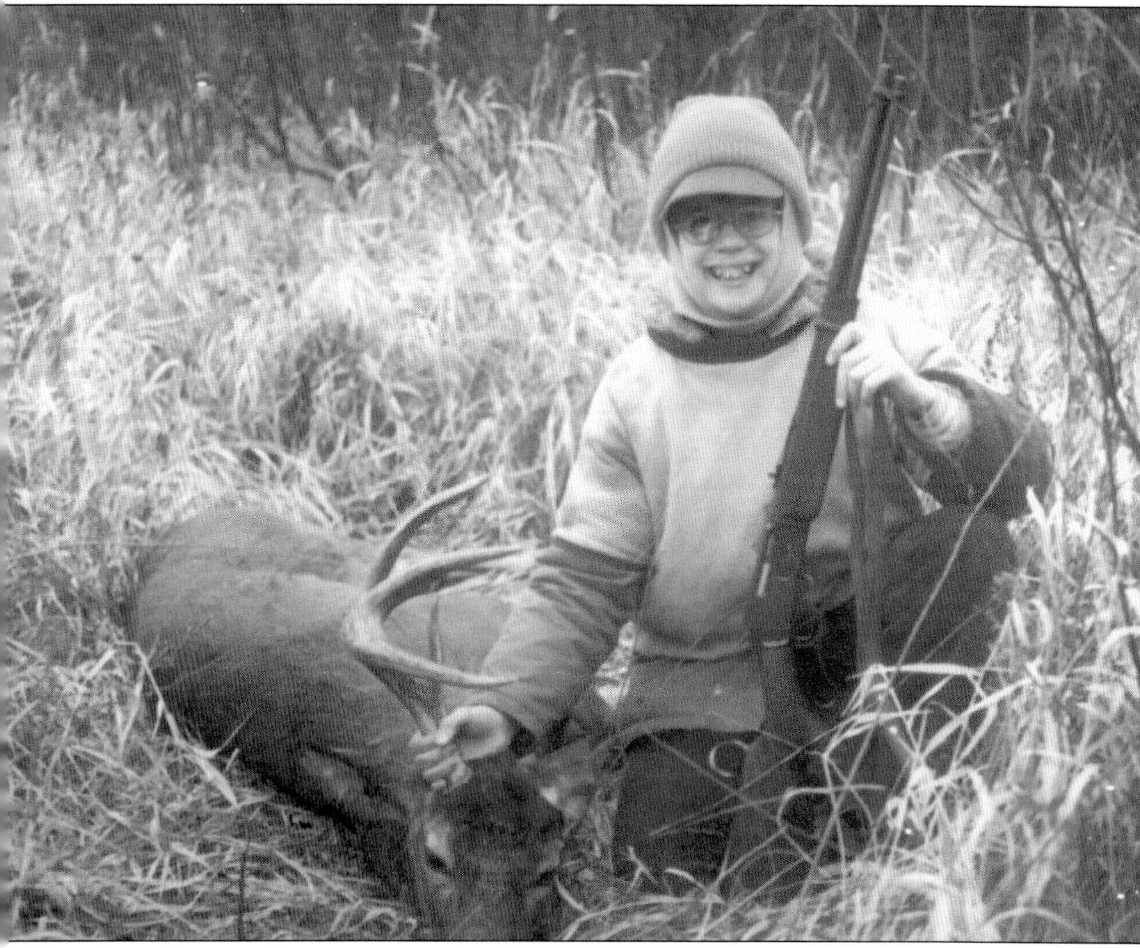

One of the joys of living in or visiting Juneau County is the excellent hunting it offers. Ryan Zenk is 12 years old in this picture. This is his first hunting season with a gun. Hunting is a tradition in his family, and he has learned to respect and appreciate animals and the environment they live in. His family will eat venison from the deer. The deer's hide may be made into gloves or slippers or saved to make a jacket. Some day his younger brothers will hunt. But today, he can share his hunting story with them. He has proven his ability to the men in his family, his father and uncles, all hunters like him. (1975, Jacqueline Ann.)

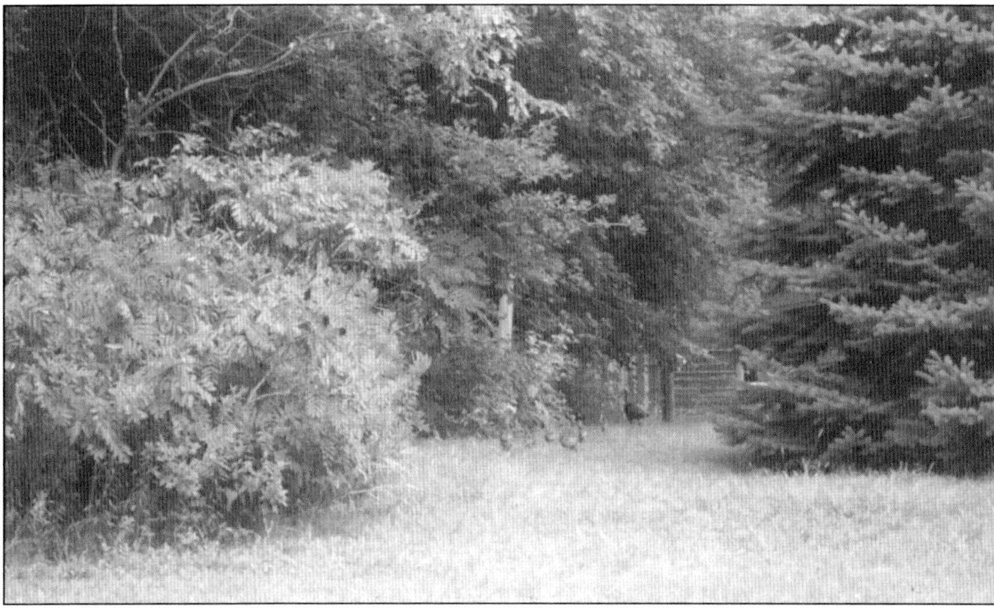

A family of wild turkey is pictured here enjoying the yard of a farm on County G near Wonewoc. The tom turkey snuck off into the woods before the picture could be taken, but the two hens and their babies continued walking around. (2000, Sheila Z.)

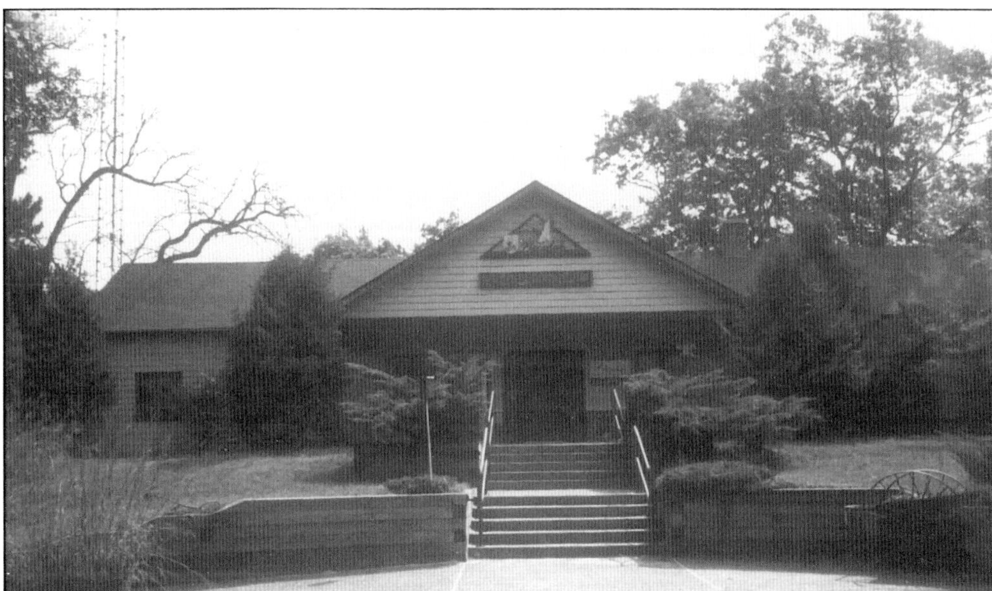

This is the Necedah National Wildlife Refuge main office building. The refuge runs beside Highway 80 from Highway 21 to Highway 173. The refuge is a vast peat land with dry ridges of sand. In 1939, Franklin Roosevelt signed an order establishing Necedah Migratory Waterfowl Refuge. It was to be a refuge and breeding ground for migratory birds and other wildlife. Today, it also preserves a variety of plants and helps endangered plants and animals. There are many opportunities at the refuge for people to learn about the natural world through experiences like hiking, hunting, fishing, and going to programs about local animal and plant life. (2000, Sheila Z.)

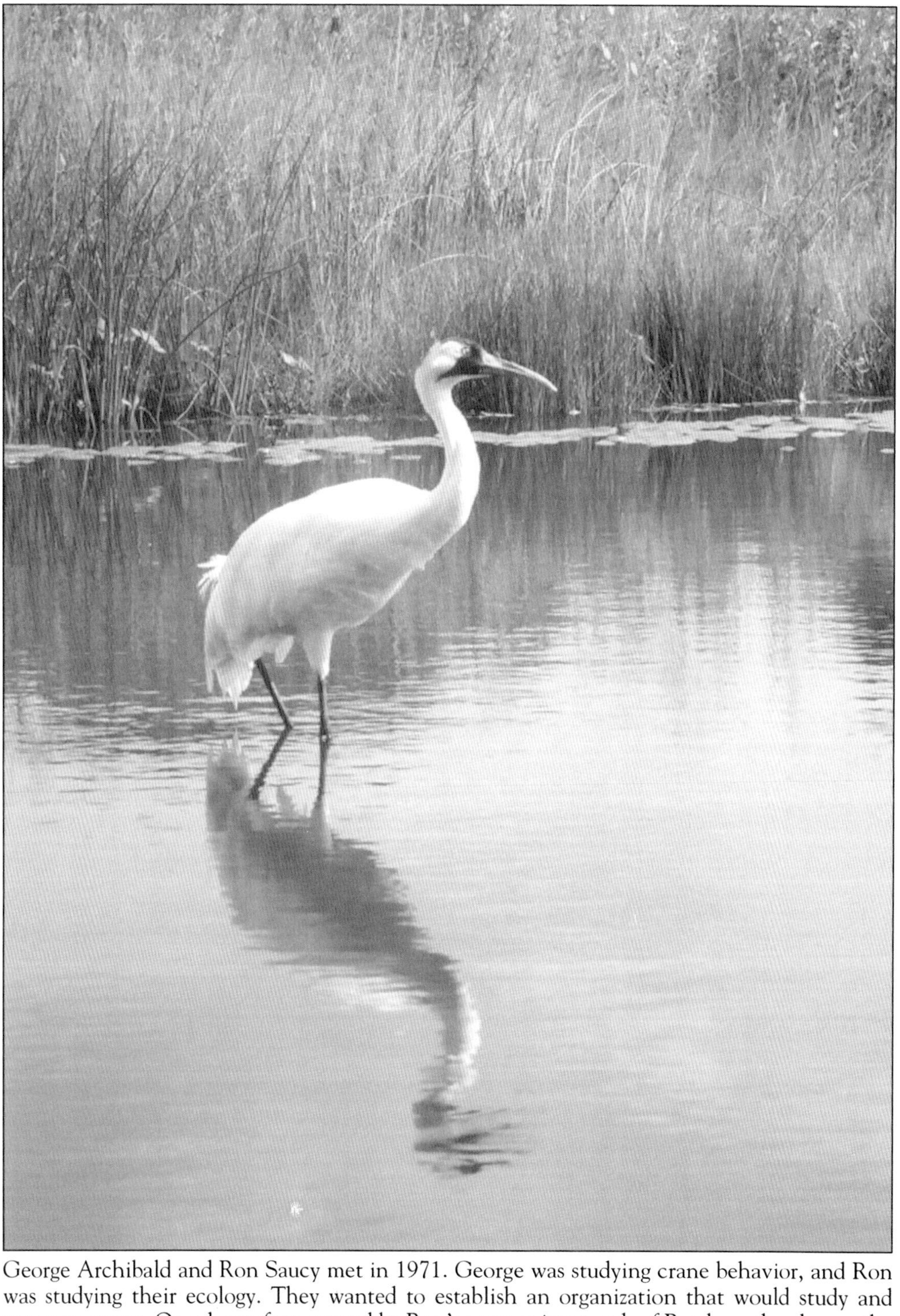

George Archibald and Ron Saucy met in 1971. George was studying crane behavior, and Ron was studying their ecology. They wanted to establish an organization that would study and preserve cranes. On a horse farm owned by Ron's parents just north of Baraboo, they began the International Crane Foundation. The foundation focuses on the following areas: education, research, habitat, restoration, and preservation. (2000, Sheila Z.)

Seven

NATURAL BEAUTY

The variety of plant life in these counties often attracts groups from the University to study the plants, and on Blackhawk Island alone, where there is a deer enclosure, there are 40 different native plant varieties. Some of the scenic rivers and lakes portray power while others embody calm and peace. The woods change with the seasons, brilliant with color in the fall, and an untouched world appears every new snowfall. Unbreakable rock bluffs suggest strength and endurance. Residents think of these counties as gardens or parks.

And in your natural beauty,
We have not money for the pocket,
But riches for the spirit.

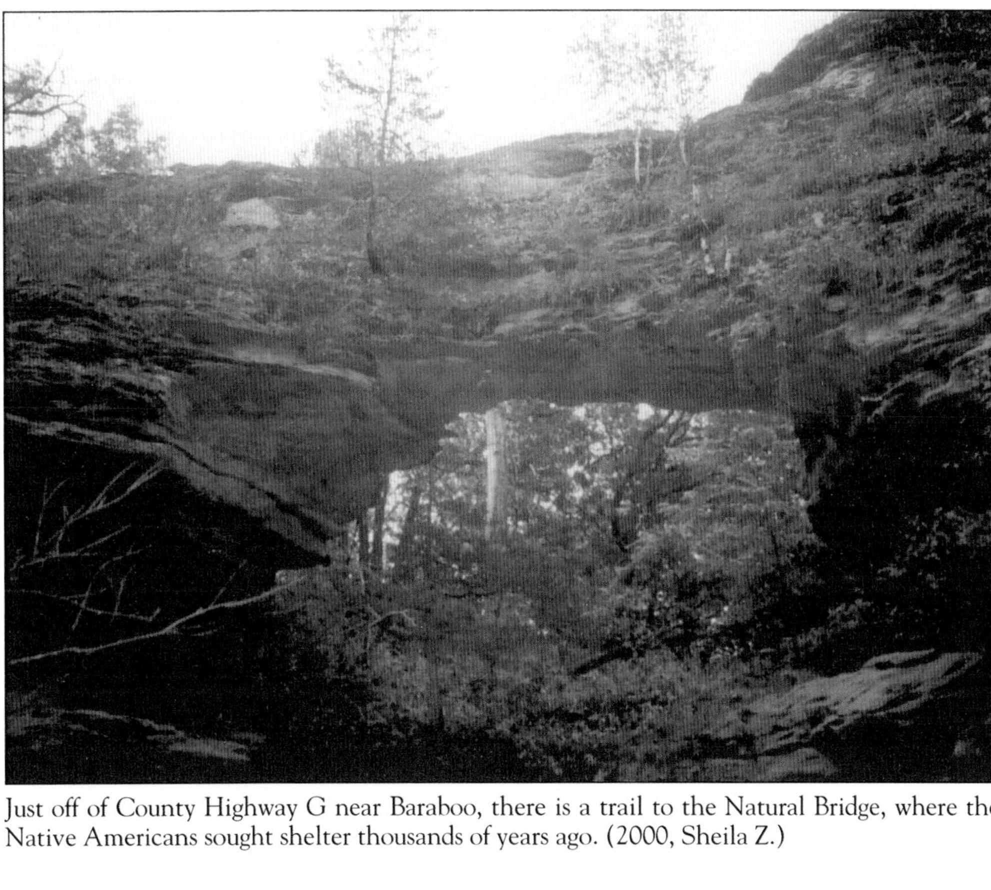

Just off of County Highway G near Baraboo, there is a trail to the Natural Bridge, where the Native Americans sought shelter thousands of years ago. (2000, Sheila Z.)

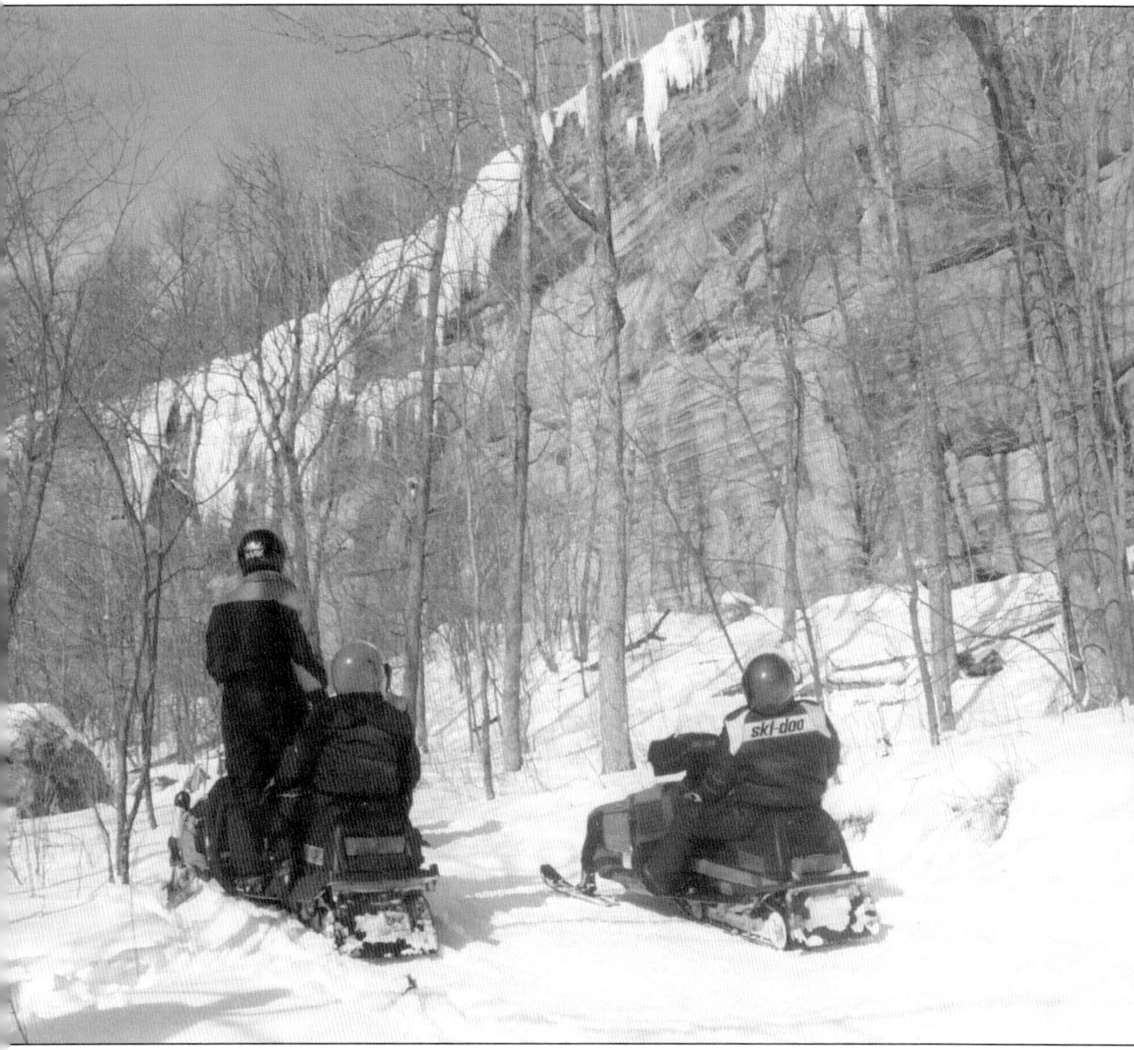

This photographer and her husband walked in snow up to their knees to see the ice on this stonewall in the woods between Wonewoc and Mauston. To their surprise, they found three snowmobilers had also stopped to look at the majestic ice-capped rock wall. (1987, Barb Ott.)

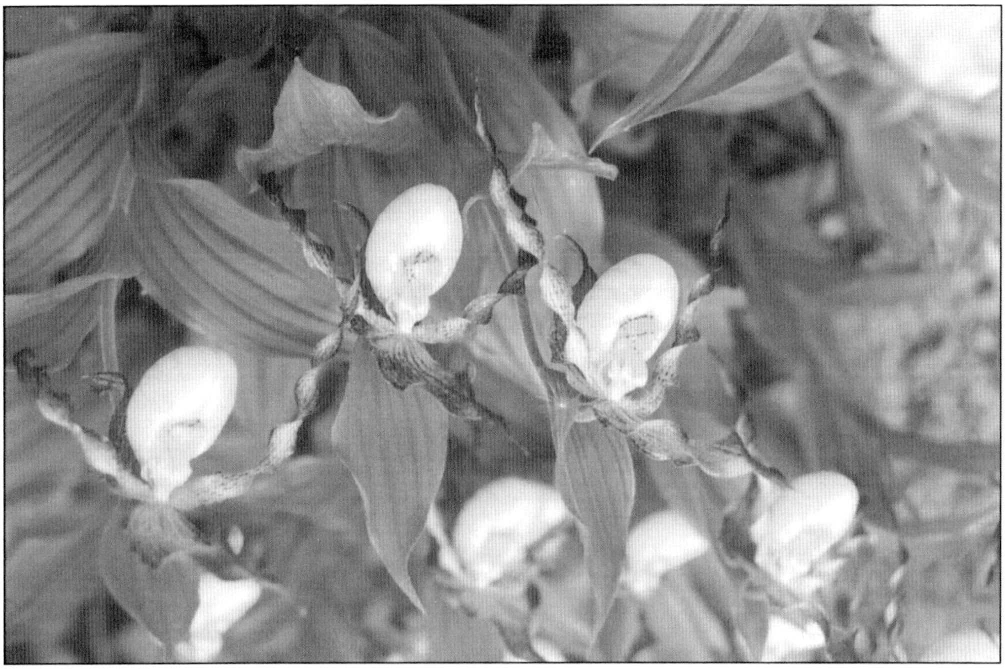

These counties always have room for gardens and space for flowers. These yellow lady slippers were photographed in Kate's back yard in Wonewoc. Her flowers were her joy. One day, two neighbors went to check on her. Kate had been sitting for a long time in her yard by her flowers; that June morning Kate was 99. One neighbor asked, "What's the matter?" "Nothing," she replied, "I want to plant my Zinnias." Kate was trying to dig a trench with a butcher knife. The neighbor dug the trench, and they all planted Zinnias. Kate had the happiness of planting her Zinnias but not the pleasure of seeing them bloom. She died that June. (1990s, Barb Ott.)

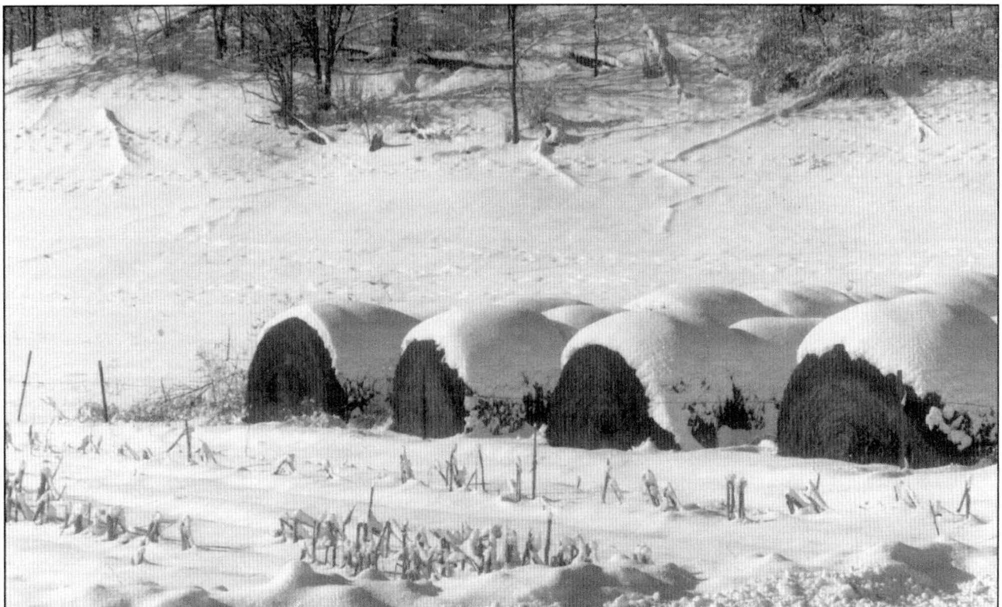

Someone frosted the hay loaves and no one's licked the frosting off yet. (1990, Barb Ott.)

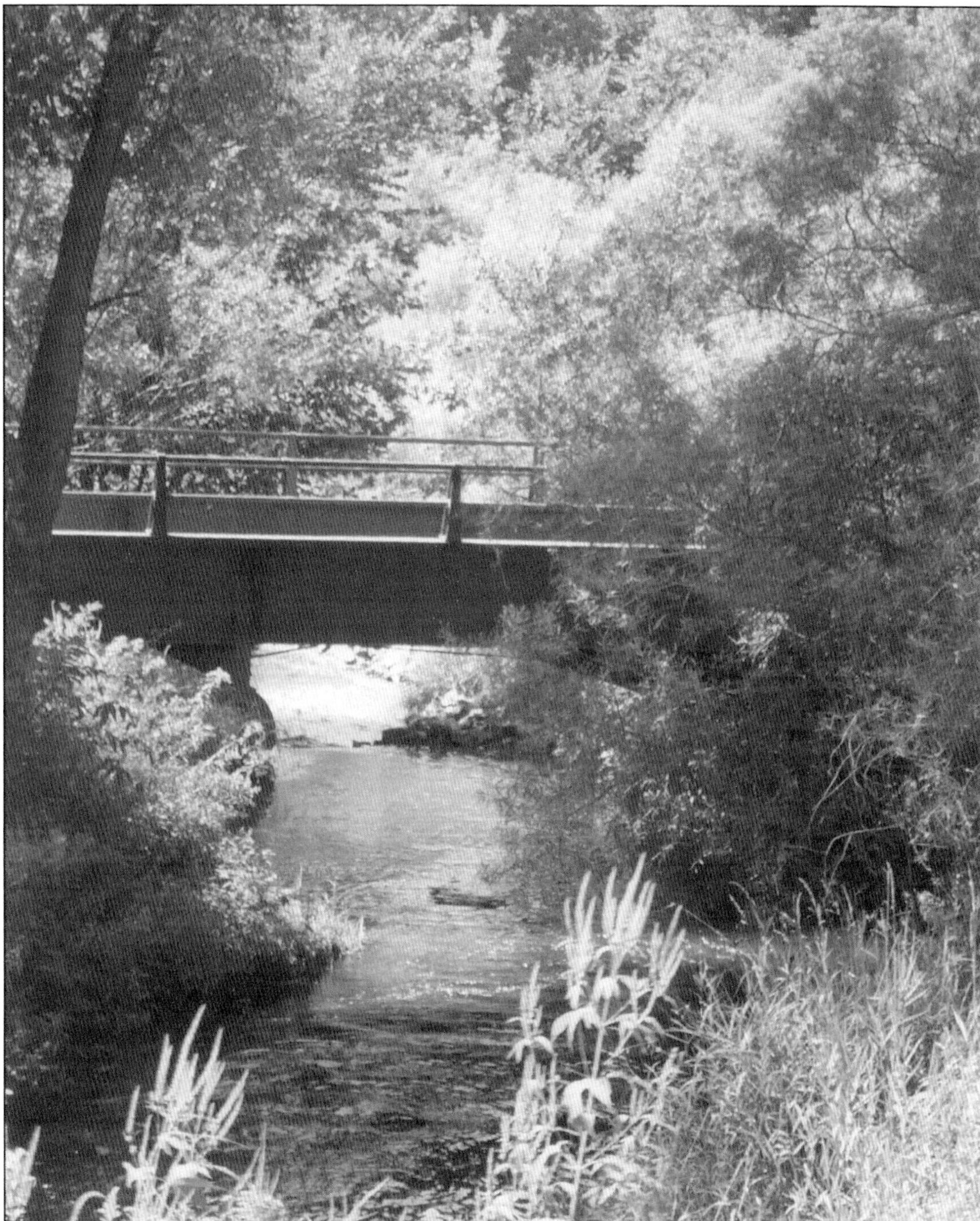

This bridge over Lake Redstone was the picture featured in the Sauk County telephone book in 1993. (1993, Barb Ott.)

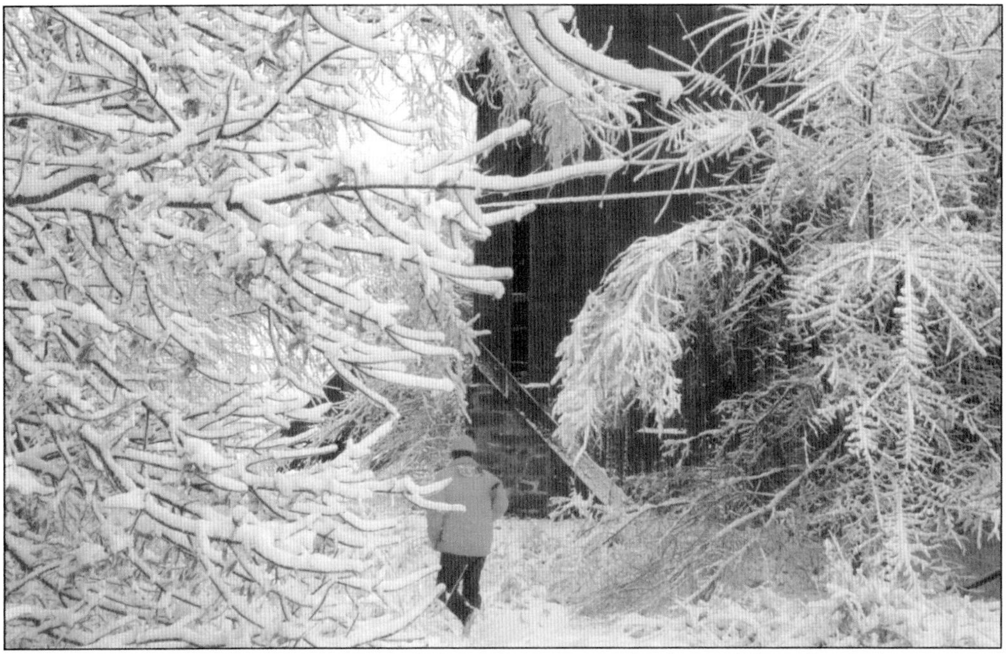

This hunter sees the transformation of the ordinary into the beautiful in the fresh snow. He probably paused on his doorstep a moment and blew moist droplets of breath out to hang suspended in the air as he viewed the beauty of an early winter morning in Juneau County. (1993, Barb Ott.)

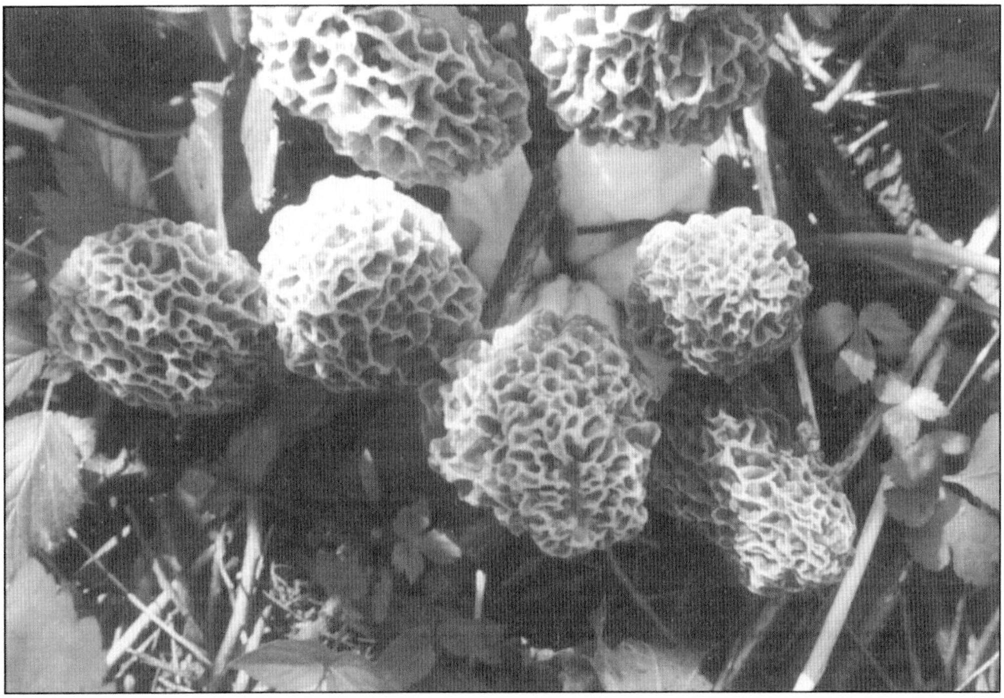

It is May 4, 1996, and the morels must be out. Local residents explore the woods looking for this caviar of the mushroom family in damp, shady spots near dead elm trees. (1996, Barb Ott.)

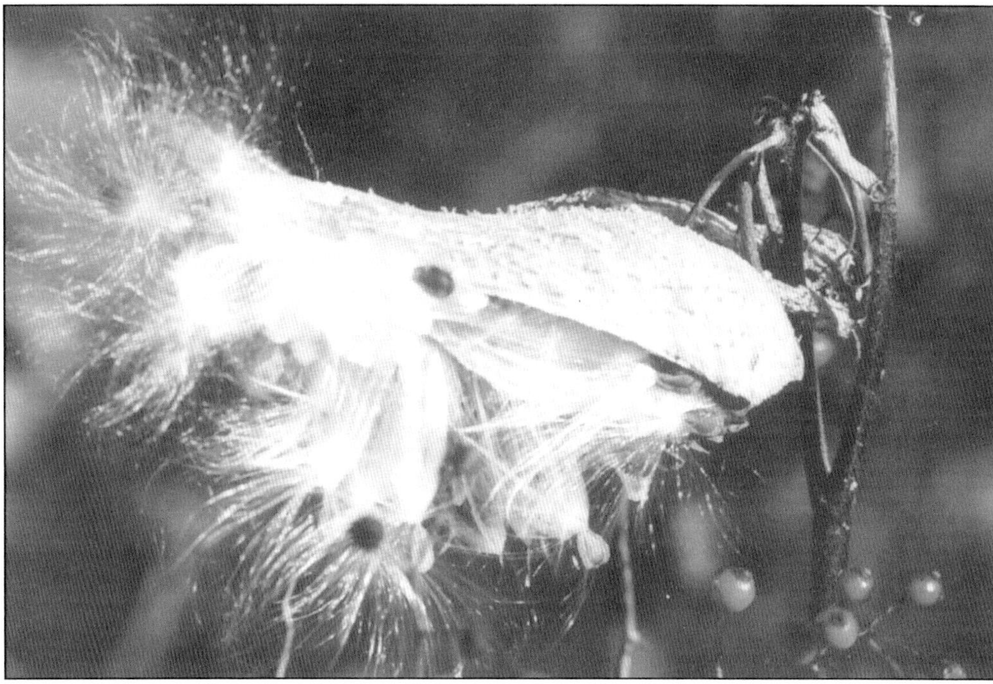

It is time for the milkweed seeds to leave their snug home. The silky hairs will ride the wind with their precious cargo to a fertile spot where the seeds can grow. (1997, Barb Ott.)

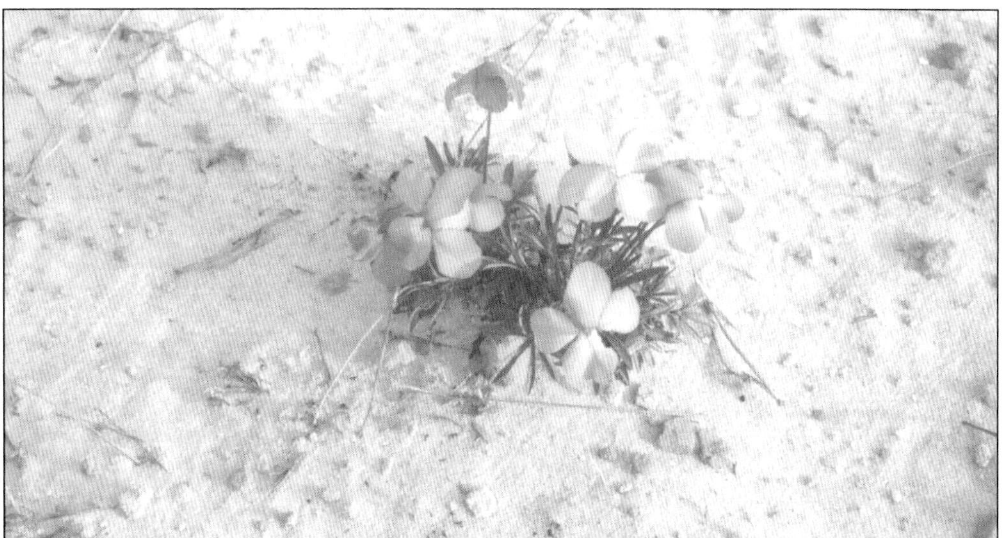

In May, the wild flowers push through Juneau's sandy soil, creating beautiful natural gardens along the roadways and uncultivated areas. Ferns join lupines, jack-in-the-pulpit, bloodroot, honeysuckle, bleeding heart, hepatica, Dutchman britches, violets, and trillium in these gardens. When people drive from Mauston to Reedsburg on Highway K, they see ditches blanketed with trilliums. Some families have a tradition of picking wild flowers to decorate their loved ones' graves for Memorial Day. Walkers, joggers, and travelers who pull off on country roads can see and appreciate the beauty of plants like this violet, which one day appeared in soil thought too dry and sterile for any plant. (1999, Bill Zenk.)

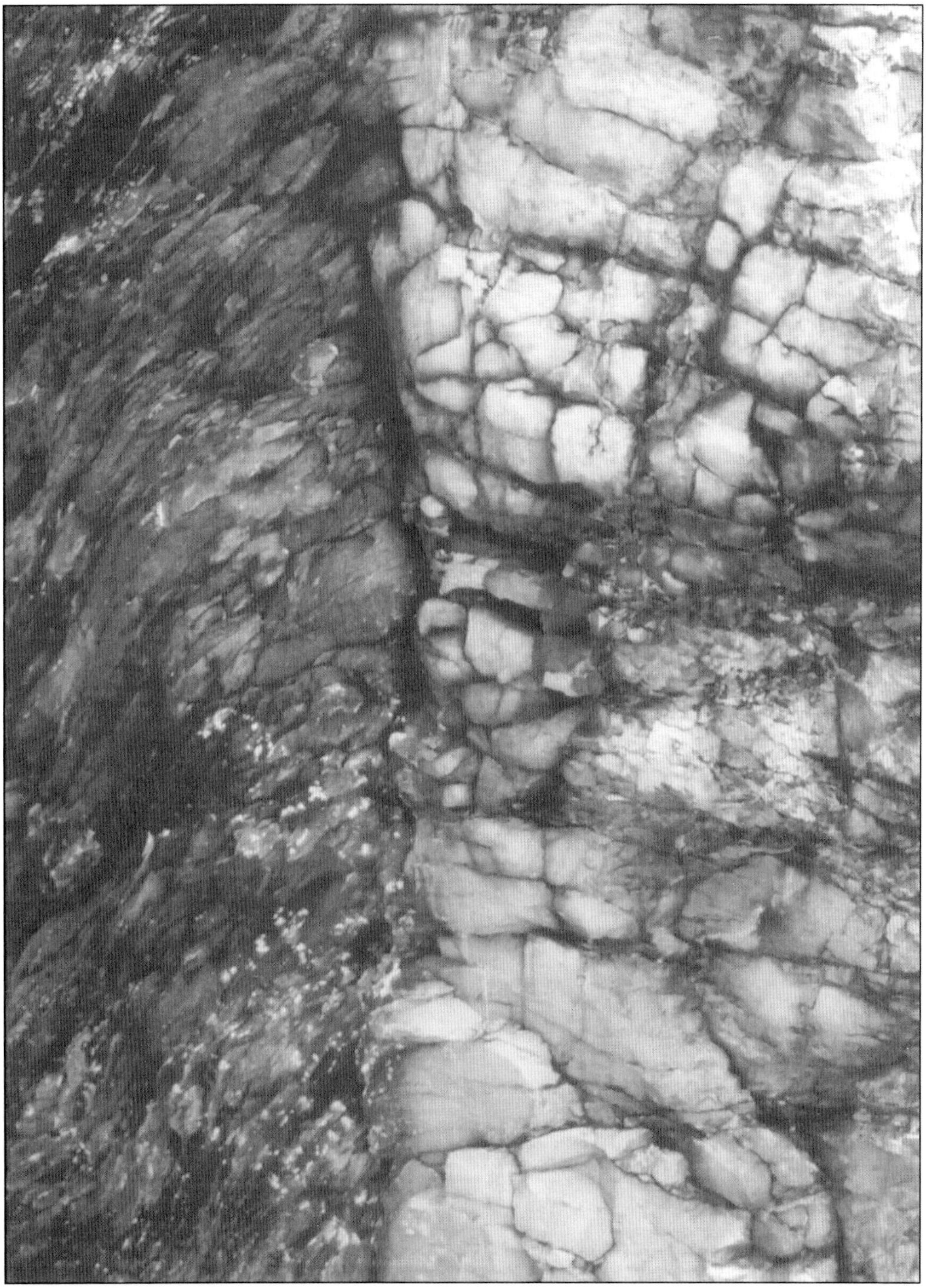

This is a picture of quartzite from the Rock Springs area, a village in Sauk County. There are different kinds of quartzite. The white rock is extremely hard and difficult to work with. It is used on abatements and walls. The pink lady is more easily crushed and used under highways and railroad tracks. Many rural driveways in Juneau and Sauk County are covered with the pink lady. (2000, Sheila Z.)

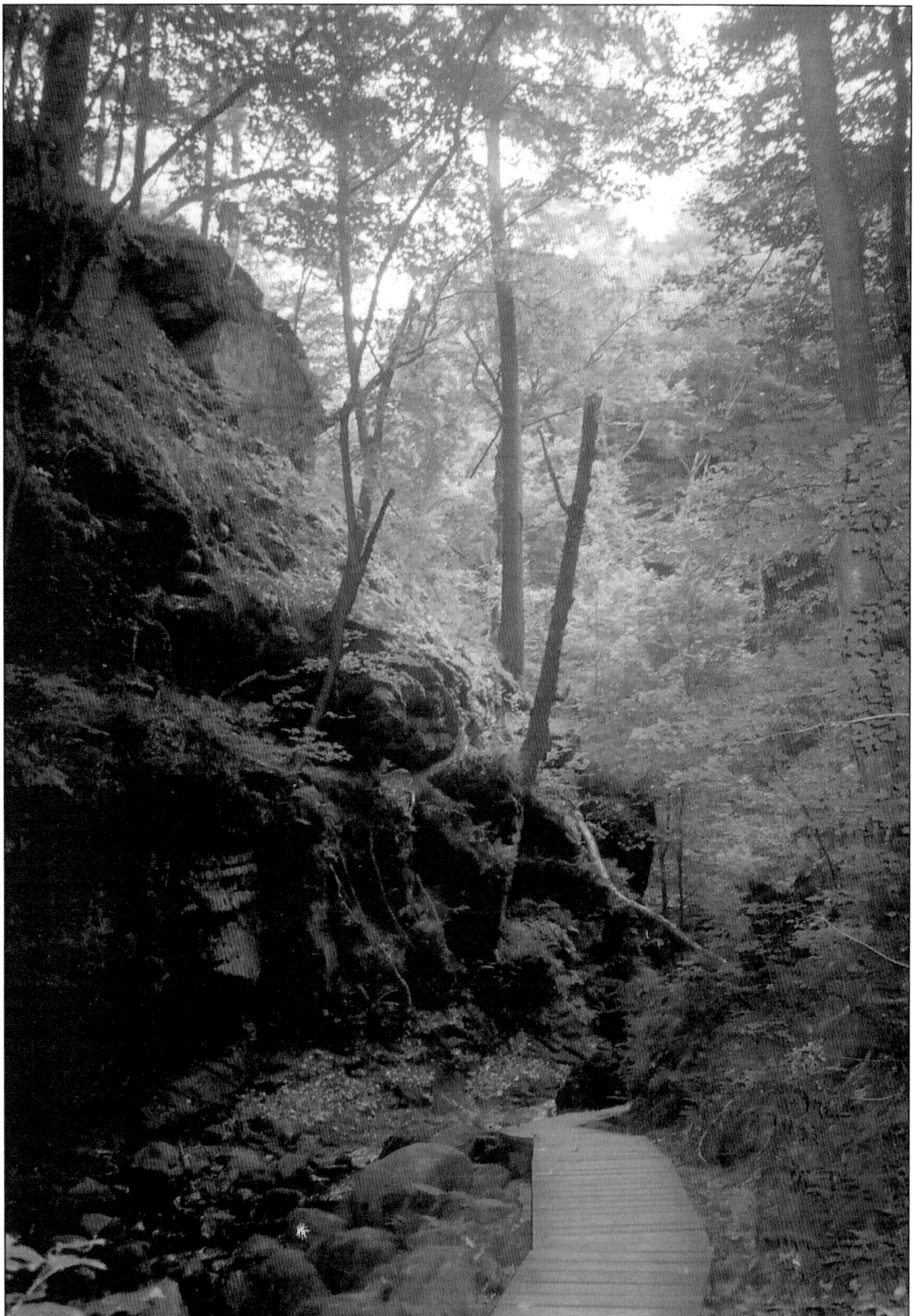

Parfrey's Glen is a tiny valley, with 100-foot-high sandstone and quartzite walls, located at the junction of Narrows Creek and the Baraboo River. The Glen's 168 acres are explored by University students and enjoyed by tourists and hikers. (2000, Sheila Z.)

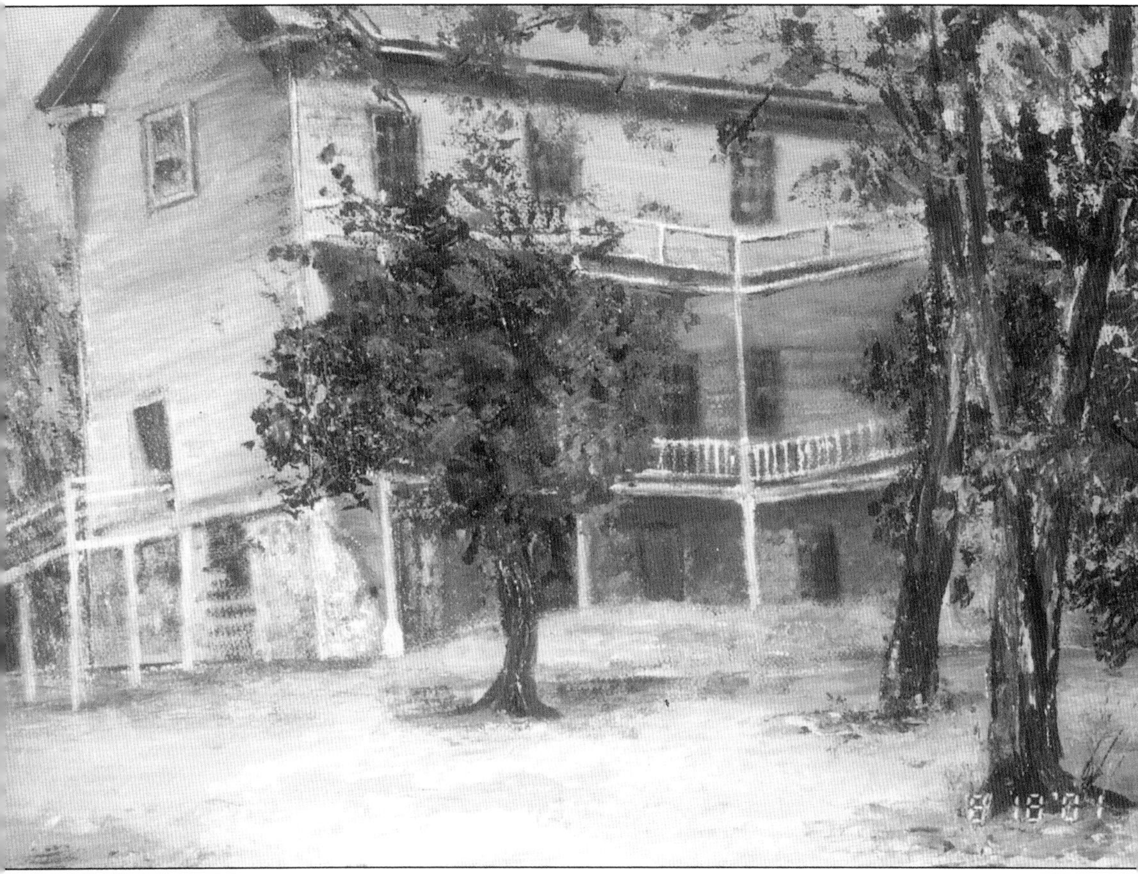

The Dells House was built on the south end of Blackhawk Island in 1837. The purpose was to have a lodging where the raftsmen could sleep and eat. Rumor suggests it was also a saloon and whorehouse. The house was abandoned in 1895 and burned in 1899. When the dam was put in at Kilbourn (Wisconsin Dells) in 1907, it raised the water level at the island 15 feet. The old Dells House root cellar foundation can be discovered a few feet from the water's edge. Two large stones from the house's foundation can be seen in the shallow water lapping the shore. (2001, Kathryn Wu.)

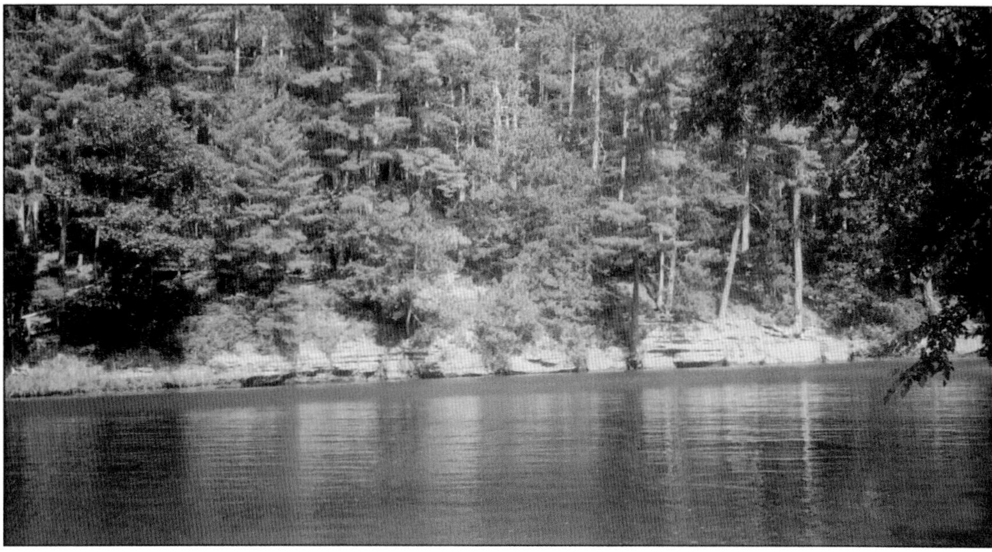

In 1909, Horace and Mary Upham bought 310 acres of what was called the "Dells of Wisconsin." They wanted to preserve the natural beauty of the area, especially 200 acres of their purchase, which was called Blackhawk Island. Blackhawk Island was named after the brave Sauk Chief who, with his followers, tried to defend their lands from the white settlers and the army. The entire parcel of land called "Upham Woods" is on the edge of a driftless area, land untouched by the glaciers. (2001, Kathryn Wu.)

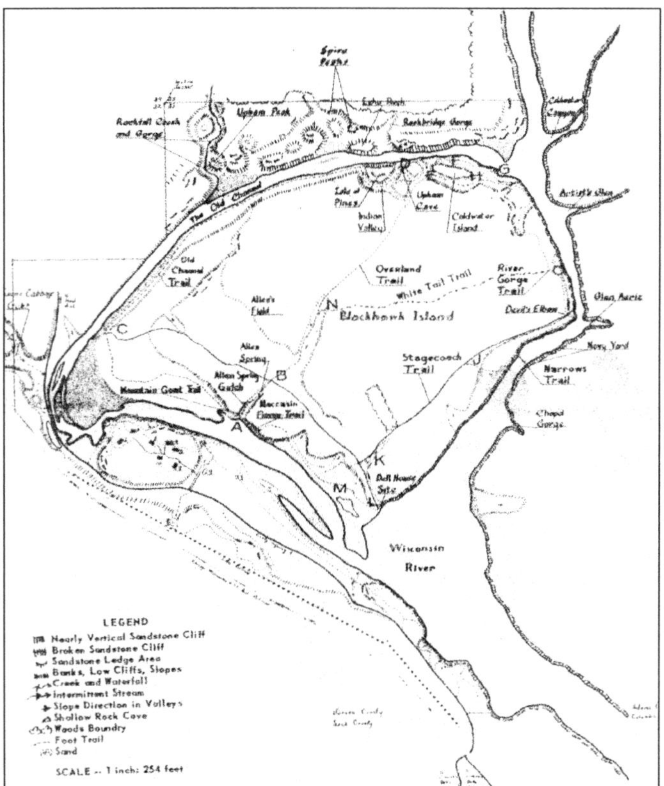

Devil's Elbow is on the right side of the map pictured here. Lumber rafts were being sent southbound from northern mills like Necedah. Before reaching the Narrows (the part of the river that remains narrow because the rocks are too hard for the river to wear them away), the lumberjacks took the rafts apart and directed the pieces around difficult spots like Devil's Elbow. Many raftsmen lost their lives. Leroy Gates, a raftsman from 1849 to 1858, as the story is told, was quite skillful. A bridge had been built at Blackhawk's Leap, and Leroy, in top hat and tails, would direct "rapids pieces" around Devil's Elbow. People were charged 5¢ a person to go out on the bridge and watch him. (1969, Upham Woods.)

This is the "Stagecoach Trail" across Blackhawk Island. It was built, along with the bridge across Blackhawk's Leap, in 1850 so that one of the first stagecoach roads could cross the island from southeast to northwest. The small trees on the trail have grown up since the route was discontinued. The large trees pictured here would have been at the edge of the stagecoach road. (2001, Kathryn Wu.)

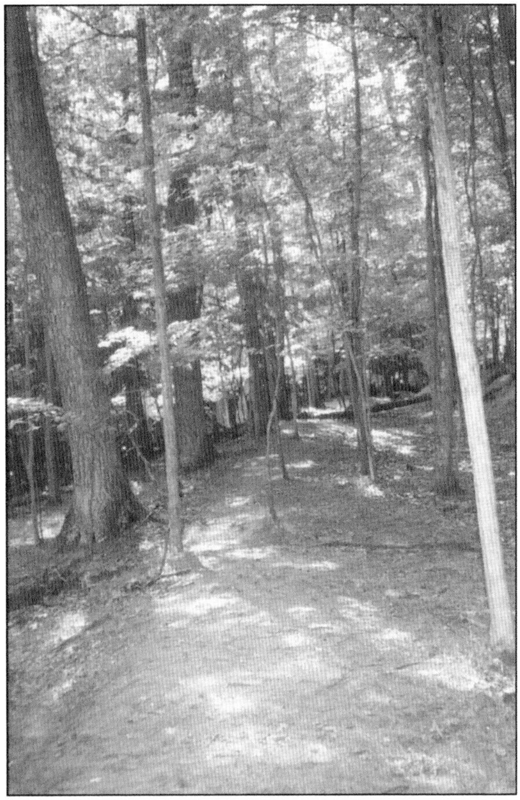

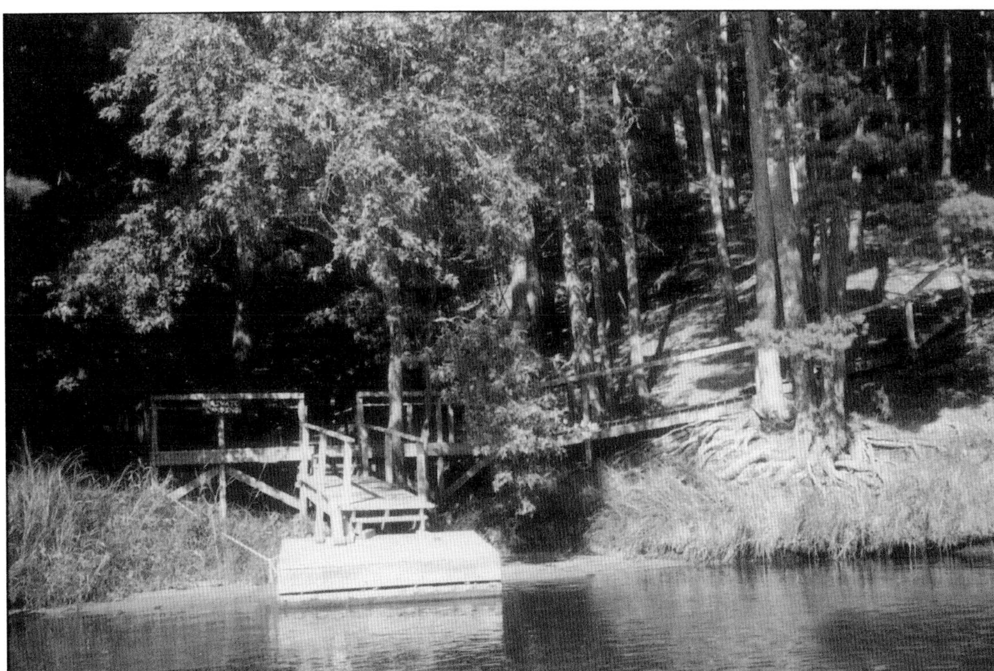

Pictured here is the landing where the boats are docked when visitors come to Blackhawk Island from the 110 acres of Upham Woods located on the main land. (2001, Kathryn Wu.)

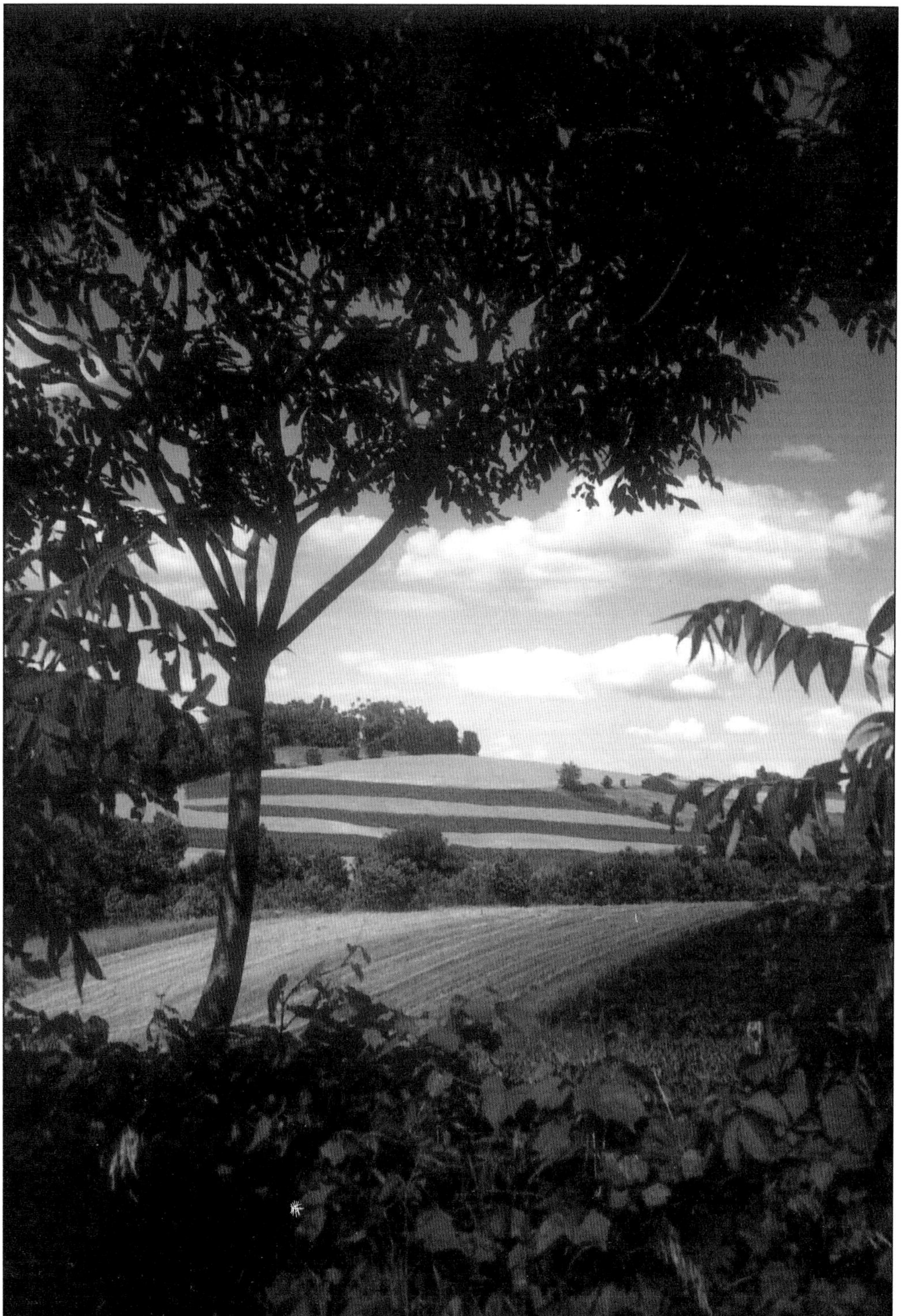

This is the way this photographer saw her farm as she looked across the crops of hay and alfalfa one early morning on her Juneau County farm. (2001, Barb Ott.)

Eight

Culture

A fine arts program called the "Lively Arts Series" brings a variety of programs to Baraboo. A dance theater is performing *A Rainforest Odyssey*. Other music includes the Madison Boys Choir, A Night of Harmony (Barbershop Quartet), the Baraboo High School Choir and Band Concert, a Gospel Concert, the Preservation Hall Jazz Band, the Baraboo High School Holiday Concert, a mandolin player,Peter Ostroushko, and a guitarist, Dirk Freymuth.

On October 19, 20, and 21, a fall art tour is held where well known artists invite visitors into their studios in Mineral Point, Spring Green, Dodgeville, and Baraboo. Most villages in Juneau and Sauk Counties have public libraries with dedicated librarians, ready to help with research projects. Home talent shows have always had a healthy existence in these communities.

A program called "Exploring Cultural Diversity in Southwestern Wisconsin," focusing on Monroe, Vernon, Richland, Adams, and Juneau Counties, was held in October 2001, at the Mauston Technical College. Interest in the fine arts and historical roots and growth is common among the adults in these counties.

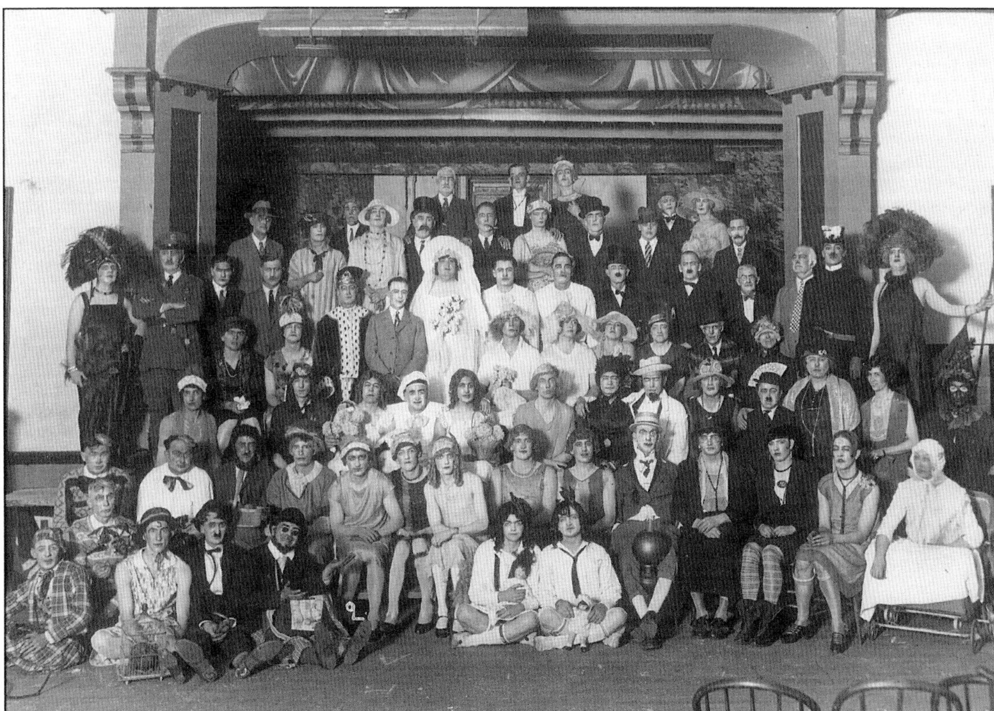

The *Womanless Wedding* was performed at the opera house in Mauston, Wisconsin. (Early 1900s, Juneau County Historical Society.)

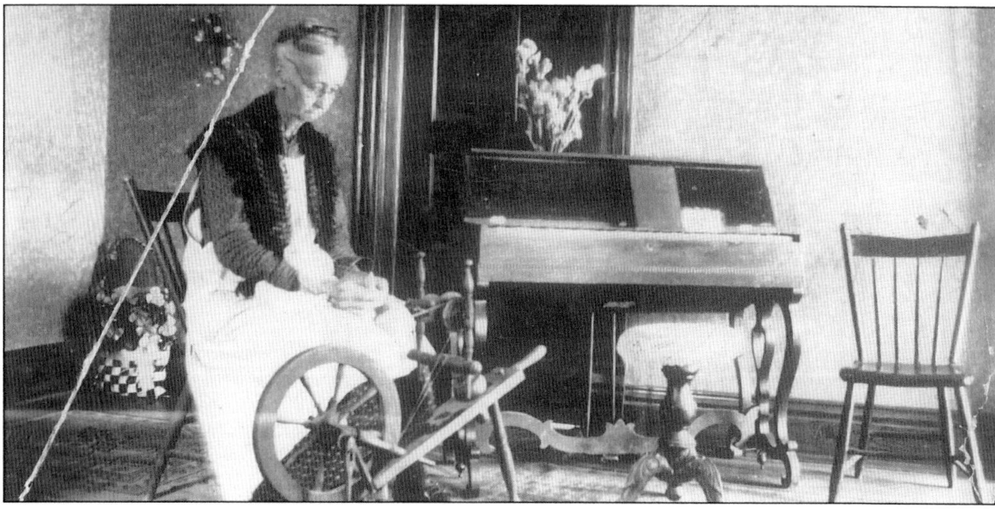

Mary Severance is pictured here *c.* 1897 with her spinning wheel and the first melodeon brought to the town of Mauston. Mary's father, a farmer named Ervin Briggs, served as a soldier in the Civil War. He was captured while on picket duty near Chattanooga, Tennessee, on April 12, 1864. His fourth daughter was born the day he was captured. Mary was seven years old. Ervin died in Andersonville Prison, Georgia, attempting, along with his fellow soldiers, to dig a tunnel out of the open-air prison. Only one soldier out of the group escaped. (Jacqueline Ann.)

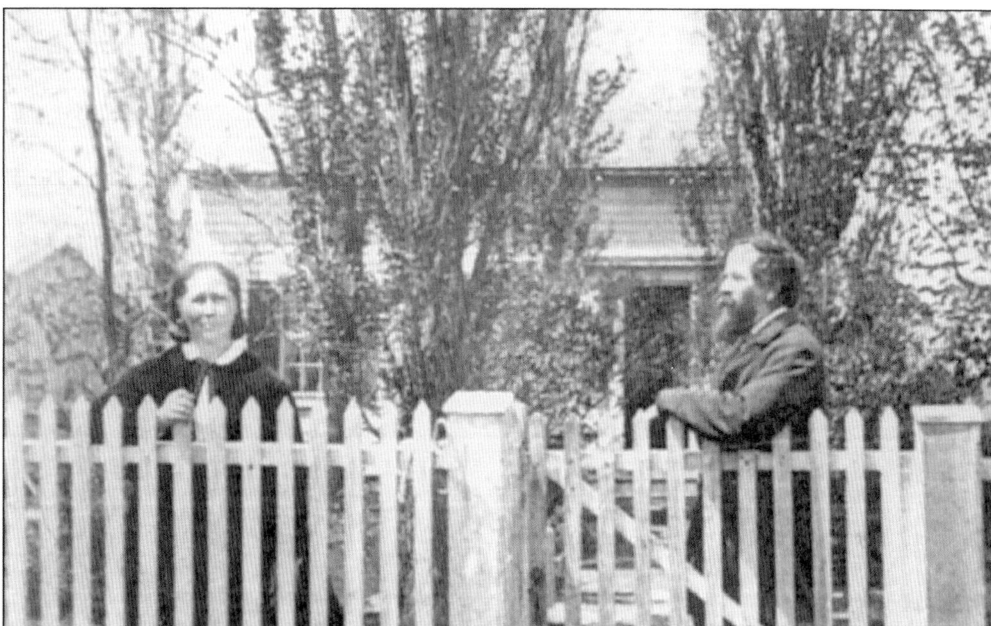

Edward Schroeter was a speaker for the Sauk City Freethinkers. German immigrants started the Free Congregation of Sauk City in 1852. They had no belief in God or any creed; they only expressed belief in reason and humanism. Mr. Schroeter said, "The first purpose of the Free Congregation must be clear thinking, for mere acceptance leads to stupidity." According to August Derleth, the freethinkers set the tone for cultural life in Sauk City for years. He felt they had the reputation of being godless but that they were wonderful Christians. (1990, Sauk County Historical Society.)

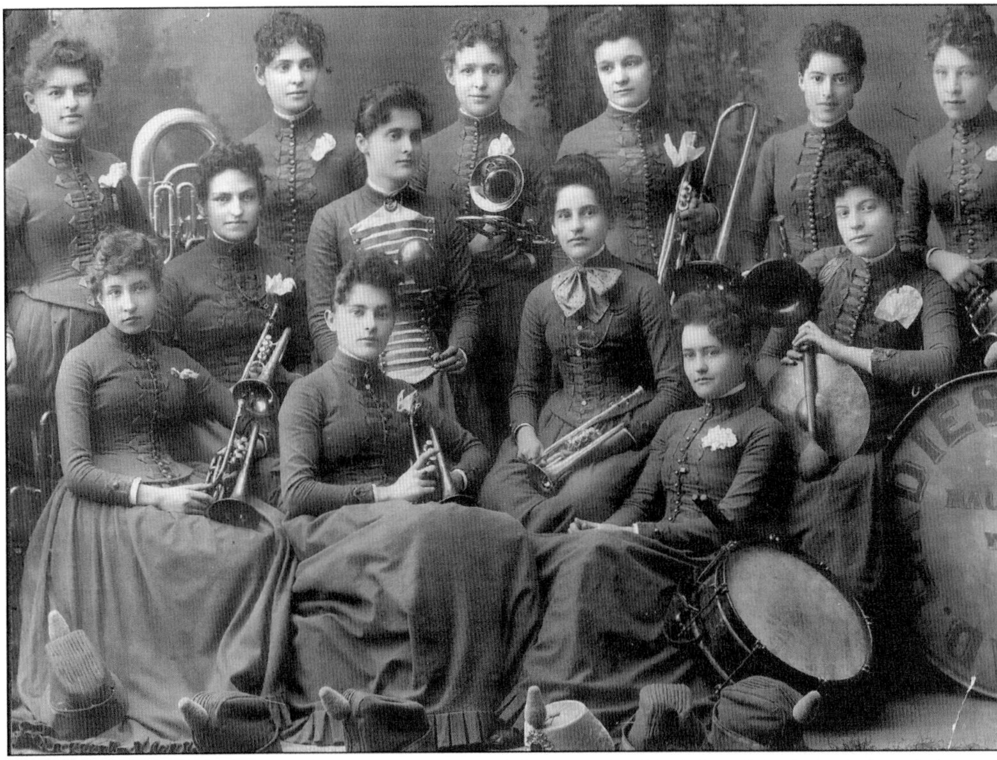

The Ladies Ideal Band of Mauston is pictured here, *c.* 1888. They liked their band dresses. Notice their band hats on the floor in front of the band. Their director was J.G. Bates. Not all the ladies could get to the appointment for the picture taking. Emma Bury, the drum major, is pictured in the second row. Mattie Sykes and Jessie Grimmer played the snare drum, and Dora Wells played the bass drum. Adleade Parker, Ella Schall, Allie Stewart, Inez Witherby, Emma Anderson, and Jessie Hinton played cornets. Nettie Priest and Grace Baldwin played trombones. Mattie Burrough and Bertha Stewart played altos. Nora Hall played Bass, and Emma Priest played the baritone. (1888, Juneau County Historical Society.)

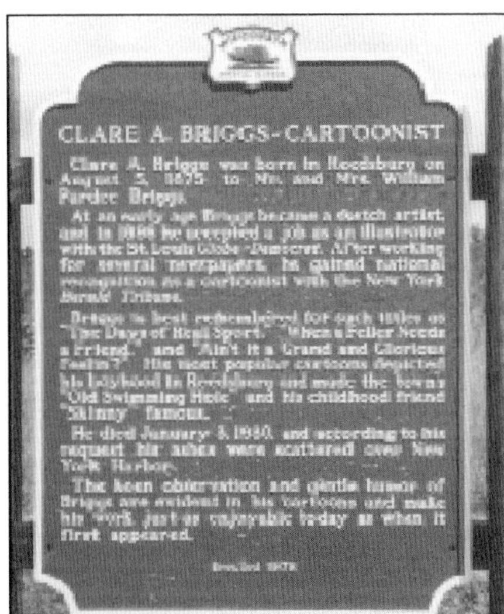

This sign is on the same property as the Pioneer Village and the Reedsburg Historical Museum. (2000, Sheila Z.)

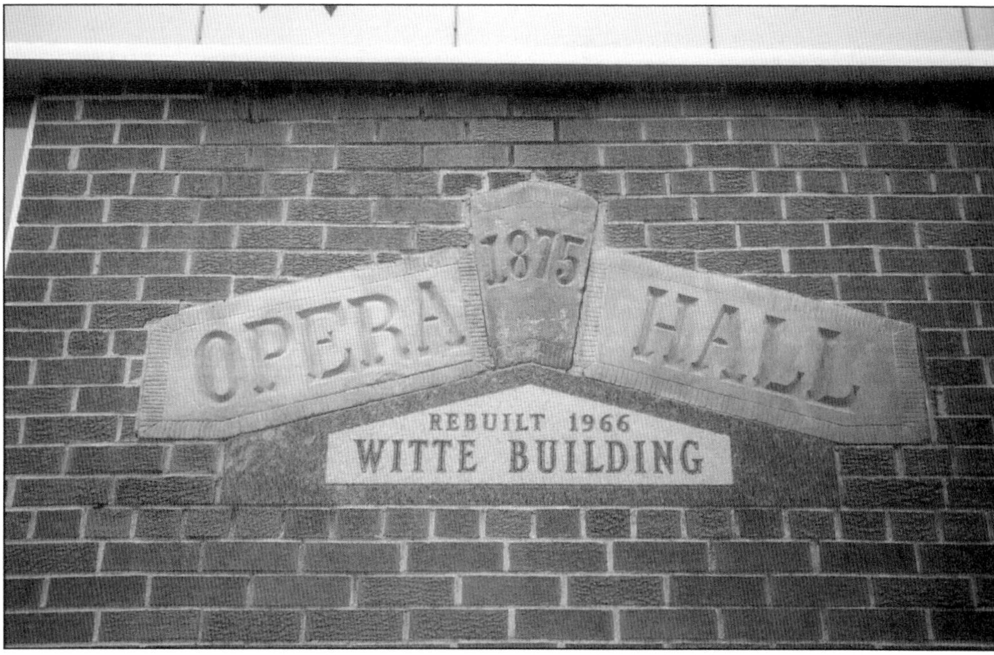

Most villages in the late 1800s and early 1900s had an Opera House. The top sign in this picture is on the building that was formerly the Mauston Opera House. Businesses operated on the ground floor of the building. The second floor was open and had a stage at one end. It was used for home talent shows, band concerts, traveling shows, and lectures. (2001, Sheila Z.)

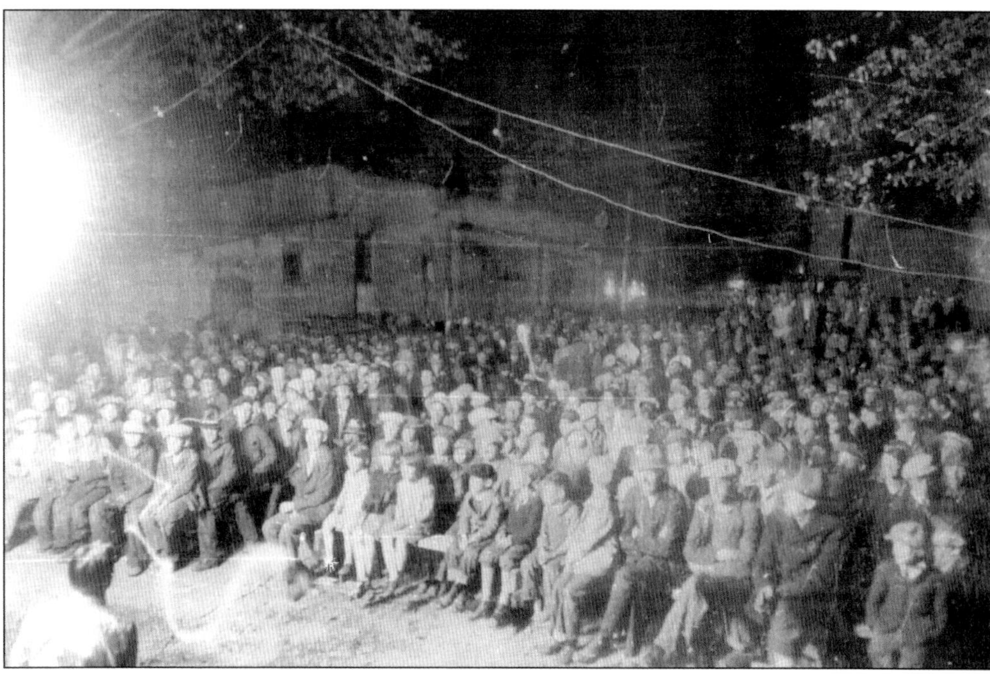

A free show in Hustler is about to start. The big screen is set up on the vacant lot and all the plank seats are full. After a while, some folks will probably go down to the trailer and get popcorn. (1930s, Claire Ness.)

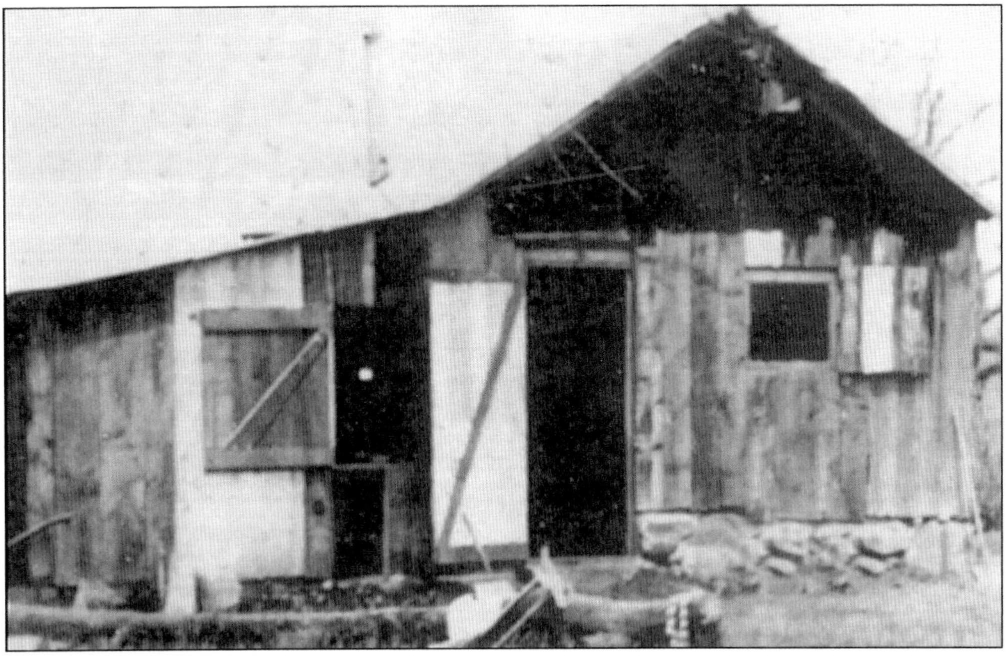

Aldo Leopold wondered why the poor farmers on sand farms in central Wisconsin didn't want to leave their farms when the government was trying to help relocate them. He bought a sand farm in Sauk County to help himself understand, and he and his family spent weekends, vacations, and hunting trips there. He called it "the shack." Here, he learned his "land ethic" from nature and wrote *The Sand County Almanac*. (Late 1940s, Sauk County Historical Society.)

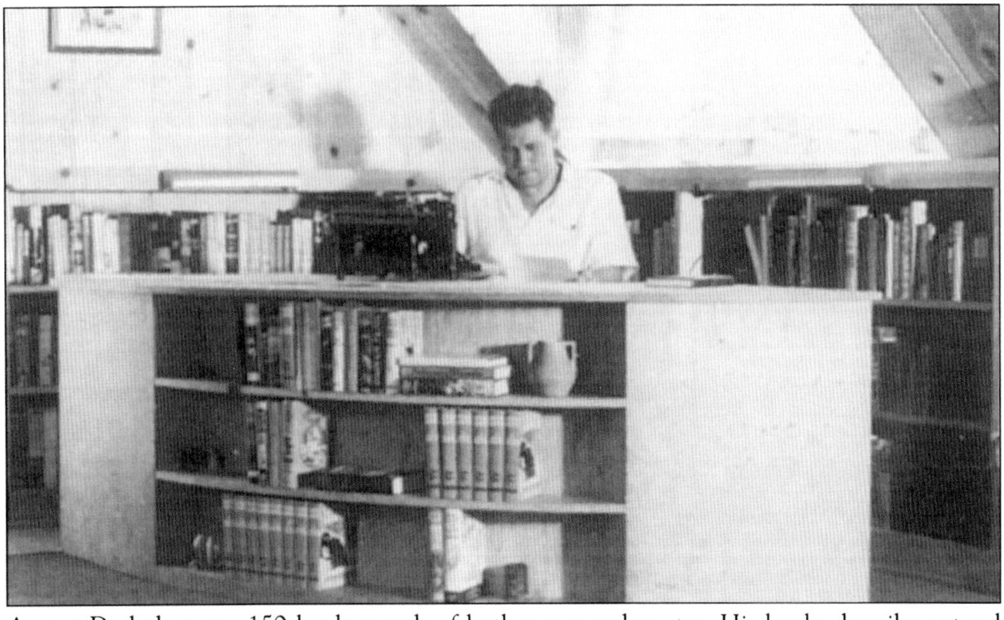

August Derleth wrote 150 books worth of both prose and poetry. His books describe natural beauty, birds, animals, and flowers. In 1940, he built his home, "Place of the Hawks," across from the Sauk City Cemetery. He was born on February 24, 1909, and died July 4, 1971. (Sauk County Historical Society.)

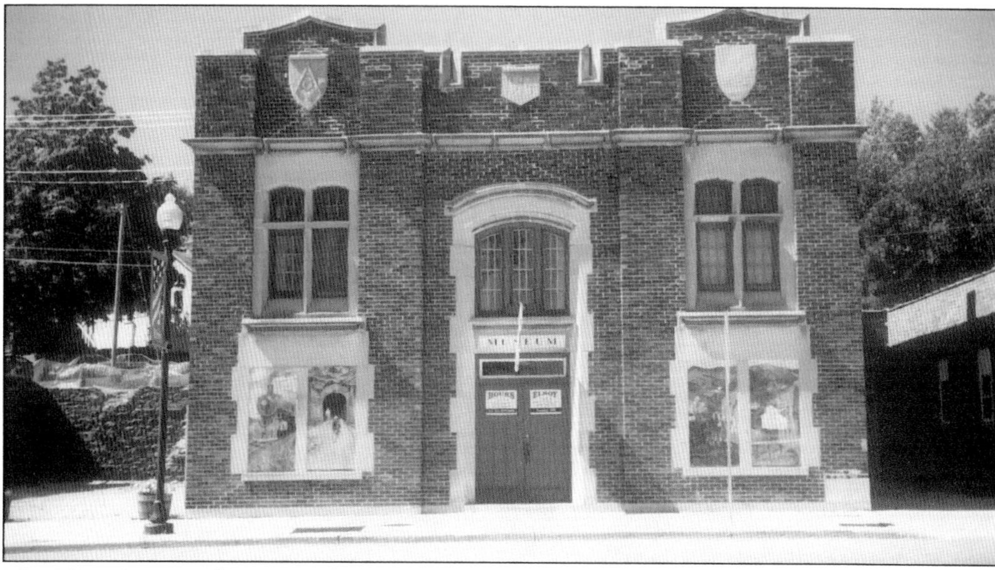

The Elroy Historical Museum has a miniature model of the 1930 train depot at Elroy. The exhibit is on the lower level of the museum. Upstairs, visitors can take a walk down Elroy's main street and see the 1930s shops and offices reproduced in individual settings. People in this community have spent a great deal of time and effort gathering materials and organizing them to provide this wonderful historical resource. (2001, Sheila Z.)

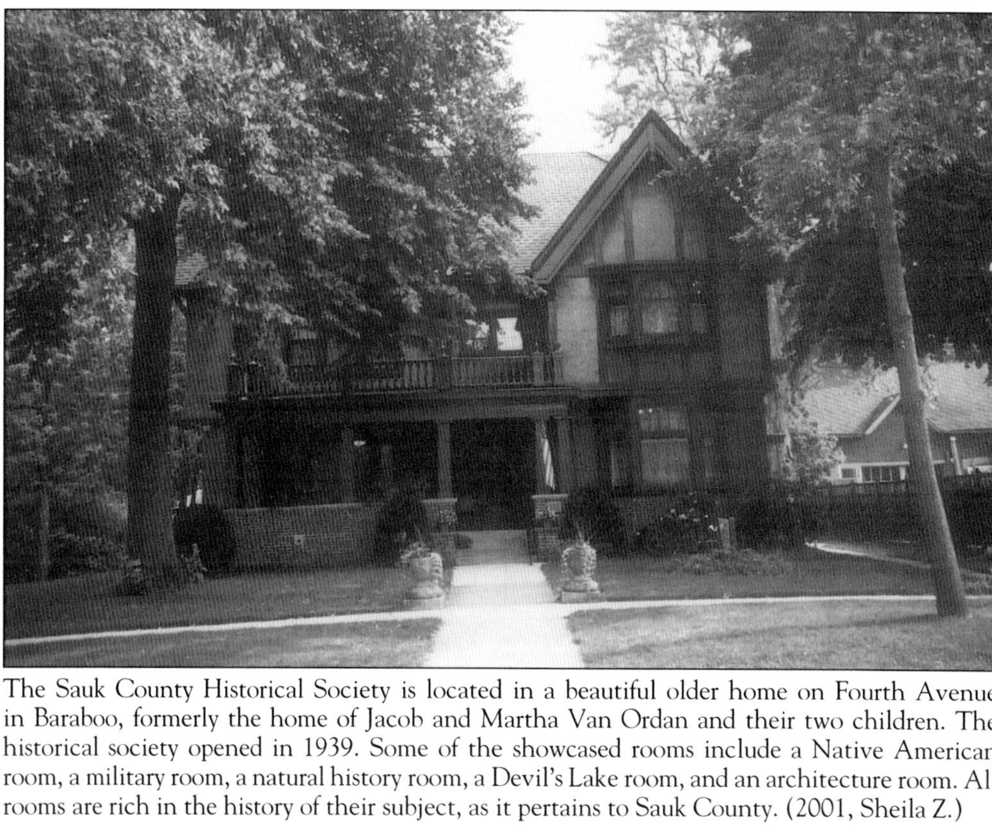

The Sauk County Historical Society is located in a beautiful older home on Fourth Avenue in Baraboo, formerly the home of Jacob and Martha Van Ordan and their two children. The historical society opened in 1939. Some of the showcased rooms include a Native American room, a military room, a natural history room, a Devil's Lake room, and an architecture room. All rooms are rich in the history of their subject, as it pertains to Sauk County. (2001, Sheila Z.)

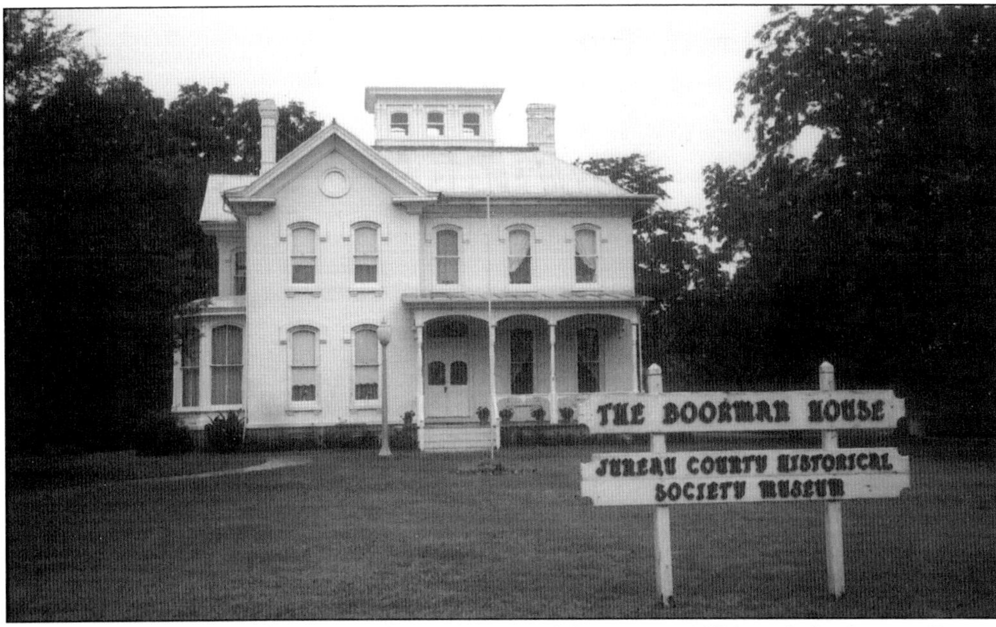

Ben Boorman built this home on Union Street in Mauston in 1876, and the Juneau County Historical Society purchased it in 1987. The museum is called the Boorman House, Juneau County's Historical Society. The rooms address different aspects of Juneau County history. There is a school room, medical room, military room, and clothing room, showcasing clothing from different eras. There is also a large library and a study room. (2001, Sheila Z.)

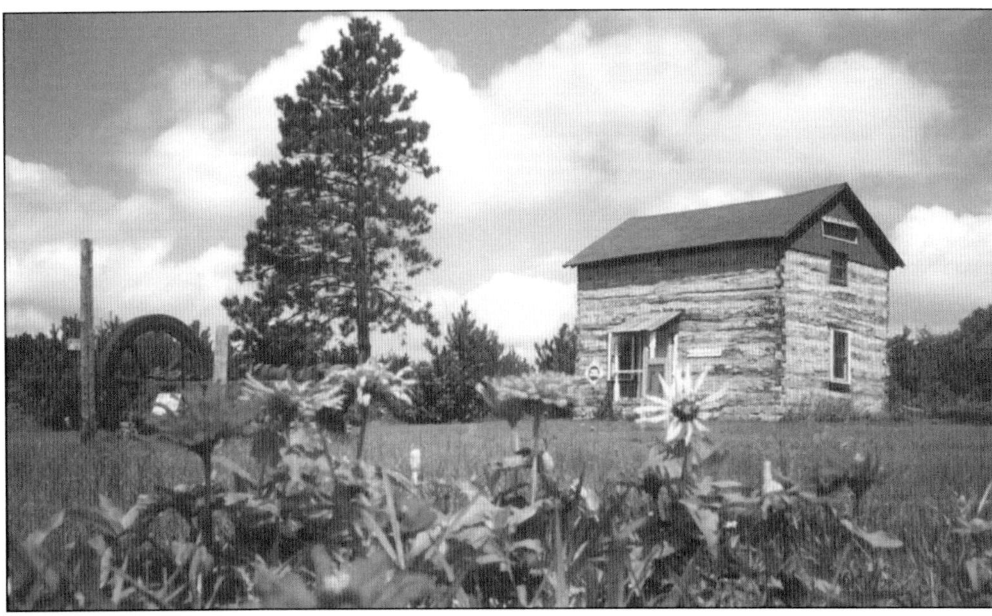

The Pioneer Village Museum is operated by the Reedsburg Area Historical Society, which began in 1965. One of their goals was to preserve remaining log buildings in Sauk County. Six log buildings are on the property, and a seventh building is being reconstructed. The buildings are dated from 1850 to 1880, and include homes, a school, and a church. Other historical subjects are showcased in a museum on the property. (2001, Sheila Z.)

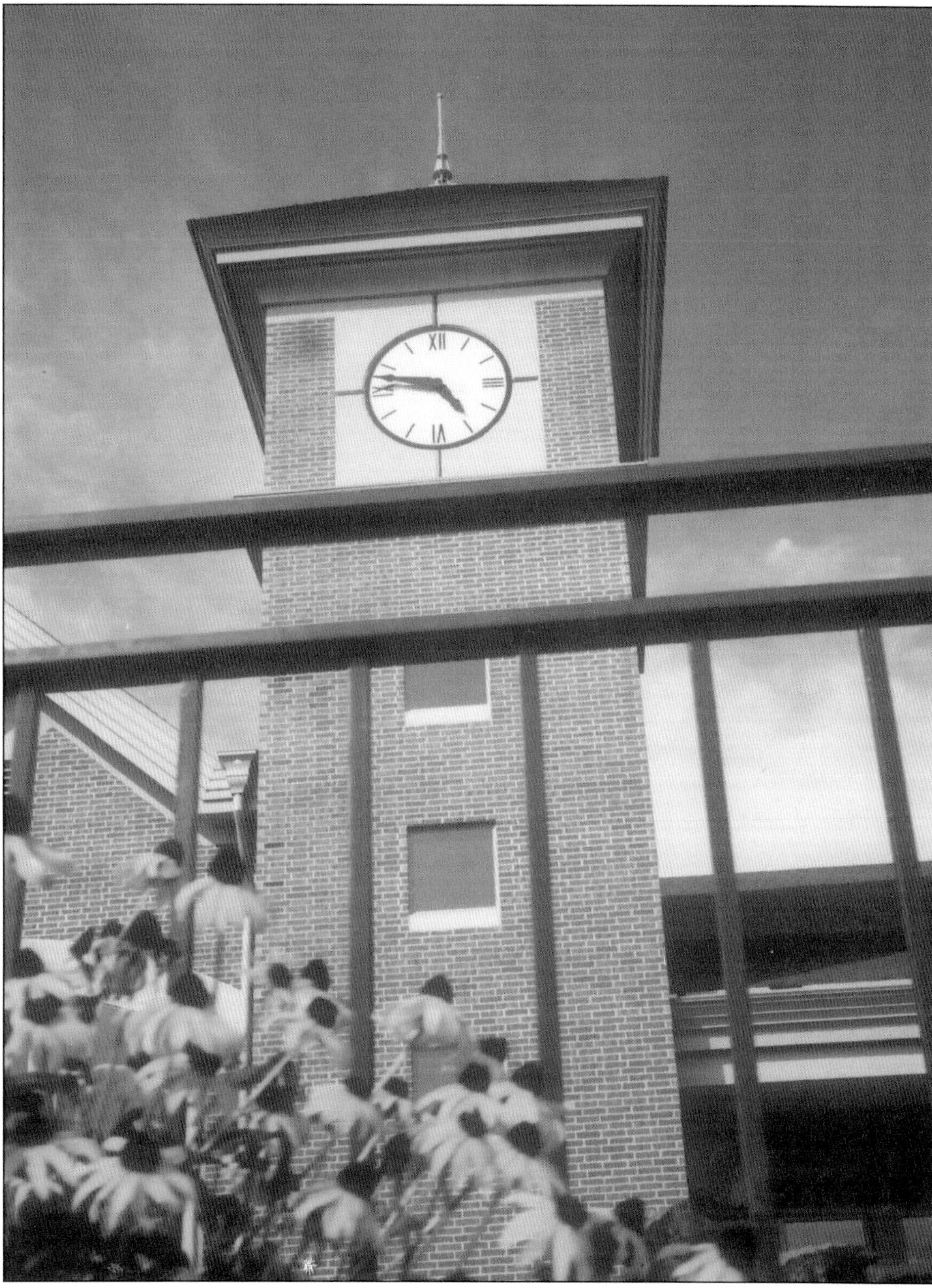

The Hatch Public Library's ribbon-cutting and dedication was May 21, 2000. The building is beautiful and a joy to use. Space is well-planned to accommodate both children and adults. The adult reading room and the children's story hour room both overlook the Lemonweir River. The Heritage Room aids research into genealogy and history. Groups of ten and others can use the private conference room. Many other special features have been incorporated into the library. (2001, Sheila Z.)

Nine

PROHIBITION

The Volstead Act of 1919, commonly known as Prohibition, was not popular in Juneau and Sauk Counties. There may have been more people breaking the law than following it. Small-town beer makers had a good business. The stills up in the hills could not be detected easily because they were too far away for authorities to pick up the scent of the liquor. Revenue agents did make raids, but as soon as one still was dismantled, another still sprang up. Bootleggers were not spending a long time in jail, only about six months plus fines. Usually, their stretch gave them notoriety and attracted more customers to their places of business.

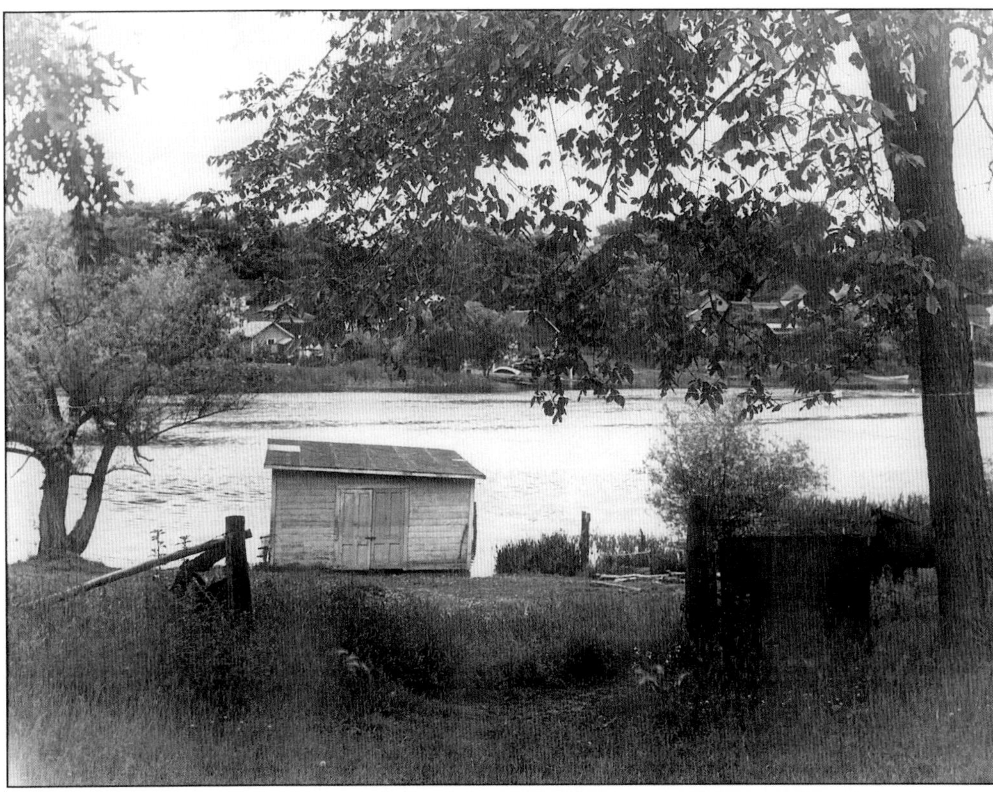

The shotgun used to kill Clinton Price, Mauston's district attorney, was found in the water near this boathouse on the Lemonweir River. Two theories were suggested for the murder. One theory claimed that Price was involved in bootlegging and turned on his co-conspirators by leading a raid on the "big still." The other theory suggested that revenge was the murder motive because Price was doing his job and led the raid. (1931, Juneau County Historical Society.)

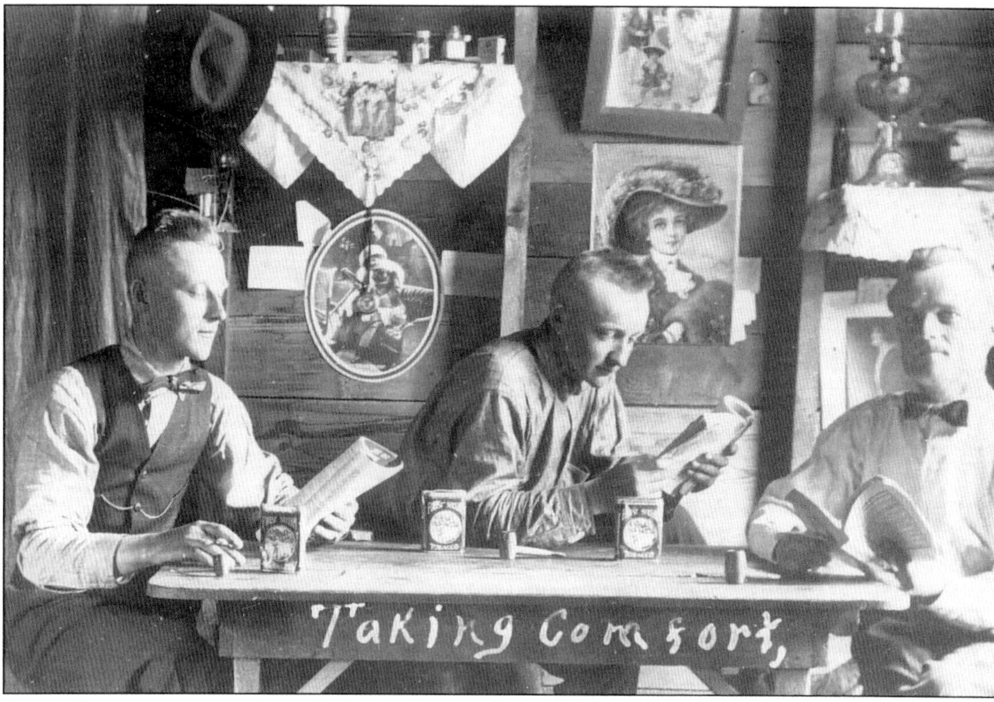

Sam Albertson came to Canada from a farm in Juneau County. He homesteaded in Canada and put up a little shack. He had a tractor and did some work for others, but times were pretty hard. His brother Andrew came and brought his nephew, Melvin Quamme. The prohibition law was in effect in the U.S. and Sam had a chance to do some liquor runs. He did it and was caught, but he did not mind the short time he spent in jail. (1920s, Claire Ness.)

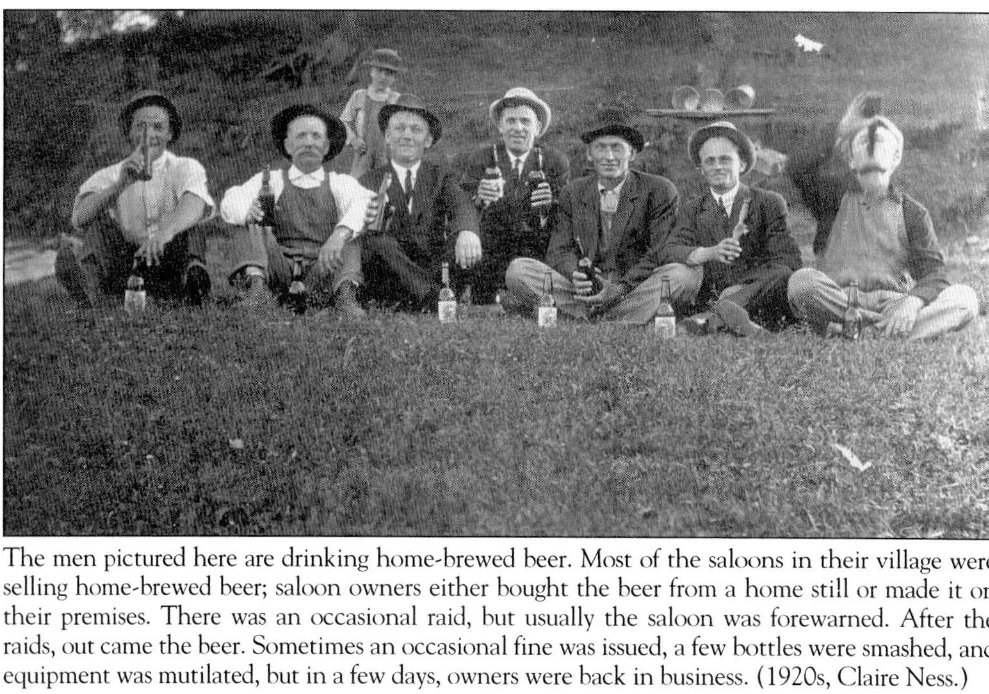

The men pictured here are drinking home-brewed beer. Most of the saloons in their village were selling home-brewed beer; saloon owners either bought the beer from a home still or made it on their premises. There was an occasional raid, but usually the saloon was forewarned. After the raids, out came the beer. Sometimes an occasional fine was issued, a few bottles were smashed, and equipment was mutilated, but in a few days, owners were back in business. (1920s, Claire Ness.)

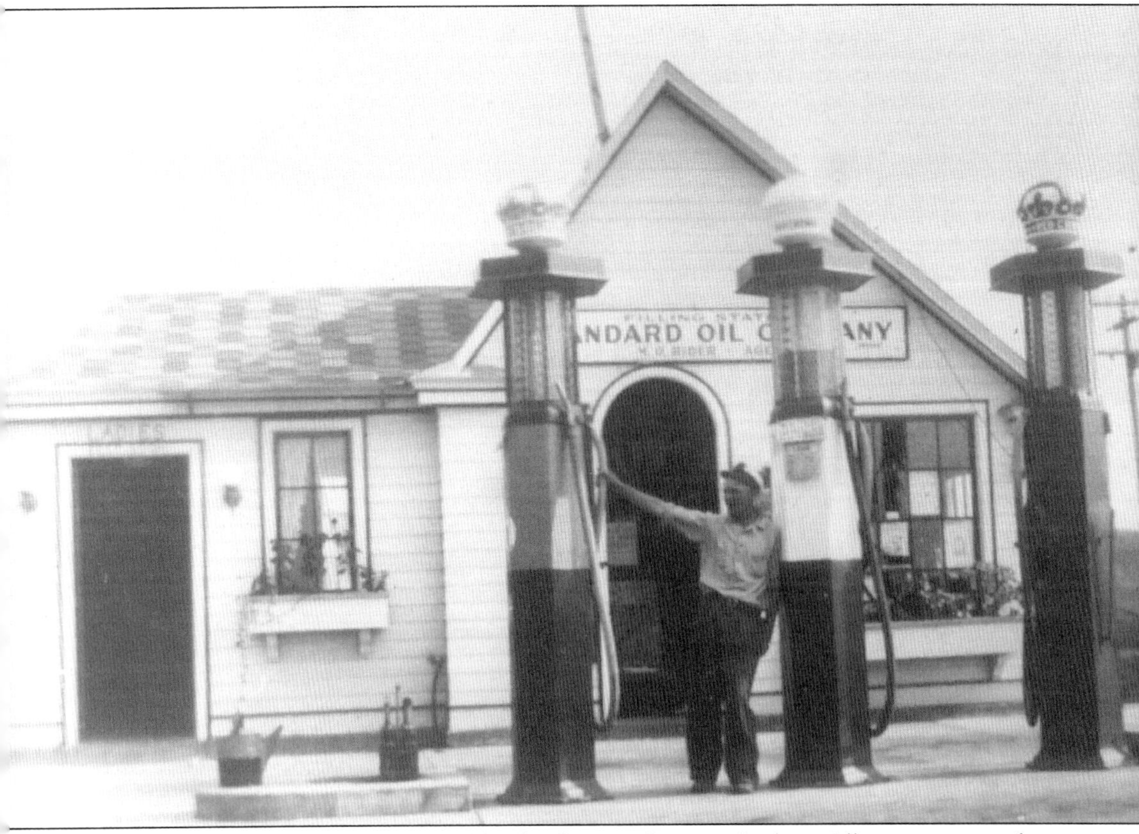

Morg Rider opened a filling station in Hustler, Juneau County. Andrew Albertson was working for him. One day, two trucks pulled in. One man held Andrew at gunpoint as liquor was transferred from one truck to another. (1920s, Claire Ness.)

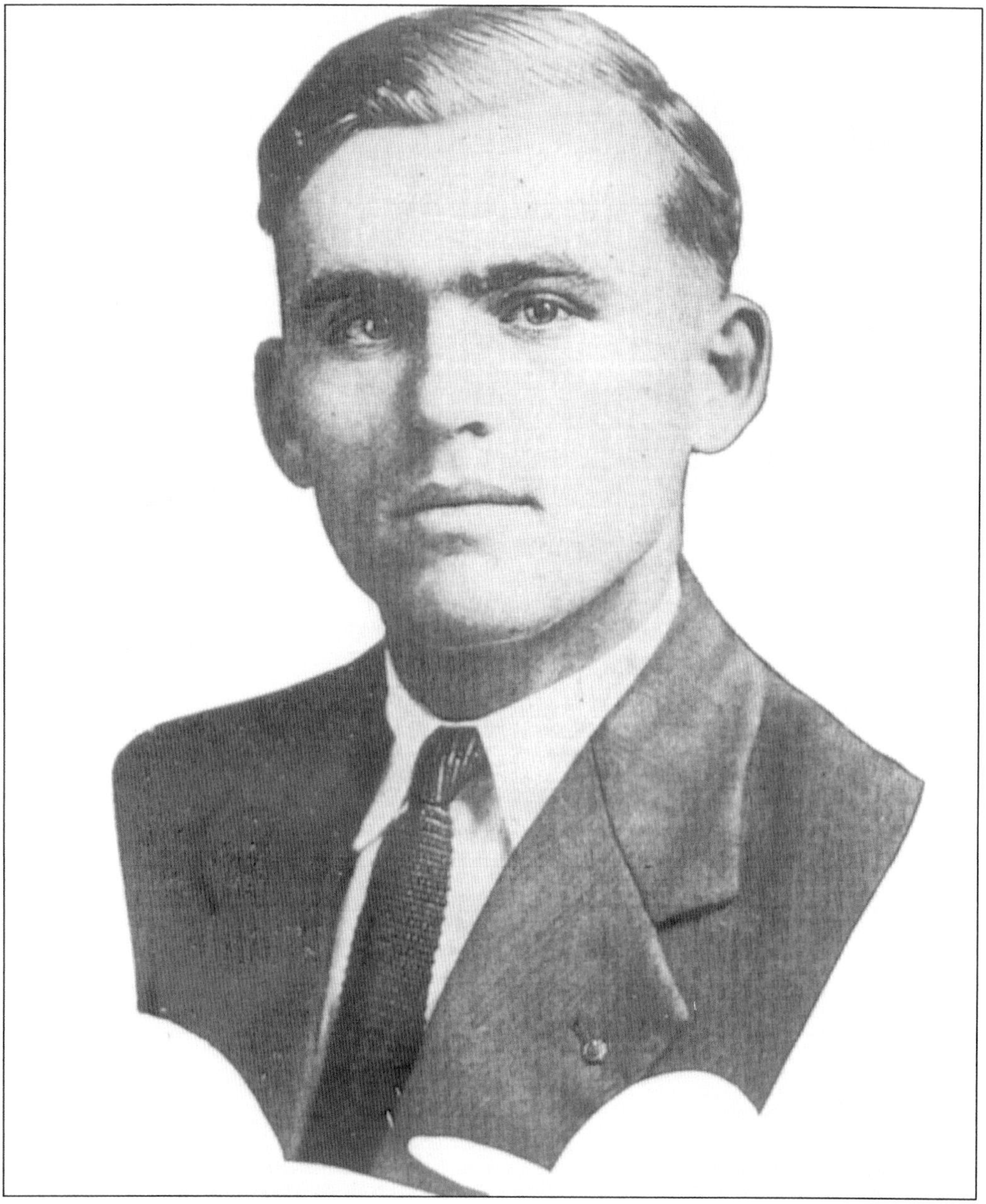

Lyall Wright, called "The Boy Sheriff of Juneau County," was elected in 1926, when he was 26 years old. He achieved fame in office for capturing a robbery gang and for obtaining a confession from William Coffey. Coffey murdered his second wife (never having divorced his first wife), cut up the body of the woman he murdered, and buried the parts near Platteville, Wisconsin. Near the end of his term, Sheriff Wright was accused of conspiracy to violate the Volstead Act. He was later found guilty of having the biggest still in Wisconsin under his protection. According to the Sheriff's testimony, Clinton Price, Juneau's district attorney who led the raid on this still, had received protection money, but was angry about the amount of money he received. Clinton Price was murdered, and Sheriff Wright was accused of the murder. The prosecution claimed a trail of blood led form the murder scene to the Sheriff's home. The evidence was circumstantial, and Sheriff Wright was acquitted. (1928, Jacqueline Ann.)

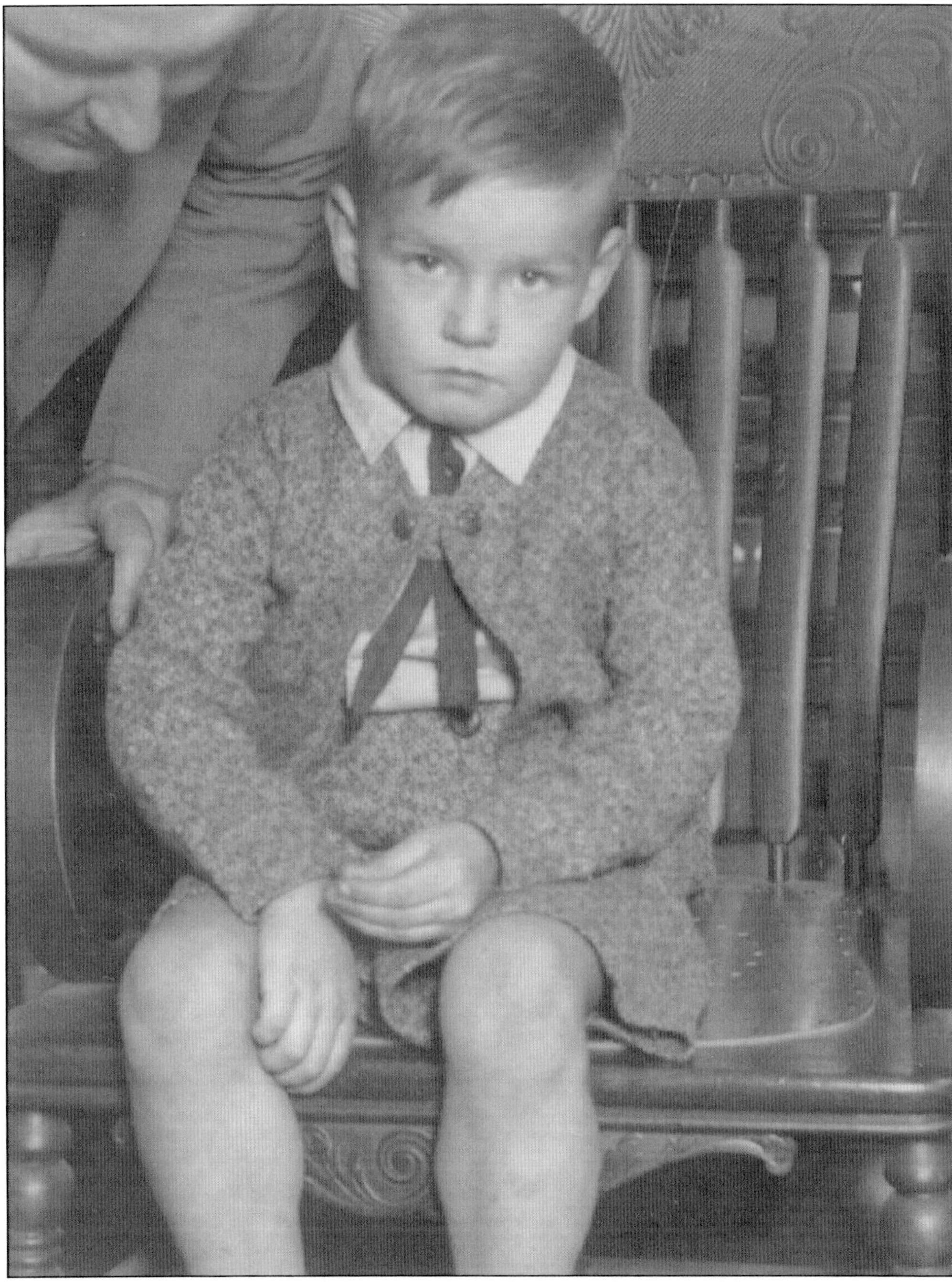

Lyall's son Harry testified at his father's murder trial. He was four years old. Harry said he broke a bottle in the alley behind their second floor apartment, and cut his hand on the bottle. His hand bled a lot. He shook his hand as he went up the stairs because his hand hurt, getting blood on the railing and stairs. Some of his blood made a mess in the kitchen and bathroom. Mom took care of his hand. Harry's mother took him from the witness stand to where the jury sat. She had him open his hand, showing the jury the palm. She walked with him in front of the jury pointing with the tip of her pencil to a long thin scar across the hand's palm. (1930, Harry Wright.)

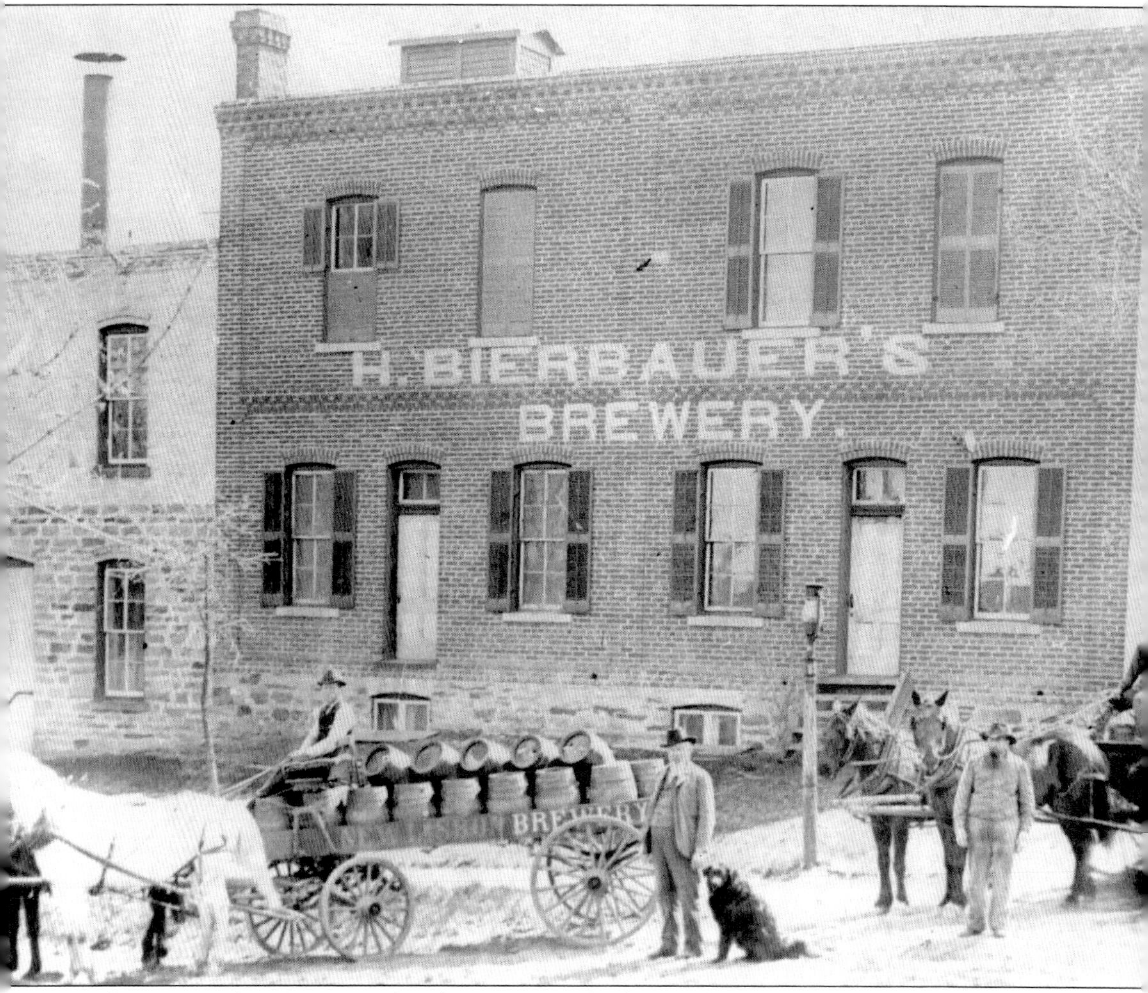

The New Lisbon Brewery closed in 1941. It had started in 1857. During Prohibition, the brewery sold ex-beer, or "near beer." They sponsored a baseball team called the "Ex-Brews." The Bierbauer brewery's embossed glasses became collector's items. They were used from 1901 to 1924. (1920s, Juneau County Historical Society.)

Ten

PROFILES

The people in this chapter developed the gifts they were born with. Doing this required self-sacrifice, love for their neighbors, and commitment. Seeing the order in nature and being aware of natural beauty contributes to good attitudes and values that can be applied to all areas of life.

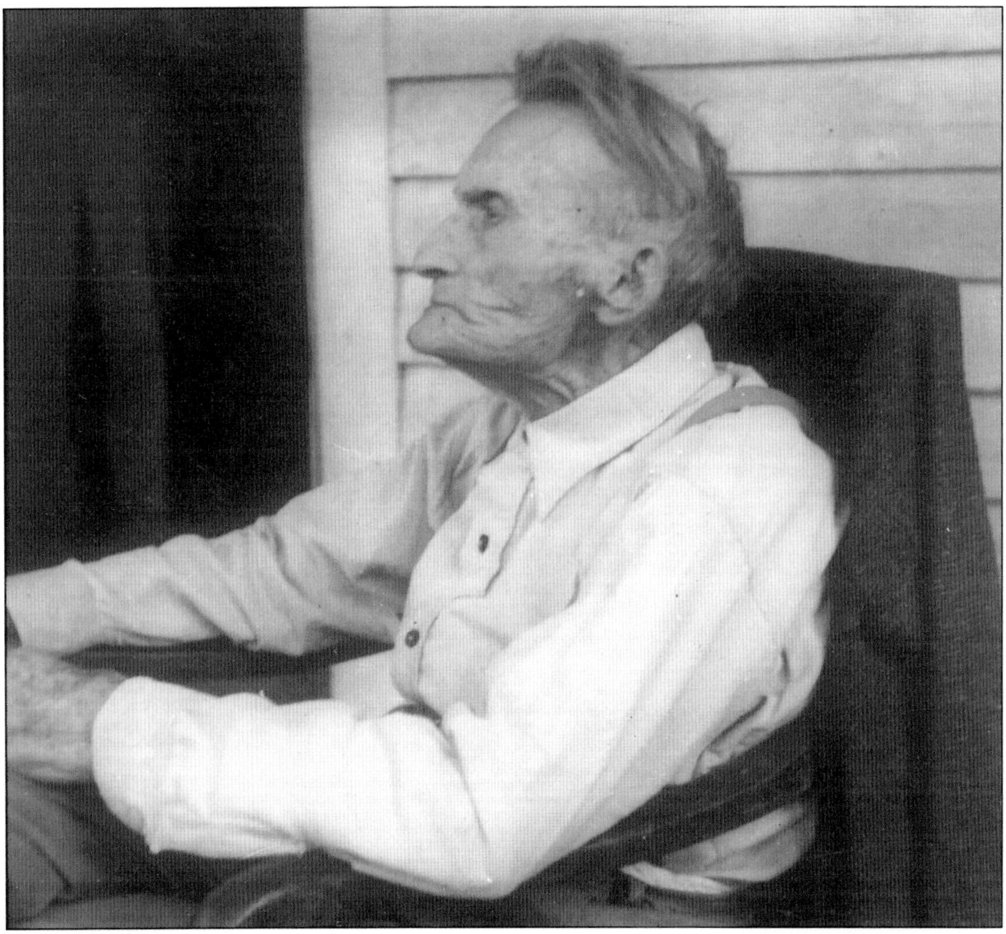

Vernon Wright's Yankee parents homesteaded near Lyndon Station. Wright was born in a log cabin and lived in Juneau County all his life. He was a farmer, justice of the peace, salesman, and school teacher. He always supported family, county, and country. In a newspaper article written about him, the reporter commented, "Vernon Wright reminds one of an old warrior."

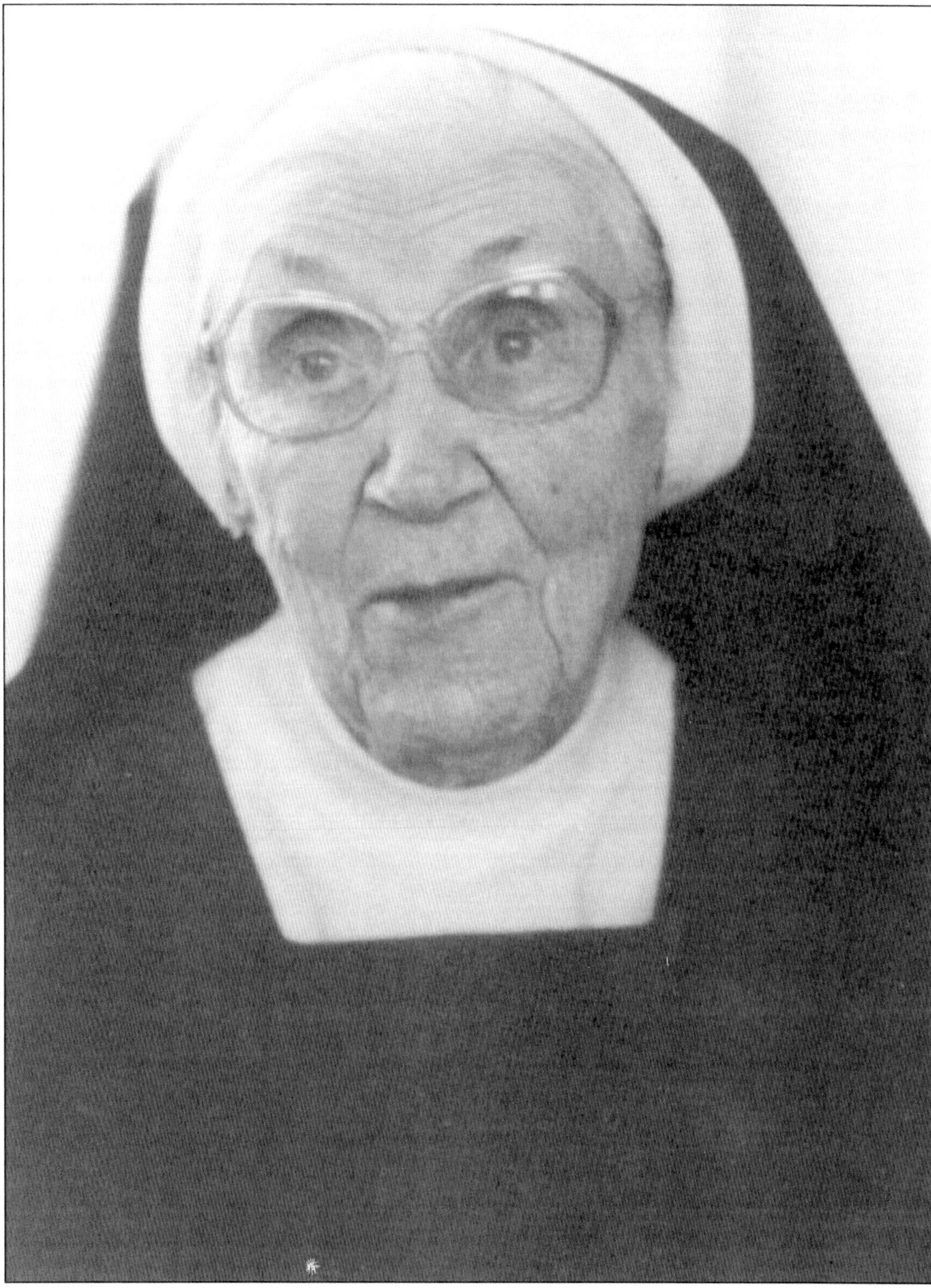

Jessica Powers was born in Cat Tail Valley, Juneau County, in 1905. She spent her first 31 years on a farm. During this time, she wrote over one hundred serious poems, most of them published. From 1936 to 1941, she lived in New York, wanting to be closer to the literary world. In New York she published a book of poetry, *The Lantern Burns*. In 1941, she entered the Carmelite cloister in Milwaukee. She was given permission to continue writing. In the next 47 years she published four books and hundreds of poems. (1988, Mary Jean Cauley.)

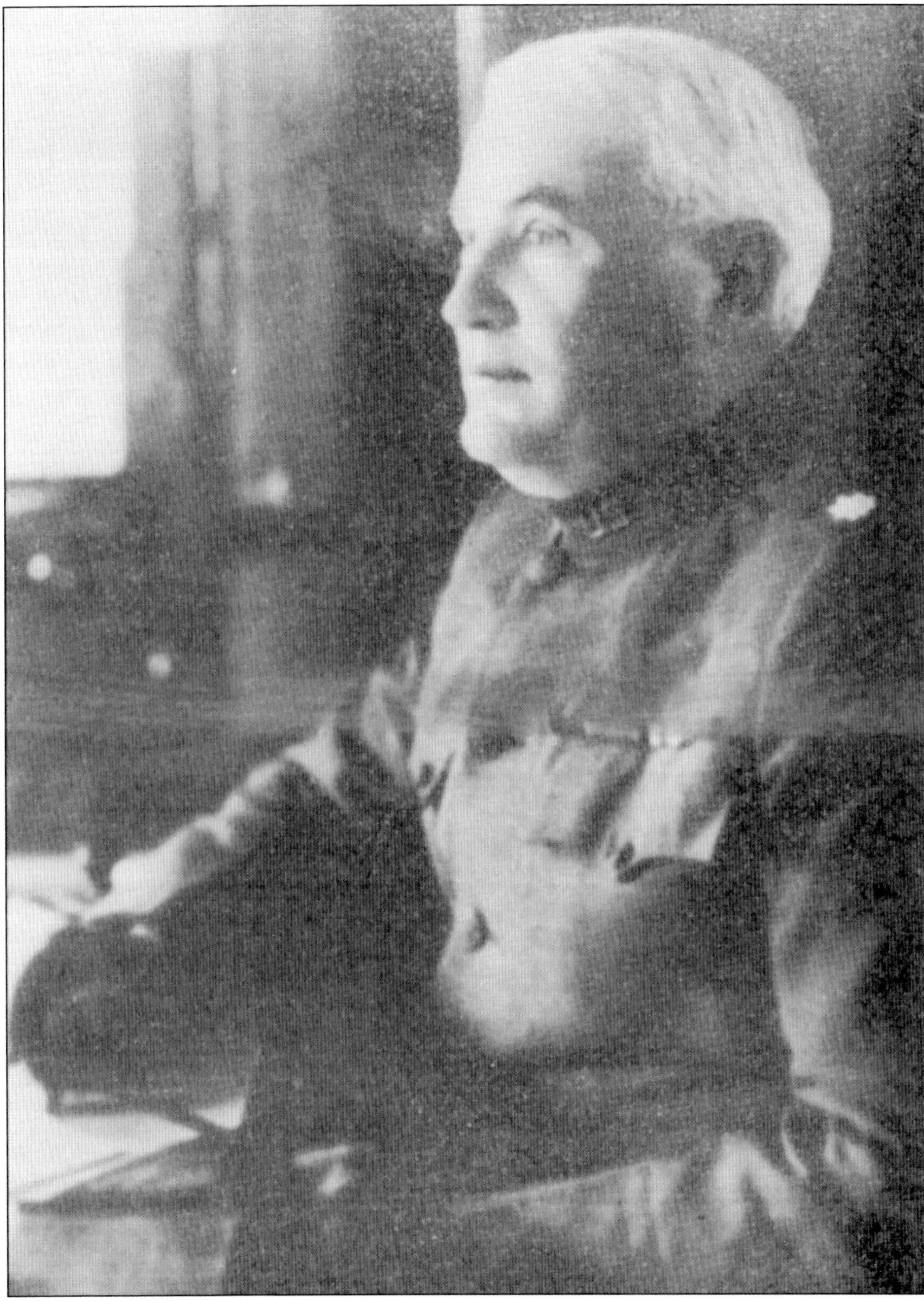

Lieutenant Colonel Williams was at the military reservation now known as Camp Williams for about 29 years. He was there during the camp's early development. In recognition of his service, the Wisconsin State Legislature voted to permanently name the camp after him. Lieutenant Colonel Williams died September 15, 1926, and is buried in a cemetery on the reservation. His son is buried in the same, small graveyard. (Early 1920s, Claire Ness.)

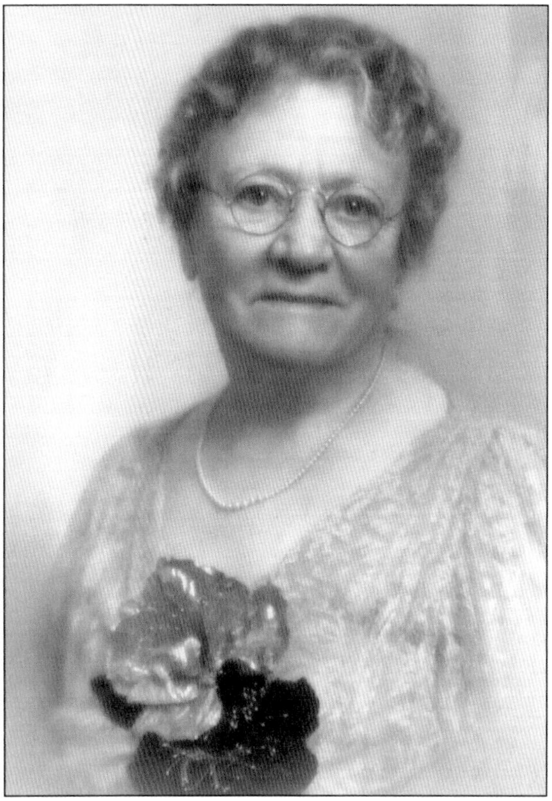

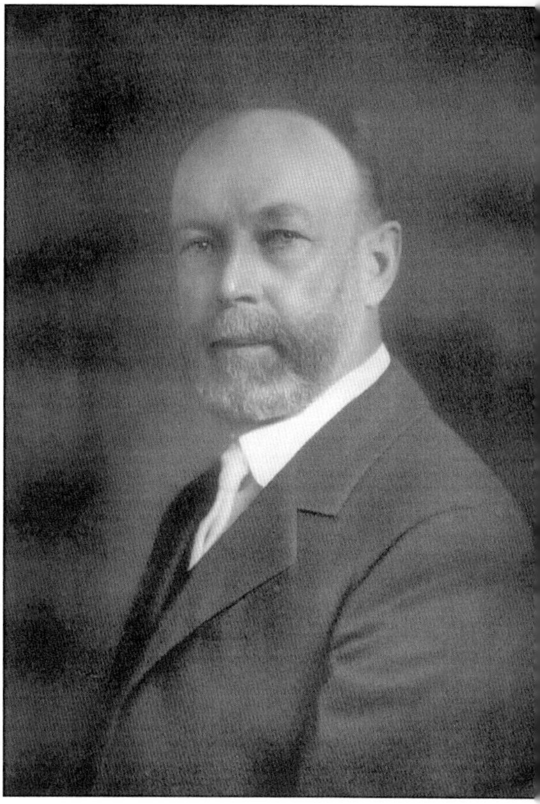

Horace and Mary Greene Upham taught their love and appreciation of the beauty and forces of nature to their daughters, Elizabeth and Caroline. The family spent their summers at their summer home, 400 acres on Highway 13 near Wisconsin Dells, and also on the 310 acres now called Upham Woods. Elizabeth and Caroline donated the 400 acres of land on Highway 13 to Camp Waubeek, a camp where people with disabilities can experience nature in a beautiful, natural setting. Camp Upham Woods is used as an outdoor laboratory for youth clubs like 4-H, scouts, school classes, and for agricultural and rural conservation. (1900, Camp Waubeek.)

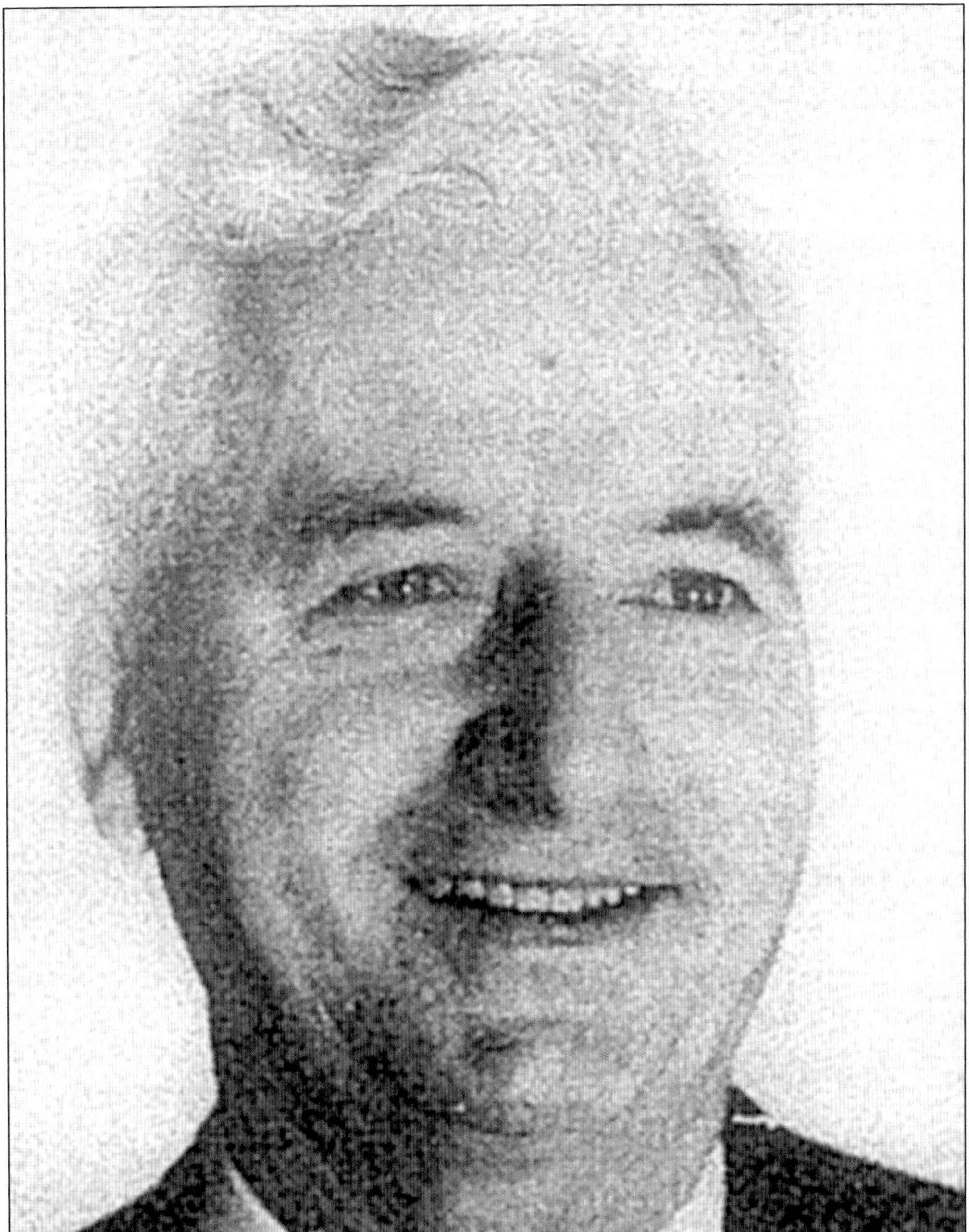

Winfred Scott Cunningham grew up on a small farm, north of Camp Douglas. He went to school in Camp Douglas through his junior year. In 1916, at the age of 16, he was appointed to the United States Naval Academy. A line from his yearbook reads, "He came to the Naval Academy from that well-known town of Camp Douglas, Wisconsin, but Winfred does not seem to have been raised on hops." Rear Admiral Cunningham was the commander of Wake Island when the Japanese captured it at the beginning of World War II. After the island was captured, he spent the rest of the war as their prisoner. (1976, Claire Ness.)

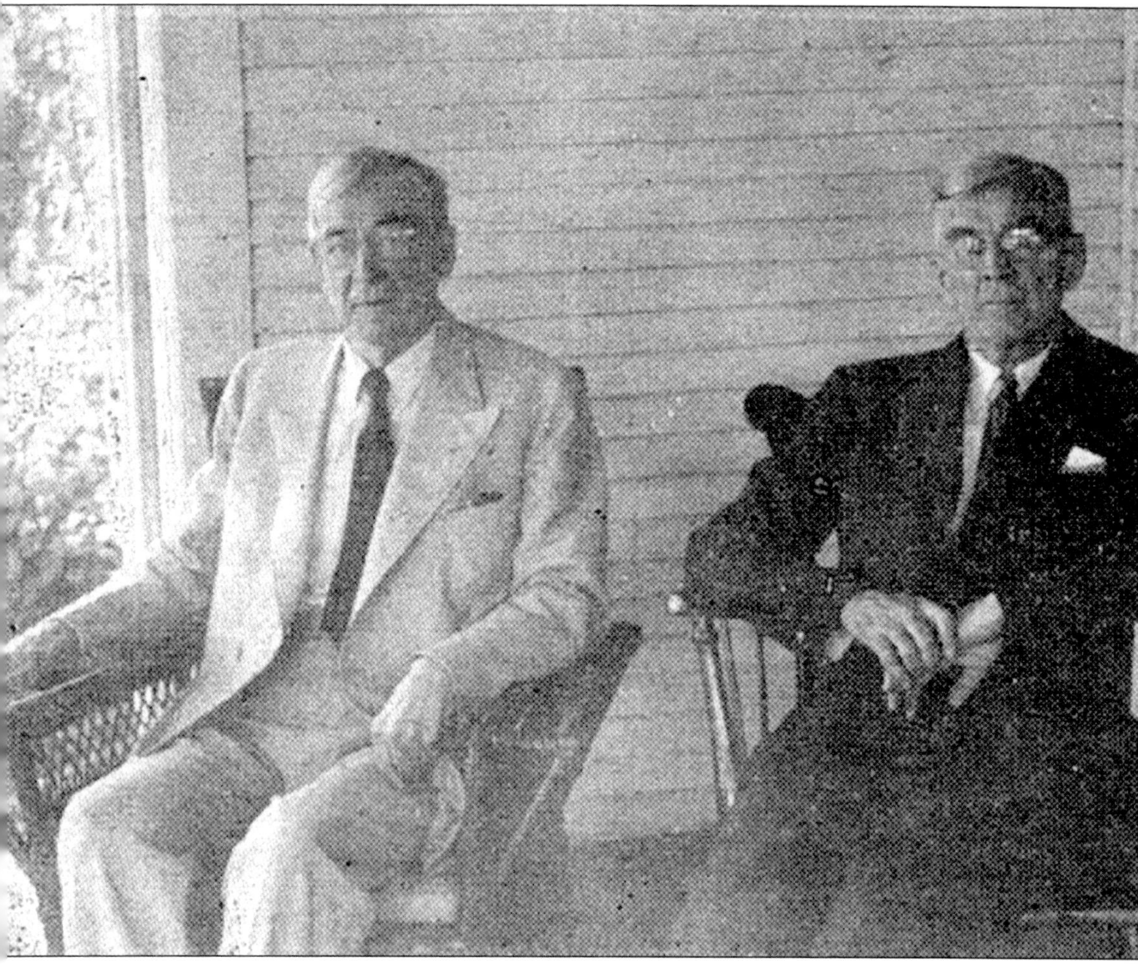

For 40 years, two brothers, Dr. Carl and Dr. Clarence Vogel, shared a medical practice in Elroy. Dr. Carl came to Elroy in 1904 and Dr. Clarence came in 1908. The men used all means of travel to reach their patients except airplanes and snowshoes. They sometimes did their surgery on kitchen tables. When Dr. Carl was in the service during World War I, Dr. Clarence had to care for the patients of the flu epidemic alone. (1940s, Elroy Historical Society.)

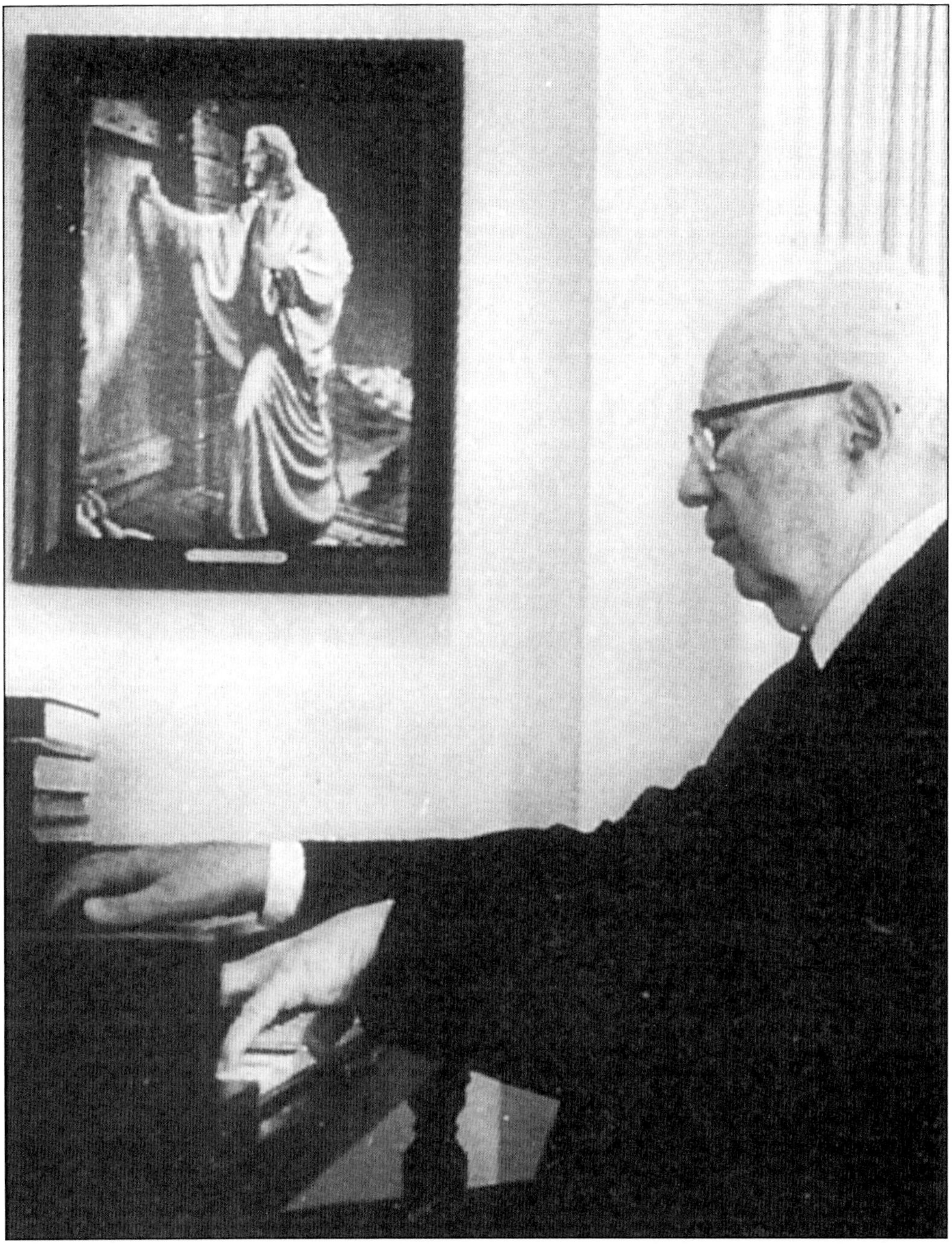

Arthur Colby lived 5-miles north of Reedsburg as a preschooler; he became blind when he was under a year old. When he was five, he left home to attend the school for the blind in Janesville during the school year and then stayed at an orphanage in Lacrosse during the summer. His mother had been left to raise five small children. It was more than she could handle. Art's teachers recognized and encouraged his musical genius, and he eventually became a music teacher. His wife also supported and encouraged him. Art, his wife, and three daughters moved to Reedsburg, where he and his wife both taught. Art died in 1996. (Reedsburg History Committee.)

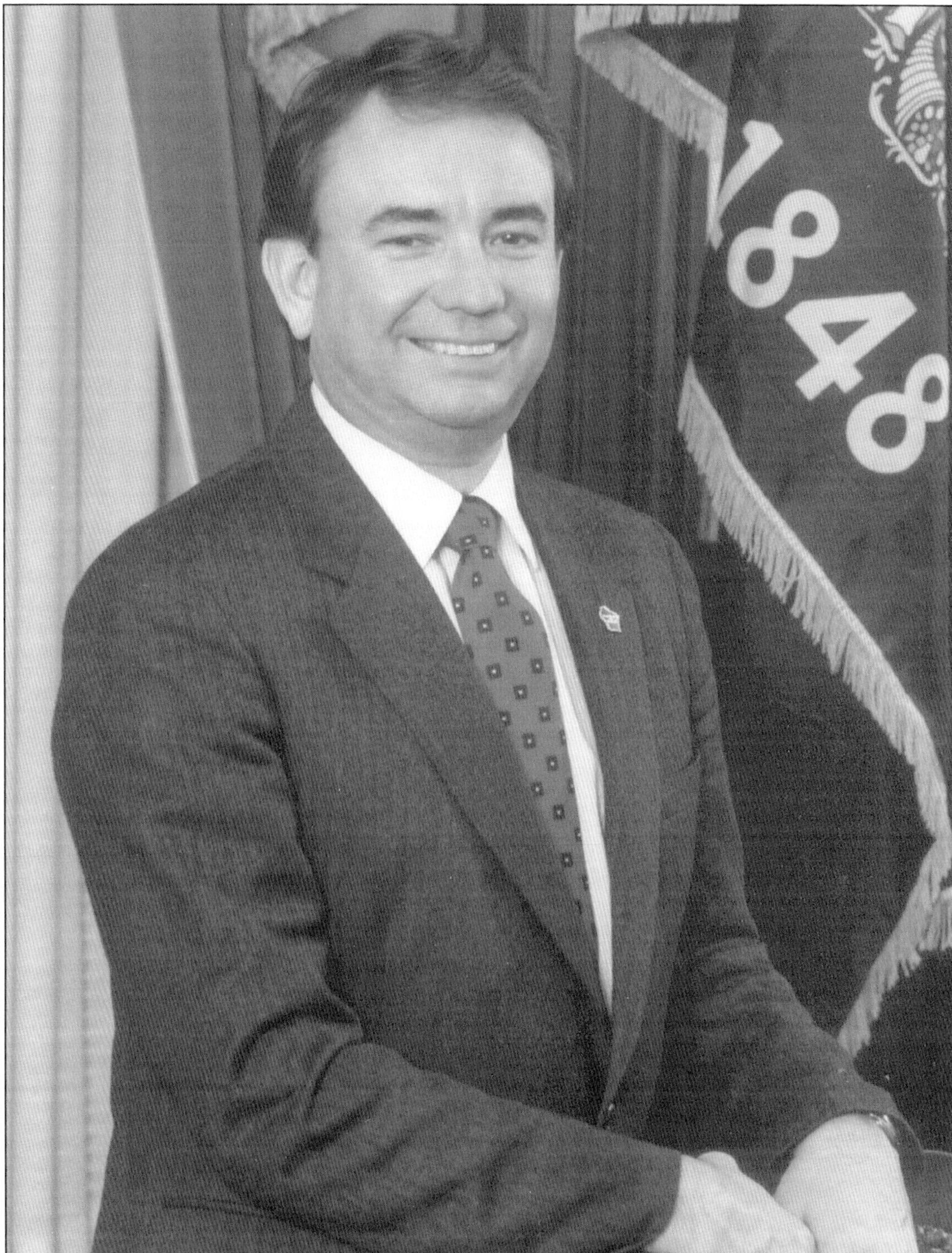

When Tommy Thompson was born, his father said, "His name will be Tommy," assuming the doctor would put Thomas on the birth certificate. She didn't. Tommy Senior was on the Juneau County Board, and lots of political talk went on at his store. The young Tommy listened as he pumped gas and worked in the store, becoming interested in the issues being discussed. Juneau County was in Tommy Thompson's district when he was elected to the Assembly in 1966. The announcement that Tommy Thompson was running for governor was made at the courthouse in Juneau County. (Elroy Historical Society.)

ACKNOWLEDGEMENTS

The authors of this volume would like to thank the following for their help in collecting information and for the access to their private collections of photographs for this book:

Barb Ott, Chad Weberg, Claire Ness, Elroy Historical Society, Gert Scully, Harry Wright, Hazel Owen, Henry Hajek, John and Delores Stastny, Juneau County Historical Society, Karna O. Hanna, Kathryn Wu, Larry and Donna Raun, Leo and Natalie Steiner, Lucille Nichols, Lynn Geitz, Marie Geitz, John Geitz, Marilyn Celeschi, Mark Miller, Mary Jean Cauley, Muriel Waarvik, Norma Scott, Peter Shrake, Rose Clark, Sauk County Historical Society, Sheri Butler, William Schuette.

A special thank you to everyone we may have missed. Your contributions are all greatly appreciated.

DEDICATION

JACQUELINE ANN would like to dedicate this book to her grandparents, Henry Gardner Briggs and Josephine Delap Briggs, Vernon Wright and Flora Mills Wright for their love and appreciation of Juneau County.

SHEILA Z. would like to dedicate this book to her husband, Patrick Zenk, for his love and encouragement and to her great grandma, Atsy Deitzman Bauer, for her creative spirit and love for natural beauty in all living things.

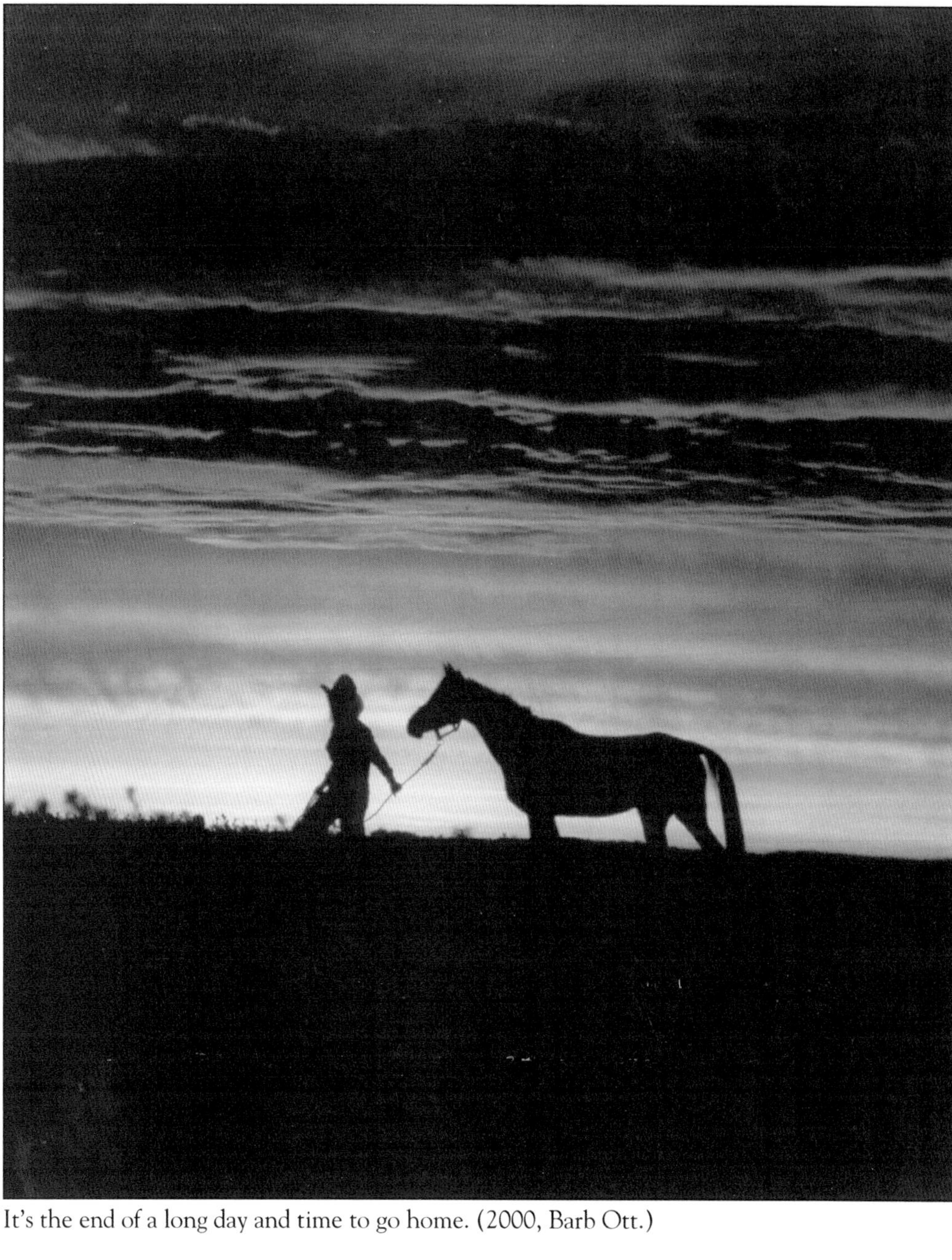

It's the end of a long day and time to go home. (2000, Barb Ott.)